# NEW MARTINSVILLE GLASS, 1900-1944

## JAMES MEASELL

Author's note: This book is an enlarged, revised edition of two publications by Everett R. and Addie R. Miller: *The New Martinsville Glass Story* (1972) and *The New Martinsville Glass Story, Book II, 1920-1950* (1975).

# TABLE OF CONTENTS

ACKNOWLEDGMENTS........................................................................................iv

INTRODUCTION...............................................................................................v

NEW MARTINSVILLE GLASS, 1900-1907 ...............................................1

THE FISHER YEARS .......................................................................................21

THE CLARKE YEARS......................................................................................52

DESCRIPTION OF COVERS .........................................................................90

COLOR PLATES ..............................................................................................91

THE McELDOWNEY YEARS.......................................................................139

RECEIVERSHIP AND RENAISSANCE .....................................................153

NEW MARTINSVILLE GLASS, 1938-1944...............................................185

BIBLIOGRAPHY.............................................................................................218

INDEX ...............................................................................................................219

VALUE GUIDE ...............................................................................................231

# ACKNOWLEDGMENTS

A book is the product of the effort and involvement of many individuals. This book is no exception. David Richardson, president of Antique Publications, was personally involved with this project in many ways—ranging from the hands-on aspects of photography to the leadership essential to a quality product. Dave and Antique Publications' staff photographer Deana Wynn are responsible for the excellent color photos in this book. Ronda Ludwig took charge of design and layout with both care and competence.

The following people graciously loaned glassware photographed in this book: Susan and Lee Allen; Roy Ash; Olive Barth; Kenneth Bole; Christine and Larry Brown; Carole and Bob Bruce; Harold and Jackie Clapp; Wilfred Cohen; Dorothy Frayzee; Jean Giddings; Art Gilbert; Addie Miller; Dianne and Paul Miller; Cheryl and Bob Pietrasz; Dean Six; Tony Topp; Philip and Frances Webb; Sarah Wolfe; and Berry Wiggins. Articles were also borrowed from Dalzell-Viking Corporation, the Fenton Museum and the Huntington Museum of Art. Eason Eige and Lorraine Kovar made special trips to Marietta with items needed for photography.

The Corning Museum of Glass granted permission to photograph two original New Martinsville catalogues with important color illustrations. Librarian Norma Jenkins of Corning's Rakow Library handled requests for assistance and information with both enthusiasm and dispatch.

Kenneth Dalzell, president of Dalzell-Viking Corporation, allowed access to storage areas in the New Martinsville plant, and he loaned valuable historical materials. Longtime New Martinsville employees Charles Mason and Harold Ruble recalled many former workers, and they helped search the factory's nooks and crannies for glassware and old records. Mrs. Herbert Kappel shared memories of her time as an office employee. Mrs. June Hill provided information about her mother, Ruth Karcher Quinet, who worked as a decorator at the plant in the 1920s.

Access to various public documents was made easy by the cooperation of the staff at the Wetzel County Courthouse in New Martinsville as well as the New Martinsville Public Library. The files of the National Association of Manufacturers of Pressed and Blown Glassware were opened through the courtesy of Frank M. Fenton.

Mr. Stan Eveson provided information about the family of Joseph Webb. Miss Emma Lou McEldowney contributed a photograph of her father and shared family memories. Information about Harry Barth came from Mrs. Olive Barth and Miss Mable Barth. Mr. O. O. Brown loaned many items from his files on Wetzel County's history. Mrs. Ruth Wells helped locate people to interview about glassmaking at New Martinsville.

# INTRODUCTION

Everett and Addie Miller were pioneers. In the late 1960s, years before many students of American pattern glass were scanning microfilm of trade journals and searching for other information, they had traveled from their home in Rives Junction, Michigan, to the Library of Congress. They made friends with executives of the Viking Glass Company, thus gaining access to important factory catalogs and other original records. They were allowed to dig at the factory site and brought home buckets of glass fragments to be studied in conjunction with the other information they found. Everett and Addie also corresponded with dealers and collectors in and around New Martinsville as well as across the country.

The results of their labor of love were two books, *The New Martinsville Glass Story*, published in 1972, and *The New Martinsville Glass Story, Book II, 1920-50*, which appeared in 1975. Both were printed by Richardson Printing Corp. in Marietta, although the Millers retained the copyrights. These volumes were quickly recognized as the definitive sources on New Martinsville glass, and the Millers also wrote numerous short articles and gave many informative talks on their favorite subject.

As diligent researchers, Everett and Addie maintained contact with dealers and collectors as well as with the Viking firm, which sold both of their books in its factory gift shop. The Millers' auction business thrived, and they regularly added pieces of New Martinsville ware to an extensive collection of American glass. Their children, daughter Jean and son Paul, shared their enthusiasm for New Martinsville glass, although they were far away in California pursuing careers. When the late William Heacock was working on a book devoted to ruby-

**Everett and Addie Miller posed for this photograph shortly after their first book on New Martinsville glass was released in 1972.**

stained pattern glass, the Millers were quick to loan research materials and to offer support and good wishes. Everett Miller died on April 23, 1990.

Collector interest in New Martinsville glass remained strong, even after the two books were out-of-print. Letters and other inquiries came regularly to Addie. She decided to offer the copyrights for sale to Antique Publications. The project took shape quickly and decisions were made: new photography would be done and the two books would be combined into a single volume covering the firm at New Martinsville from 1901 through 1944, when it became the Viking Glass Company. Incidentally, Viking operated until 1986, when the plant was sold to Kenneth Dalzell, who had been associated with the Fostoria Glass Co. in nearby Moundsville; in 1987, the factory was reopened under the name Dalzell-Viking and is still in business today.

Most of the photography was done at the Millers' home in Rives Junction, Michigan. Son Paul and his wife Dianne drove across the country from California with boxes of New Martinsville glass. Daughter Jean, now relocated in nearby Jackson, opened her collection. David Richardson and I spent the better part of two days carefully arranging items page by page for most of the color photos you will see here. Our task and my subsequent research was made easier by everyone's helpfulness. As luck would have it, I found a 1904 New Martinsville catalog on one of my first research days.

As I journeyed to New Martinsville several times and talked to dealers and collectors alike, more than once I was asked this quiestion: "Do you know the Millers?" My replies always began this way: "Yes, indeed. They're the pioneers."

James Measell
August, 1994

# CHAPTER ONE

# NEW MARTINSVILLE GLASS, 1900-1907

IN APRIL, 1900, two Ohio-based glassmen, Mark Douglass and George Matheny of East Liverpool, were interested in establishing a glass factory near Wheeling. They had been associated with the Specialty Glass Company of East Liverpool as well as the West Virginia Glass Company of Martins Ferry, perhaps when the latter absorbed or merged with the former. Douglass had been a manager, and Matheny was a mould-maker.

According to the April 21, 1900, issue of *China, Glass and Lamps*, Douglass and Matheny considered refurbishing the venerable Buckeye Glass Works plant in Martins Ferry. This factory had been a large and important concern in the 1880s, but it was badly damaged by an arson fire during a strike in the early 1890s. The venture did not materialize, however, and Douglass and Matheny looked elsewhere. New Martinsville soon came to their attention.

An article in the October 18, 1900, issue of the *Wetzel Republican* newspaper offered a "Retrospective and Prospective Sketch [of New Martinsville], Touching Upon Present Improvements." The writer noted that New Martinsville had a population of about 2,800. There were several references to "hustling business men ... who believe that our city is destined to become one of the greatest commercial centers in the state." The article mentioned almost in passing that "a large glass house" was to be erected in the near future. Douglass and Matheny had come to New Martinsville, and plans had been laid and approved.

By late November, 1900, the *Wetzel Republican* (November 29, 1900) carried this headline: THE NEW MARTINSVILLE GLASS Co. Not a Matter of Fancy, But of Fact, An Assured Concern For this City." George L. Matheny was singled out for particular credit. He was lauded for his "indefatiguble [sic], stick-to-a-tiveness" in surmounting "every obstacle." A stockholders meeting was scheduled for December 14, 1900 (*Wetzel Republican*, December 6, 1900). In late December, the *Wetzel Republican* noted that these officers had been elected: Samuel R. Martin, president;

George L. Matheny, vice-president; and J. W. Collins, secretary-treasurer. Other members of the board of directors were as follows: James Cooper; David Fisher; E. D. Mooney; and G. B. Woodcock. Both Mooney and Fisher became key figures in the company's history.

In late 1900, both *Crockery and Glass Journal* (December 18, 1900) and *China, Glass and Lamps* (December 27, 1900) reported that Douglass and Matheny were among a group of investors who had applied for a corporate charter to establish a glass plant at New Martinsville. According to papers filed in Wetzel County, Matheny, Douglass and Fisher held 20 shares each, while P. D. Morris had two shares and William Hamilton one share. The corporate charter was granted by the West Virginia Secretary of State and entered into the Wetzel County records on January 8, 1901. New Martinsville lawyer P. D. Morris had been given power of attorney for the fledgling organization, and the group purchased several acres of land from Mr. and Mrs. Owen Witten and Mrs. Witten's mother on December 21, 1900. *China, Glass and Lamps* carried this account:

*The New Martinsville, W. Va., Glass Co., which is being promoted by Mark Douglass and George Matheny, has applied for a charter and the factory is now said to be a certainty for New Martinsville. The application is made by Mr. Hamilton, of Wheeling, Mark Douglass and David Fisher, of Martin's Ferry, and George Matheny and P. D. Morris, of New Martinsville. All the money for the concern has been subscribed. It is the purpose to break ground for the building in less than two weeks and push it to completion as soon as possible.*

*China, Glass and Lamps* (January 3, 1901) revealed that the New Martinsville plant "will manufacture tableware, lamps, novelties and packers' goods. Work will be started on the plant at once and they expect to be in operation about March 1. They will have a 12-pot furnace and 4-ton tank." The *Wetzel Republican* reported that "the plant ... will be of the latest style and manufacture tableware and glass novelties." Douglass arranged for some fixtures to be shipped from East Liverpool to New Martinsville (*Crockery and Glass Journal*, January 17, 1901).

**This drawing of the New Martinsville plant, which appeared in the June 27, 1901, issue of the _Wetzel Republican_, was also used on the firm's letterhead stationery and bilheads.**

A banner headline—"THE FIRST GLASS"—greeted readers of the _Wetzel Republican_ on June 27, 1901. A vignette of the factory appeared, and a lengthy article recounted the "commencement of what we believe will be an era of great prosperity" concluding that "this large concern ... is a valuable addition to the city of New Martinsville and deserves the support of every progressive citizen." Apparently, some additions had already been made to the firm's board of directors, for two other names were mentioned—Jacob Koontz and Thomas Mooney. The bookkeeper was listed as "R. Ruggles." Mark Douglass was factory superintendent, and David Fisher assistant superintendent. The article noted that the plant's fixtures included "one decorating layer [sic, should be lehr]," an indication that the firm was making gold-decorated and/or ruby-stained ware. The first glassware was made by presser Elzie Miller, a young man destined to work in the plant for half a century and whose family was associated with glassmaking in New Martinsville for four generations.

By early August, the New Martinsville Glass Manufacturing Company's stock had been increased from $50,000 to $100,000 (_Wetzel Republican_, August 1, 1901). Frank W. Clark was now president, and Samuel R. Martin was vice-president. John Stender and F. C. Wells were added to the board of directors. The skilled glass-workers organized themselves, and Local Union No. 16, an affiliate of the American Flint Glass Workers Union, was chartered in New Martinsville on August 10, 1901.

On August 22, 1901, this story appeared in the _Wetzel Republican_:

_Saturday we paid the New Martinsville Glass Mf'g. Co.'s plant our first visit since it has been put into operation. The concern presented an active scene and one which was pleasant to us as it represents the commencement of other manufacturing concerns in this city._

_About 150 persons were busily engaged in the manufacturing of different lines of ware including blowers, pressers, mixers, off-bearing boys [carrying-in boys], girls in the packing department, shippers, polishers and mould-makers._

_The factory proper is under the supervision of Mark Douglass, an experienced and competent glass worker. An elegant line of colored and plain ware was being made, including tumblers, lamps, large and small fruit dishes, shades and other lines of various designs and patterns. The furnaces were in full blast and everything was run with a precision and nicety that was surprising considering the short time the factory has been in operation and the fact that most of the boys and girls were new and had not thoroughly learned the details of the work._

_The packing department, under the management of Mr. Fisher, was busy preparing shipments of ware, and is kept quite busy filling orders. In fact orders at present are coming in faster that they could be supplied if the factory was running to its fullest capacity._

_The mould-room was equally as busy and interesting as the other parts of the plant. Mr. G. L. Matheny has charge of the mould-room and designs the patterns for the ware. This department is running several hours extra each day in order to complete the moulds for a full line at the earliest possible time._

_In the business department, Mr. J. W. Collins, secy., and Mr. Ruggles, treas. and bookkeeper, were busy looking after the business details of the concern. Both gentlemen are very pleasant, but strict business men with a weather eye always on the lookout for any advantages they might secure._

At a stockholders' meeting in October, 1901, subscriptions to stock were still being sought, as the firm needed more capital. A story in the _Wetzel Republican_ (October 17, 1901) noted that "an addition for decorative ware has just been completed," yet another indication that the company was involved in making gold-decorated and/or ruby-stained glassware. Readers of the _Wetzel Republican_ were informed that the "success of the Glass plant has exceeded the most sanguine expectations of its promoters" and citizens of Wetzel County were urged to purchase stock in "the best opportunity for an investment now offered in this section ...."

Surprisingly, Mark Douglass' tenure at New Martinsville was short-lived, and he resigned in

December, 1901. He was replaced by Joseph Webb, an English emigrant in his late 40s who had been making colored glass in the United States for about 18 years. News of Douglass' departure was carried in the *Wetzel Republican* (December 5, 1901). George L. Matheny probably left about the same time. He later became foreman of the mould shop at H. Northwood and Co. in Wheeling and may have been involved with the rumors surrounding the formation of the West Virginia Optical Glass Co. in Wheeling.

The New Martinsville Board of Trade held its first annual banquet in mid-April, 1902, at the Brast Hotel. The group convened first at the home of board president Jacob Koontz, who was also a member of the board of directors of the glass company. In fact, most of the 40 men in attendance at the banquet were probably stockholders of the New Martinsville Glass Manufacturing Company, and a number were officers of the concern. The *Wetzel Republican* (April 21, 1902) mentioned that a "splendid display" of glassware graced the center table in the Brast Hotel's dining room. After the meal "coffee and cigars appeared," and Frank W. Clark, who was vice-president of the Board of Trade and president of the New Martinsville Glass Manufacturing Company, "told of the fine plant possessed by the Glass Company, of the high character of the men at the head of its departments, and of the splendid business which it had built up in less than one year ...." Glass company vice-president Samuel R. Martin also spoke, as did the firm's manager, James W. Collins.

## PRESSED PATTERN GLASS, 1901-1907

For the first seven years of its life, the New Martinsville Glass Manufacturing Company depended upon pressed pattern glass for much of its financial success, although Webb's Muranese ware, which is discussed later in this chapter, contributed greatly to the firm's growing reputation. Fortunately for today's glass collectors, the company's patterns were generally well-advertised, often with illustrations, in such trade publications as *Crockery and Glass Journal* or *China, Glass and Lamps*. In addition to these important materials, three other sources are available to document products made during this period: a billhead from April, 1902; an unillustrated "Net Price List" issued by the firm in January, 1903; and a large company catalogue from 1904. A few glass articles are illustrated in catalogues from major wholesale

houses, such as Butler Brothers and G. Sommers & Co.

The company introduced a wide array of patterns, and many of them were decorated with gold and/or ruby-stain. Heacock thought that the New Martinsville firm may have begun decorating operations in 1905 or 1906, but the Net Price List from 1903 mentions gold band tumblers and pattern No. 600 with gold decoration, as well as tumblers and vases in decorated (probably hand-painted) opal glass. The 1904 company catalogue shows gold-decorated articles as well as the No. 600 line with an attractive hand-painted floral decoration. This section will discuss the pattern lines known to have been introduced between 1901 and 1907.

The Millers obtained their copy of the billhead to Josephus Clark (see next page) from the archives of the Viking Glass Company, the modern successor to the New Martinsville Glass Manufacturing Company. Few factory records seem to have survived the March, 1907, fire which destroyed the plant, so this billhead is a valuable record, indeed. Clark was a well-known merchant in New Martinsville, since his large store was located in town, and he advertised regularly in the various newspapers which served Wetzel County.

Several glass colors are mentioned: Venetian (once abbreviated "Ven."), Muranese, Blue, Ruby, and Turquoise. The #150 water set is the lone entry for ruby, and the wholesale price for a dozen sets ($8.50) is $1.00 more than the other colors listed for these sets on the first line. This price differential suggests that the ruby is indeed ruby glass made from a formula containing gold, for such ware was typically more expensive than other colors. The #155 molasses jugs are called "Opalescent," but this likely refers simply to flint opalescent glass rather than to colored ware. The articles for which color is not mentioned are surely crystal glass, and some are further described as "stain" or "stained" (presumably, both terms refer to ruby-stain). The entry "Dec." means decorated ware, probably crystal glass with gold rims or edges. Some shapes are also mentioned, such as "Flared" and "Sqr." (square).

On October 30, 1902, James W. Collins applied for a design patent on what was to become the New Martinsville firm's "Rock Crystal" line (collectors today often call this line Floral Panel). Collins described the ware as "having a body provided with vertically-extending curved panels or

THE New Martinsville GLASS MFG. CO.

PRESSED AND BLOWN GLASSWARE, LAMPS ETC.

NEW MARTINSVILLE, W. VA. *Apr. 28 1902*

SOLD TO *Josephus Clark,*

TERMS | 60 DAYS NET OR 2 % OFF IF PAID IN 30 DAYS.

*City*

| | |  | | | |
|---|---|---|---|---|---|
| 1 | 1/6 | Doz. #150 Water Set Ven. Crys & Blue | 7.50 | 1 | 25 |
| | 1/6 | " #700 Finger Bowls, Muranese | 3.00 | | 50 |
| | 1/6 | " 700 " Venetian | 1.85 | | 30 |
| | 1/12 | " #700 Berry Set Muranese | | 1 | 13 |
| | 1/2 | " #200-8" Berry | .70 | | 35 |
| | 1/4 | " #200-8" " Stain | .95 | | 24 |
| | 1 | " #200-4½" " Gro. 1.90 | | | 16 |
| | 1 | " #500-4½ | .30 | | 30 |
| | 1 | " #150 Custards | .50 | | 50 |
| | 1/2 | " #400-7" Berry | .75 | | 37 |
| | 1/2 | " #400-8" Berry | 1.06 | | 53 |
| | 1 | " #400-4" " Gro. 2.75 | | | 23 |
| | 1 | " #400-4½" " " 3.25 | | | 27 |
| | 1/2 | " #72 Soda | .45 | | 23 |
| | 1/2 | " #73 " | .40 | | 20 |
| | 1/2 | " #74 " | .40 | | 20 |
| | 1/2 | " #150 Water Set Ruby | 8.50 | 4 | 25 |
| | 3 | " Corn Tumbs asst. 57 & 63 | .18 | | 54 |
| | 2 | " #51 Tumbs | .37 | | 74 |
| | 1 | " 60 " | .37 | | 37 |
| | 1/6 | " #600 Jugs | 2.60 | | 43 |
| | 1/6 | " #600 " Tank | 2.75 | | 46 |
| | 1 | " | .23 | | 28 |
| | 1 | " Stain | 2.35 | 1 | 17 |
| | 1/6 | " #600 Nut Bowls | .90 | | 15 |
| | 1/6 | " #60 Mol. Jugs Turquise N.S. | 1.00 | | 17 |
| | 1/6 | " #155 Mol. Jug Opalescent | 1.25 | | 20 |
| | 1/6 | " #200 Jugs | 1.30 | | 21 |
| | 1/6 | " #600 Berry Florid | .90 | | 15 |
| | 1/6 | " #600 Crimpled Berry | .90 | | 15 |
| | 1/6 | " #600-7" | .90 | | 15 |
| | 1/6 | " #600-7" " Sqr. | .90 | | 15 |
| | 1/6 | " #400-8" " Sqr. Dec. | 3.00 | | 50 |
| | 1 | " #400-4½" | .80 | | 80 |
| | 1 | " #400-7" Berry Set Dec. | 7.30 | 7 | 30 |
| | 1 | " #63 Tumb asst Dec. | .40 | | 40 |
| | 1/6 | " #600-7" Berry Set Dec. | 7.30 | 1 | 21 |
| | 1/12 | " 600-Nut Bowl Dec. | 1.65 | | 14 |
| | 1 | " #54 S & P. Dec. Gro. | 5.25 | | 48 |
| | 1/2 | " A Lamps | .90 | | 45 |
| | 1/8 | " B " | 1.10 | | 56 |
| | 1/2 | " C " | 1.35 | | 67 |
| | 1/2 | " D " Sewing | 1.65 | | 83 |
| | 1/6 | " D " Stained | 1.25 | | 29 |
| | 1/6 | Doz. C Lamp Stained | 1.45 | | 24 |
| | 1/6 | " B " " | 1.20 | | 20 |
| | 1/6 | " A " " | 1.00 | 17 | 30 50 |

This billhead, dated April 28, 1902, reveals many New Martinsville products.

columns with ornamental designs in intaglio or sunken in the glass." This technique was in contrast to much American pattern glass of the times, wherein patterns were typically raised from the surface. The phrase "rock crystal" was well-known in the Stourbridge area of England at this time, and several firms there produced items whose graceful floral motifs might have been Collins' inspiration (see Charles Hajdamach's excellent book, *British Glass, 1800-1914*, esp. pp. 234-248).

Collins' design patent (#36,170) was granted on December 16, 1902, and illustrated ads for Rock Crystal began to appear. The pitcher was shown in a December, 1902, issue of *Crockery and Glass Journal*, and an individual cream and "cup custard" were shown in early 1903. In July, 1903, *Crockery and Glass Journal* quoted an optimistic J. W. Collins as follows: "I see nothing to interrupt us in having a fall trade of unusual proportions. Never have we known such prosperity as we have now, everyone is engaged at good wages, which means consumption of an enormous volume of both the fancy and staple lines of ware, so I cannot but think the coming season will be a record breaker" (July 25, 1903). The *Journal* also disclosed that "orders to the amount of $50,000 remained unfilled at the close of last fire," a clear indication of the firm's success.

This ad appeared in *Crockery and Glass Journal* (February 5, 1903).

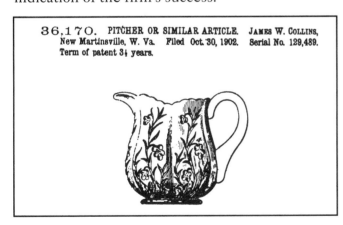

Design patent for New Martinsville's Rock Crystal line.

An ad in the December, 1903, Holiday Number of *Crockery and Glass Journal* alluded to "many new articles in Rock Crystal" without elaboration. The 1904 company catalogue featured the pitcher on its cover (see p. 93), and the line was available in crystal, in crystal with "Heavy Gold Edge" (designated No. 6), or decorated with all-over gold (designated No. 49; see p. 97). The all-over gold deco-

ration was introduced in early 1904, and the New Martinsville firm had this to say about it in the January 16, 1904, issue of *Crockery and Glass Journal*: "Our Rock Crystal Line has been much enlarged and improved since put on the market a year ago; and as the beautiful Rock Crystal cuttings are becoming more popular with the few who are able to buy this very artistic but expensive class of ware, so will this remarkable production in pressed glass become more appreciated."

In January, 1903, the New Martinsville Glass Manufacturing Company had issued an unillustrated, twenty-page "Net Price List" which featured "crystal and fancy colored table glassware, lamp, gas electric shades, etc." Several pages were devoted to the common beer mugs, goblets, soda tumblers and inkwells made by many American firms, but the rest of the price list records the various patterns then available to the wholesale buyer. Pattern lines were typically identified only by number, of course, and the following were listed (today's popular collector's names are given in parentheses): No. 200 (Beaded Diamond; see

Kamm 7, p. 37); No. 400; No. 500 Wetzel (Star of David); No. 600; and No. 800. Some 21 pieces in the Rock Crystal line were also available.

In addition to the pattern lines noted in its 1903 Net Price List, the New Martinsville Glass Manufacturing Company also offered "blown water sets" in crystal, blue and green as well as an extensive line of lamps with plaster collars. Condiment articles, such as molasses cans and salt/pepper shakers, were available in opal glass and turquoise. Lighting shades for both electric and gas fixtures were being made in crystal, cora-line and opal glass, and the crystal shades were apparently available with ruby stain.

In late 1903, the New Martinsville firm's pattern No. 100 (Celtic) made its debut [see Figs. 166 and 277-278]. A reporter from *China, Glass and Lamps* visited the company's display: "The new line of the New Martinsville Glass Co., No. 100, is a figured one, in cut effect. Vertical rows of diamonds with line through centre, in imitation of light cutting, give it a pleasing effect. It is shown in crystal and heavy gold decorations" (January 14, 1904). A full page notice in *China, Glass and Lamps* appeared in December, 1903, featuring four pieces of No. 100. Another full page ad in *Crockery and Glass Journal* showed both No. 100 and Rock

TO THE TRADE:

With many thanks for the liberal patronage extended to us during 1903, we beg to announce that we have added many new articles in Rock Crystal, greatly extended our line of Hotel and Bar Tumblers and Goblets, and added a complete new line of Tableware, after style of light cut, light in weight, symmetrical in shape, and when made in the popular New Martinsville Crystal (diamonds cut to order) the effect is very pleasing.

MURANESE WARE, "the ware that made us famous," will be made in a number of new effects.

We will occupy during January, 1904, Room No. 11, first floor, Monongahela House, Pittsburg, Pa. All buyers are requested to call.

With Compliments of the Season.

## The New Martinsville Glass Mfg. Co.

**The first ad for the No. 100 line (December, 1903).**

Crystal, and No. 100 was described as "in imitation of the light dainty cutting now so popular with lovers of cut glassware" as well as "remarkably low in price."

In 1904, the New Martinsville firm issued a comprehensive catalogue of more than 70 pages. Through the courtesy of the Corning Museum of Glass, many pages from this catalogue are presented in the color section of this book (see pp. 93-100). The first 12 pages of the catalogue are given over to the sorts of staple goods that were made by many early twentieth-century glasshouses—soda tumblers, common tumblers, water tumblers, beer mugs, and various kinds of plain goblets. Some of these staples were also advertised in trade publications. Two "pressed bell sodas" were illustrated in the March 12, 1903, issue of *Crockery and Glass Journal*, and the firm invited buyers to inquire about its "full line of Table and Hotel tumblers, ground bottom, fire-polished with natural gas."

As one might expect, New Martinsville's Rock Crystal line is well-illustrated in the 1904 catalogue. About a dozen pages are devoted to Rock Crystal, including decoration No. 6, a "Heavy Gold Edge" and decoration No. 49, an unusual all-over gold treatment (see p. 97 and Figs. 43-44, 46 and 48). The No. 49 decoration on Rock Crystal must have been popular for some time, for the January 14, 1906, issue of *China, Glass and Lamps* made mention of it. The Rock Crystal spooner and celery holder moulds were also utilized to produce a series of swung vases, including one listed as No. 3, which measured 21" tall [see Fig. 45 for a vase in salmon].

Perhaps the most important aspect of this 1904 catalogue for today's collector is its decorated ware. In addition to the treatments on Rock Crystal described above, the catalogue shows the No. 600 with No. 43 gold decoration (see p. 98) as well as an attractive floral motif in red and green with blue bands, which is designated "Decoration No. 20" (see pp. 98-99). No. 100 (Celtic) is shown with gold decoration (see p. 97), although it is not numbered. Likewise, both the No. 200 line and berry dishes in the No. 400 line are shown with gold decoration.

About a quarter of the 1904 New Martinsville Glass Manufacturing Company catalogue was devoted to lighting goods of various kinds. These range from stand lamps in different lines (No. 100, No. 120, No. 200, No. 600 and No. 800) to hand lamps, night lamps, and electric and gas shades.

Some of the stand lamps were well-decorated (see p. 99). Night lamps were shown in pink, salmon and Turquoise (see p. 100). Among those identified by the Millers were Swirl Rib [see Fig. 36] and Flowering Vine [see Figs. 38 and 42]. No. 800 is now called By-the-Sea [see Figs. 37, 39 and 41 as well as the back cover]. Several of these motifs were also used for hand lamps in crystal [see Figs. 272-273]. Electric and gas shades were produced in a variety of colors, although not all were illustrated (see p. 100). Several plain hand lamps, designated No. 250, were also available at this time, although they were not illustrated in this catalogue.

**The New Martinsville Glass Manufacturing Company.**
Mr. Fisher, of the New Martinsville Company, is displaying a lot of things in his sample rooms this year. The Muranese ware which I always connect in my mind with that particular factory, and rightly so, Mr. Fisher tells me, is still making good. A new effect in the ware in blue and brown has been introduced into the dome shades of which there is an interesting array, and bon bons, pin trays and salad bowls appear in the ware.

**D. FISHER.**

Mr. Fisher's new line of general tableware is christened the "Wetzel," which is in heavy imitation cut and includes some vases larger than any put out before by the factory in a similar line. An entirely new decoration of gold and engraving on an older one makes practically a new line. In the lamps, the "locked on collar" is a new and desirable feature.

*China, Glass and Lamps* **carried this account of New Martinsville glass and a sketch of David Fisher in its January 14, 1905, issue.**

In January, 1905, the New Martinsville Glass Manufacturing Company displayed yet another new line of crystal pattern glass at Pittsburgh's Monongahela House hotel. The line was given both a number, No. 500, and a name, Wetzel, obviously derived from the firm's home county in West Virginia. *China, Glass and Lamps* (January 14, 1905) described No. 500 Wetzel as "heavy imitation cut," and a full page ad said the ware "is NOT CUT although you may think it is when you see it." A line of plain lamps with "locked collars" was also shown at this time.

By mid-spring, 1906, assortments of the No. 500 Wetzel line were appearing in Butler Brothers catalogues. These consisted of berry set, table set and water set and were available either plain or with gold decoration. Within a few months, the gold-decorated sets were offered by G. Sommers & Co., too. Some articles in this pattern were produced for quite a few years, and others were added to the line. These were offered in conjunction with assortments of later products; readers should consult the index for references in later chapters of this book [see also Figs. 257-259].

**Butler Brothers catalogue (Mid-Spring, 1906).**

The success of the firm's pattern glass lines and other wares is captured in the August, 1905, issue of *Glass and Pottery World*, which carried this interesting bit of news:

*The New Martinsville Glass Manufacturing Company has declared a 6 per cent dividend and could have made it larger if desired. This company well deserve all the success which has come to it. No man in the trade has worked harder than J. W. Collins, and he has developed a genius for patents and a taste in original designs unexpected even to his many loyal friends. E. D. Mooney and his associates in the factory have also been very much alive. The company has made good in every way and the trade will continue to look to them for new ideas in glassware, confident that they will not be disappointed.*

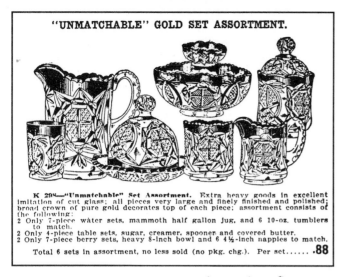
Nonetheless, James W. Collins resigned from the company in October, 1905, and went into business for himself, starting a store in Washington, Pennsylvania. The November, 1905, issue of *Glass and Pottery World* reported that veteran glassman David W. Baird, formerly of the Riverside Glass Co. in Wellsburg, had assumed the post of secretary of the New Martinsville Glass Manufacturing Company. Collins' venture into storekeeping apparently proved unsuccessful, and he returned to the glass trade at the Mound Valley Glass Company in Kansas (*Glass and Pottery World*, October, 1906).

The December 21, 1905, issue of *China, Glass and Lamps* both introduced Baird and lauded the firm's two new pattern glass lines:

*The New Martinsville, W. Va., Glass Co., now under the management of D. W. Baird, will display in rooms 156 Monongahela House two new tableware patterns and a large variety of attractive specialties. The new patterns are both figured—one heavy imitation cut, rich and massive, the other light figured—both of an excellent character for different classes of trade. Mr. Baird is at home in the regular tableware trade, and the company will undoubtedly achieve success under his efficient management.*

The imitation cut pattern is No. 700 (Pleated Oval) and the other is No. 88, which also had an original name, Carnation. The two new patterns were advertised together in the trade journals during the first several months of 1905. By March, 1906, No. 700 was no longer featured in the firm's ads, but No. 88 Carnation was prominently featured in several publications. Not surprisingly, items in No. 700 seem relatively scarce today, but No. 88 Carnation is well known to collectors.

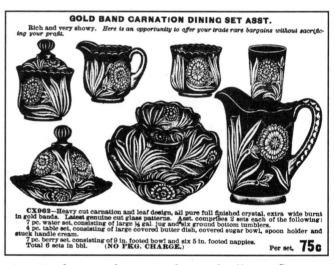
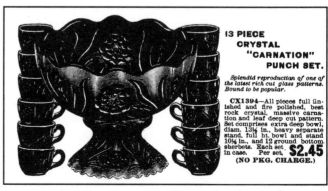

# THEY CAN'T BE BEATEN!

No. 88 Water Set.

For originality and quality our two new water sets are the trade getters of 1906.

Look at them and judge for yourself.

No. 88 Water Set.

In th epast our water sets have always attained a distinct popularity. This year's are better than ever.

Let Us Send You a Trial Order.

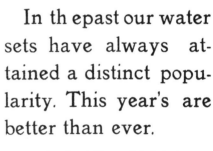

No. 700 Water Set.

No. 700 Water Set.

# NEW MARTINSVILLE GLASS MFG CO. NEW MARTINSVILLE, · W. VA.

**From *China, Glass and Lamps* (March 31, 1906).**

## GOLD CARNATION TUMBLER.

*Big special 10 center, easily worth 15c.*

**CX196**—Large full size, brilliant full finished crystal, rich deep cut floral design, 1¼ in. burnt in gold band top, ground and polished bottom. 1 doz. in box. Per dozen, **78c**

## CRYSTAL "CARNATION" TOOTHPICK HOLDER.

*Will be a fine seller if offered at 5c.*

**CX506**—Tall footed shape, fancy deep cut floral pattern, cut star bottom, clear bright finished crystal, ht. 2¾ in. 1 doz. in box. Per dozen, **35c**

## 5-IN. FOOTED FANCY DISH.

*Very latest gold carnation design.*

**CX732**—Deep 5 in. round footed shape, 1¼ in. wide burnt in gold band scalloped edge, heavy cut floral design, full finished and firepolished. 1 doz. in box. Per dozen, **78c**

**Butler Brothers catalogue (Fall, 1906).**

In its Fall, 1906, wholesale catalogue, the Butler Brothers mail order house featured New Martinsville's No. 88 Carnation among the "September Bargains in Glassware & Crockery." Berry sets, table sets and water sets were available

**CRYSTAL CARNATION SETS for the Dining Room.**
*Entirely new design, first quality ware. Quick sellers. Excellent imitation of the expensive cut glass.*

**CX939**—Massive rock crystal pattern, rich heavy cut carnation and leaf design all pieces full finished. Asst. comprises 3 sets each of the following:
7 pc. water set, consisting of large ½ gal. jug and six ground bottom tumblers,
4 pc. table set, consisting of large covered butter dish, covered sugar bowl, spoon holder and stuck handle cream,
7 pc. berry set, consisting of 9 in. footed bowl and six 5 in. footed nappies.
Total 9 sets in bbl. (NO PKG. CHARGE) Per set, **41c**

**Butler Brothers catalogue (Fall, 1906).**

in crystal and crystal with gold decoration. The tumblers and sauce dishes could be had with gold decoration for 78 cents per dozen, and toothpicks in crystal [see Fig. 291] were 35 cents per dozen! A punch set—footed bowl plus a dozen cups—was offered in crystal.

By early 1907, No. 88 Carnation was being decorated with both ruby-stain and gold on the same article. Many such pieces can be found, and the combination is very attractive, indeed [see Figs. 118-124 and 201]. This combination of gold decoration and ruby-stain was also used on later New Martinsville pattern lines. Occasionally, an item in No. 88 Carnation may be found with amber stain, but these pieces are scarce, indeed [see front cover]. The January 14, 1906, issue of *China, Glass and Lamps* had carried a mysterious reference to the New Martinsville's "Red Raven Split" decoration. This is surely ruby-stain and could refer to the ruby/gold combination found on the No. 88 Carnation line.

In July, 1906, the New Martinsville firm introduced the first of a long series of patterns designated with numbers in the 700s. According to *China, Glass and Lamps* (August 25, 1906), "The New Martinsville, W. Va., Glass Mfg. Co.'s factory is certainly a very busy place. They are running twelve shops, six on each shift, with plenty of orders both for decorated and plain ware. Prospects for a successful season at this plant are very bright."

The new line, No. 702 (Long Leaf Teasel), was shown in full page ads which appeared in the August, 1906, issue of *Glass and Pottery World* and in the August 4, 1906, issue of *China, Glass and Lamps*. No. 702 was available in "plain or decorated." This line seems to have been short-lived, and articles are relatively scarce today [see Fig. 275].

In October, 1906, the company was nearly ready to introduce two more pattern glass lines to the market. No. 704 (Placid Thumbprint) was a relatively plain line, but No. 705 [see Figs. 149-152, 226-228 and 256], which also carried the name Klear-Kut, was a heavy, imitation cut line in the tradition of No. 500 Wetzel and No. 700 (Pleated Oval). No. 704 occurs in crystal [see Figs. 270-271], but the most desirable items are ruby-stained [see Figs. 132, 155-156, 167-168 and 196-199]. No. 704 salt/pepper shakers are known in opal glass, usually with hand-painted decoration [see Figs. 51-52]. Some pieces in this pattern, such

# New Martinsville Glass Manufacturing Company

### New Martinsville, West Virginia

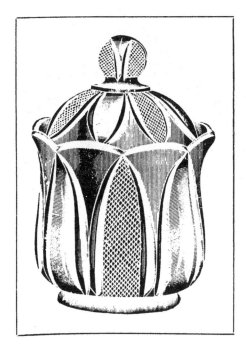

Manufacturers of

### Gold Decorated Tableware

### Lemonade and Water Sets

### Tea Sets, Tumblers

### Goblets and Specialties

## LAMPS PLAIN AND DECORATED

### Night Lamps

### Molasses Cans

### Shakers

### Bar Goods

*Our No. 702 Line of Ware Just Ready for the Market is a Beauty, either Plain or Decorated*

---

**From *Glass and Pottery World* (August, 1906).**

# New Martinsville Glass M'f'g Co.,
## NEW MARTINSVILLE, W. VA.

No. 705 Butter and Cover

No. 705 Sugar and Cover

No. 704 Butter and Cover

No. 704 Sugar and Cover

Full Lines of this ware, both plain and decorated can be seen at the *MONONGAHELA HOUSE, PITTSBURG, Rooms No. 139 and 140* during all the month of *January, 1907.*

From *China, Glass and Lamps* (December 29, 1906).

as berry bowls and articles from the table set, may be marked with a typographically backwards "N" above a block "M", both of which are enclosed in a thin circle.

The October 13, 1906, issue of *China, Glass and Lamps* carried this report on the firm's past success and prospects for the future:

*The New Martinsville Glass Co., New Martinsville, W. Va., are maintaining their reputation in the production of pressed tableware, stemware, tumblers, glass lamps with lock collars, and some lines, we believe, that are not made by any other firm. They have largely increased facilities, and besides turning out great quantities of ware decorated in colors and gold the distinctive feature at this institution is the peerless Muranese ware in which many beautiful patterns are produced. Their 702 line which came out in July has met with surprising favor. Their two latest lines 704 and 705 that will [sic] be out at the first of the year stand equally high in beauty and finish. They will also produce a handsome line of German beer mugs with covers. One 12-pot furnace and two day tanks are being operated.*

The German mug was futher described in the November 10, 1906, issue of *China, Glass and Lamps*: "The cover of the stein is transparent, being made of glass, upon which the initials of the owner of the mug is inscribed. The mugs are made in barrel shape and make an attractive article."

When they were displayed in January, 1907, at the Monongahela House, the two new patterns, No. 704 and No. 705 Klear-Kut, made quite an impression upon the trade press. The writer from *Glass and Pottery World* (January, 1907) described No. 704 as "a good Colonial table line" and said that "no buyer should miss seeing" No. 705 Klear-Kut. The reporter for *China, Glass and Lamps* (January 5, 1907) penned this enthusiastic account:

*The palm for the best imitation cut pattern at this year's exhibit will be awarded by a great many to the New Martinsville Glass Co. David Fisher has a line this year that he can well be proud of and just as eloquent as he likes in praising it without saying a word too much. The No. 705 pattern is pronounced by a great many to be the nearest approach to cut glass yet seen. In every particular has the cut pattern been followed, and so closely has it been copied that there is not a feature that one could mention that would exist in the cut pattern which is not present in the imitation. The line is complete*

*and instead of nappies we find the regulation cut glass bowls, which brings it that much nearer the appearance of the real thing. Another feature which its producers have not overlooked is the weight which they have put into it. Most of the imitation cut glass lines of this year are lighter in weight than formerly, but this one is massive and extremely brilliant. By the way, there has been a new name coined for New Martinsville glass, and it is now known as Klear-Kut. Don't forget it when visiting the displays. There is nothing too strong that can be said in commendation of this line, and while this may sound as rather extreme, the line deserves all of it. This line is shown in plain and also in the gold decorated, for which this company is well known. Hardly less praiseworthy, and some might even say more praiseworthy, is the colonial line of this company's No. 704. This is a wide panel pattern with punty and star effect. To lovers of the colonial style this will appeal without doubt and will make a strong bid with the buying public. ... Mr. Fisher is located on the fourth floor, but if there were no elevators a climb even to the fourteenth story would be worth while.*

Before long, the No. 705 Klear-Kut line was to be found in Butler Brothers catalogues along with No. 88 Carnation. In the spring, 1907, Butler Brothers catalogue, gold-decorated berry sets, table sets and water sets in No. 705 Klear-Kut were offered at 95 cents per set, about a dime more than comparable sets in No. 88 Carnation. There are two varieties of pitchers in No. 705 Klear-Kut. Those which are ruby-stained [see Fig. 150] are plain below the top rim, while those which are gold-decorated have a bit of geometric pattern [see Fig. 152].

A printed *Wetzel County Directory*, which was issued in December, 1906, listed over 50 men under a special heading, "Flint Glass Workers." In similar directories of larger cities and towns, only the most prominent businessmen (store owners, attorneys, druggists, doctors, etc.) were given such recognition. The following list reflects the importance of these workers to the economic wellbeing of New Martinsville:

| | |
|---|---|
| David Baker | Albert Charton |
| W. R. Belford | Frank Cheffy |
| David Baker | R. H. Combs |
| W. R. Belford | G. C. Crimmel |
| J. C. Bess | W. M. Deighton |
| William Bishop | G. W. Elson |
| A. L. Bowers | J. F. Forbes |
| George Bresock | William Forbes |

Henry Fox
Harry France
Michael Gaffney
George Garrett
W. T. Garrett
John Gillett
Cyrus Grandon
John Gruntz
C. F. Hassner
W. D. Hassner
John Herrigan
C. R. Hommell
C. N. Huggins
Jackson Jacobs
Daniel Kavanaugh
M. J. Kavanaugh
Henry Kern
William Kunzler
W. Lamberton
D. L. Lehew
Lewis List

Joseph Medley
E. E. Miller
Frank Miller
George Mooney
W. L. Mooney
S. M. Murry
W. E. McCormick
Carl Nelson
C. W. Oldham
Henry Oneacre
Thomas O'Donnell
G. W. Pegg
Theodore Saladin
C. E. Shurtliff
Howard Shurtliff
G. E. Smith
John Smith
William Smith
Clyde Swaner
Joseph Vickers

## JOSEPH WEBB AND THE MURANESE LINE

The creator of New Martinsville's unique Muranese glass was Joseph Webb (b. March 5, 1852, d. December 29, 1905), an Englishman who emigrated to the United States about 1883, probably with his younger brother, Hugh Fitzroy Webb (1855-1939). Two other men—E. D. Mooney and Martin Kavanaugh—may also have been involved in making various Muranese effects after Webb left New Martinsville in 1904.

The Webbs were sons of the British glass manufacturer Joseph Webb (1813-1869), whose cousin was Thomas Webb, proprietor of the famous Thomas Webb & Sons glassworks in Stourbridge, England. Before joining the fledgling New Martinsville firm in December, 1901, Joseph Webb made a name for himself at other glasshouses in the United States. Much of his work involved various yellow and rose-pink glass formulas.

Joseph Webb was employed at the Phoenix Glass Co. in West Bridgewater, Pa., from 1883 to 1893. The October 11, 1883, issue of *American Pottery and Glassware Reporter* noted that Joseph Webb "is now superintending the manufacture" of finger bowls and gas shades in "plain and crackled glass of every shade and color—blue, green, amber, canary, lemon, citron etc." While at the Phoenix, he patented techniques for making "fancy glassware" (U.S. Patents #345,265 (1886),

#363,190 (1887) and #379,089 (1888)). Webb also registered a design for Ivory finish glass, #17,664 (1887). The March 29, 1893, issue of *China, Glass and Lamps* reported that Webb, "for many years metal maker for the Phoenix Glass Co., ... has resigned to accept a place with the Libbey Glass Co., Toledo, Ohio." Apparently, Webb was engaged to take charge of the Libbey exhibit at the World's Fair in Chicago during 1893.

Webb's employ with Libbey was short-lived. An obituary report (*Crockery and Glass Journal*, January 11, 1906) said that Webb went to Dithridge's Fort Pitt Glass Works in Pittsburgh; the March 8, 1894, issue of *China, Glass and Lamps* noted that Webb was indeed working at the Fort Pitt at that time, crediting him with "making some marvelously beautiful things in colored glass." In April, 1894, this company introduced a color called "Rosina," which shaded "from deep to light rose" (*China, Glass and Lamps*, April 18, 1894). The next mention of Webb in the trade journals is a note in *China, Glass and Lamps* (November 16, 1899) to the effect that he was then with the Tarentum Glass Co. and "making as fine a ware as was ever turned out in the state." At this time, the Tarentum firm was making an opal line called Georgia which came in lemon yellow, pomona green and a deep rose-pink (*Crockery and Glass Journal*, September 21, 1899; *China, Glass and Lamps*, September 28, 1899).

By late 1900, Joseph Webb and Hugh Fitzroy Webb had established the Webb Decorative Glass Works at Coudersport, Pa. In mid-1901, this firm was marketing "Pompei Ware" through the Frank Miller showroom at 25 W. Broadway in New York City. These wares were available "in a variety of shapes with a greenish gold iridescent effect, at surprisingly low prices," according to *Housefurnisher: China, Glass and Pottery Review* (June, 1901). This enterprise did not last long, however, and the Webb brothers looked toward West Virginia. The November 9, 1901, issue of *China, Glass and Lamps* revealed that Webb had submitted a proposal to the board of trade in Sistersville, West Virginia, for a glass plant to be called the Tyler County Glass Company. This project did not materialize.

Webb started in at New Martinsville in December, 1901, replacing Mark Douglass, who had gone to the Cooperative Flint Glass Co. in Beaver Falls, Pa. (*Wetzel Republican*, December 5, 1901, and *China, Glass and Lamps*, December 21,

1901). Within two months, Webb's Muranese line was on the market, a clear indication that he probably revived color effects he had made earlier in his career. Under the headline "New Ware Being Made at the Glass House," the *Wetzel Republican* (February 6, 1902) carried this extraordinary account of Webb's glassware line:

*Saturday, through the courtesy of Mr. Joseph Webb, superintendent of the New Martinsville Glass Manufacturing Company, we were shown the new ware which the company is adding to its line. It does not require a connoiseur to appreciate the beauty and perfection of these goods.*

*The general terms for the ware is opaque, opalescent and iridescent, yet very little conception is gained from these terms. Various color effects are obtained in the ware, ranging from full colors to the most delicate tints and shadings, many of which are changeable in rays of light, and many pieces have the effect of hand decoration.*

*Not only has the company commenced the manufacture of fancy ware, but is extending its line in crystal and also continuing the goods formerly made.*

*It is impossible to convey an idea of the beauty of the ware being made, and the primary and sole object of this article is to interest you sufficiently to inspect the ware yourself. You will find any of the managers of the company willing and pleased to show you around. The result of your visit will be pleasant and instructive to you and also surprising. That is, you will be surprised at the beauty of the ware, the effects in colors and shades. The closest and minutest inspection of the ware heightens its merits and convinces one that in Mr. Webb the company has a superior glassmaker. For several generations past Mr. Webb's ancestors have been engaged in the manufacture of glass in England, where he acquired his knowledge, which he has perfected through study and investigation. He has a reputation which sells the goods made under his supervision.*

*Mr. Webb has just perfected a new ware, which is unrivaled for beauty. The ware has been named "Muranese," and will be made in water sets, finger bowls, berry sets, vases, etc. The outside finish is a dead gold, while the inside is burnished gold of brilliant luster, with iridescent effects. The ware can be made in a variety of colors.*

*To even a casual observer, there has been a decided improvement in the general conduct of the plant, though before it seemed to be almost perfect, and everything argues a very successful business life for the concern.*

In May, 1902, a brief note in *Housefurnisher: China, Glass and Pottery Review* said that Webb's Muranese line rivalled Venetian glassware. In August, 1902, the same trade publication had this to say when comparing New Martinsville's Muranese line to Tiffany glass:

*In the way of novelty, the glass being made by the New Martinsville Glass Mfg. Co., of New Martinsville, W. Va., is one which buyers should not overlook. The artistic effects which their colorer has been able to obtain gives the completed product a distinctive appearance. It resembles in some respects the Tiffany favrile. When made up in electric globes, it possesses the quality of transparency to a marked degree.*

After leaving New Martinsville in 1904, Webb was at the Haskins Glass Co. in Martins Ferry before becoming general manager of the Byesville Glass Company near Cambridge, Ohio. This ill-fated firm, which suffered substantial windstorm damage within a month of its opening in 1901, had originally been known as the American Art Glass Company, so Webb may have been hired to establish its reputation in the art glass field. Unfortunately, Webb died on December 29, 1905, but *China, Glass and Lamps* noted that his "glassmaking receipts have been turned over to Messrs. Schott and Brooks" of the Byesville firm.

The *Wetzel Republican* reported Webb's death on the front page of its January 4, 1906, issue and offered this personal portrait: "Mr. Webb was a very pleasant gentleman. One who had traveled extensively, read much and was an entertaining and versatile talker, and a man who by his gentlemanly and kindly manner made many warm friends, to whom the news of his death will be very sad." An obituary in the *National Glass Budget* called him "a well-known glassmaker," and *China, Glass and Lamps* said he was "a glassmaker without peer and an artist in original designing." *Crockery and Glass Journal* (January 11, 1906) carried this account of his life:

*The remains of Joseph Webb, manager of the Byesville, O., glass Co. were interred Jan. 2 in Woodlawn cemetery, Philadelphia. Mr. Webb's death followed a protracted illness which had its origin in an attack of malarial fever. The deceased was fifty-two years of age and came from Stourbridge, England, where his family had long been famed for its activity in the glass industry. When he reached the United States in 1883, he engaged with Phoenix Glass Co. He left this position to accept a berth with the Fort Pitt Glass Co. Later he removed to Cory, Pa., where he and his brother, Fitz Hugh [sic] Webb, opened a factory. He afterwards signed with the New Martinsville Glass Co. and finally with the Byesville Glass Co.*

Webb's Muranese line was made, in various forms and color effects, from about February, 1902, through March, 1907, several years after Webb had left the firm. An original factory billhead dated April 28, 1902, records that New Martinsville merchant Josephus Clark purchased "1/6 doz. Finger Bowls" in Muranese for fifty cents. The August 21, 1902, issue of *China, Glass and Lamps* called its readers attention to the New Martinsville firm's line of electrical specialties of an iridescent character that are unique and beautiful." These were probably shades from the Muranese line (see Figs. 20-26).

A full-page advertisement in the December, 1903, issue of *Crockery and Glass Journal* called Muranese "the ware that made us famous," and promised "a number of new effects." The January 14, 1904 , issue of *China, Glass and Lamps* noted that the New Martinsville firm had added "many novelties to their Muranese line, which is another of their special attractions." The 1904 New Martinsville catalogue reveals that Muranese ware was then designated as No. 900 and was being made in these colors—pink, salmon and opal. Each of these is illustrated in this book. For salmon, see Figs. 1-3, 6, 11,13, 16-17, 19-21, 33 and the front cover. For pink, see 4-5,10, 12, 13, 22, 25, 27-28, 30-31 and the back cover. For opal, see Figs. 7-9,15, 34, and the back cover. For a discussion of these colors, see p. 92. In January, 1906, *Glass and Pottery World* said that "the Muranese ware, made only by this factory, continues to sell freely. In lamp shades, it represents a class of its own in colored glass."

The Millers noted that there were several other terms used for variations in the Muranese line, such as Sunburst, Sunglow, Sunlite, etc. Among the most interesting is a nearly transparent version called "Sunrise" [see p. 92 and Figs. 23, 28-29, 31 and 34]. The Millers surmised that these names were coined by the workers, but it is interesting to note that the November 10, 1906, issue of *China, Glass and Lamps* mentioned that the New Martinsville Glass Mfg. Co. are having a good run on their "Sunlight" ware ...." Although most of the Muranese ware occurs in opal, pink or salmon, there is some indication that it may have been made in light blue or turquoise, too. The Millers unearthed fragments in blue.

It seems likely that Webb's formula and techniques were passed on to some of the workers at New Martinsville, who may have added innova-

tions of their own after Webb left the firm. In fact, the *Wetzel Republican* (August 8, 1907) reported that Webb "intrusted to Mr. [Martin] Kavanaugh his receipts and formulas for making the different kinds of ware...." Another man, E. D. Mooney, may also have known how to make the Muranese colors. Mooney corresponded with the National Association of Manufacturers of Pressed and Blown Glassware in May, 1903, regarding the costs of making "plated" shades. The implications of this correspondence are that New Martinsville's Muranese ware was relatively expensive to produce in terms of the labor involved and that Mooney sought to reduce costs.

Perhaps the most interesting account of the secrets behind Muranese ware was related by glass researcher Dr. Arthur Peterson, who visited New Martinsville in 1967 and interviewed glassworkers and others whose ancestors had worked at the plant during Webb's time. Peterson wrote an article for *Hobbies* magazine the following year, reflecting stories he had heard to the effect that a worker covertly "drilled a hole in the ceiling" in order to watch Webb at work and learn the ingredients for Muranese ware!

In January, 1907, *Glass and Pottery World* again mentioned "the celebrated Muranese [sic] ware made only by this enterprising concern." Likewise, the January 5, 1907, issue of *China, Glass and Lamps* lauded the Muranese line: "Another distinct feature of the New Martinsville display is the Muranese ware which, as usual, is produced only by them. Mr. Fisher is located on the fourth floor, but if there were no elevators a climb even to the fourteenth story would be worth while."

**GENUINE MURANESE WARE.**

It is impossible to properly describe this ware. Pure gold and silver melted together form the basis of the gloss interior finish, which reflects every color in the rainbow. Outside of delicate pink opal glass. **Muranese ware sells on sight—everybody buys it.**

K 2649.

K 2650-1.

K 2649—Muranese Bonbon or Rose Bowl. 7½ inches in diameter; 2¾ inches deep; heavily crimped edges; iridescent interior; very useful for candies or flowers. Per doz.................. 4.90
K 2650—Muranese Small Fruit or Bonbon. Diameter 8¾ inches; depth, 2½ inches; crimped edges; iridescent; an ornament for any home. Doz.. 5.35
K 2651—Muranese Fruit or Salad Dish. Extra size; diameter, 11 inches; greatest depth, 3½ inches; a very showy piece and one that will command attention. Per doz..................... 8.75

**G. Sommers & Co. catalogue (1908).**

Although some Muranese ware is shown in a 1908 G. Sommers & Co. catalogue, it seems reasonable that the fire of March 17, 1907, marked the end of its production in New Martinsville. The pieces offered by the Sommers firm (crimped bon-bons, fruit dishes etc.) were quite expensive in comparison to other "art" glassware then being advertised.

The 1904 New Martinsville catalogue features salts in "Crystal, Opal, Blue, Salmon, Green (and) Pink," and Turquoise is also mentioned (see p. 94). Most of these had original factory numbers in the 50s or 60s. The Millers identified a plain blown shaker as No. 52; these are well-known in opal glass, and there are numerous hand-painted decorations [see Figs. 49-50 and 61-62]. Another often-seen shaker, popularly called Curved Body, was made in opal glass as well as other opaque colors [see Fig. 67]. The opal examples are decorated in various ways, typically with an elaborate "S" or "P" [see Figs. 63-66, 68, and 70-71] or a simple floral motif [see Fig. 69].

C316—Tall shape with wide base, fancy floral fired decorations forming letters "S" and "P," heavy cast plated tops. Per dozen, 84c

C316, 84c Doz.

**Butler Brothers catalogue (Fall, 1906).**

Many of the following shakers from the 1904 catalogue are shown in this book [see pp. 101-102], and today's popular collector's names are given here in parentheses: No. 53 (Scroll Two Band; see Figs. 103-107); No. 54 (Palmette Band; see Figs. 80-85); No. 55 (Many Petals; see Fig. 58); No. 56 (Curly Locks; see Fig. 60); No. 57 (Vining Rose; see Figs. 98-102); No. 58 (Creased Waist; see Figs. 72-79); No. 61 (Rose Viking; see Figs. 92-94); No. 62 (Vine with Flower; see Figs. 86-91); No. 63 (Tall Aster; see Figs. 108-111); and No. 69, which has yet to be identified. Another shaker, Pillar and Flower [see Figs. 95-97], is known to have been made at New Martinsville through the Miller's fragments, although an original number or name has not yet been ascertained. Still others occur in Webb's characteristic New Martinsville colors but have been named by previous writers; among these are Rose Relievo [see Figs. 53-54] and Leaf Drooping [see Figs. 55-57].

According to the 1904 company catalogue, dec-

orated molasses cans (see p. 95) were made in opal glass as well as pink and salmon [see back cover]. Turquoise and the latter three colors were also used for a line of night lamps (see p. 100). Molasses cans were also made in crystal [see Fig. 274].

Electric and gas shades were made in a variety of colors, including coraline, pink opaque, salmon opaque, and ruby; some of these were probably etched, too (see p. 100). The April 23, 1902, billhead had mentioned both Venetian and Blue as well as a water set in Ruby and molasses jugs in Turquoise and Opalescent. Webb was probably responsible for all of these colors during his tenure at the New Martinsville firm.

**FLOOD AND FIRE**

Glass factories located along the Ohio River were always concerned about flooding, especially in the early spring when snow melting in the mountains and/or heavy spring rains often caused the river to overflow its banks. Every firm feared fire, of course, a calamity seemingly made to measure for a glass house in which the intense heat of glassmaking furnaces and molten glass is in constant proximity to tinder-dry wooden construction as well as potentially volatile chemicals. In mid-March, 1907, the New Martinsville Glass Manufacturing Company suffered a classic "double whammy" when a damaging flood was closely followed by a devastating fire.

In March, 1907, the Ohio River steadily rose to flood levels in many Ohio Valley towns, including New Martinsville. According to the *Wetzel Republican* (March 21, 1907), "the waters were over Main Street and most of the business houses flooded." The newspaper noted that the businessmen were not "seriously crippled," and predicted that "in a few days, [they] will have fully recovered from any damage, which, after all is more or less of a temporary nature." The ultimate impact on the glass factory was far more profound.

On Sunday morning March 17, 1907, the New Martinsville Glass Manufacturing Company's plant was destroyed by fire. Most accounts of the blaze reported that flood waters had come into contact with unslaked lime, a chemical used in glassmaking which generates enough heat when wet to cause combustion. The *Wetzel Republican* (March 21, 1907) carried a long story under the headline "Flood and Fire Destroy Property!" and the *Wetzel Democrat* (March 22, 1907) had these vivid details:

From the *Wetzel Republican* (March 21, 1907).

*Sunday morning, when practically the entire city was under water, fire broke out in the plant of the New Martinsville Glass Company, the principal industry of the city, and the entire building was destroyed. Nothing remained but the huge stack of the furnace which, outlined against the charred remains, told of a loss of between $40,000 and $50,000. The company carried $29,750 insurance on the building, and once this is secured, work of rebuilding the plant will be immediately commenced. The mould shop, which is a brick structure, stands some distance from the main factory and escaped uninjured. In the building is stored the molds, which represent the biggest part of the plant.*

*The New Martinsville Glass Company gives employment to about 250 people, and is one of the largest glass houses in the state. The city water tanks on Martin hill were allowed to go dry, and there was no water to fight the flames. All through the plant, there were water plugs*

From the *Wetzel Democrat* (March 22, 1907).

*and lines of hose, and had there been a supply of water the fire could have been easily put out and the city's principal industry saved. As soon as it became known that the glass plant was on fire the employees and hundreds of people in skiffs and johnboats went to the scene of the fire and helped to fight it with buckets of water.*

*The fire had gained such a progress and the building being a frame one it was impossible to extinguish the fire and attention was turned to the saving of the nitre house and mould shop, by constantly throwing buckets of water on the buildings.*

*The origin of the fire is said to have been the water coming upon unslacked lime, which set fire to the building. The loss will be greatly felt in many homes in the city, and the former employees will have to secure work in other cities until the plant is rebuilt. Several box cars standing on the B. & O. side tracks were burned.*

*Thomas Mooney, superintendent of the glass plant, had his face badly burned in fighting the flames.*

*New Martinsville can not afford to lose the factory, and should extend aid toward rebuilding it by subscribing at once.*

*The directors have held a meeting and have decided to rebuild the plant.*

Prior to the meeting, the *Wetzel Democrat* (March 29, 1907) told its readers that "the intention of the stockholders to rebuild their factory will be welcome news to the business men and citizens." Funds from insurance coverage and the sale of additional stock helped to finance the new construction, but the glass company also received loans in 1907 and 1908 from the New Martinsville Bank, of which Samuel R. Martin was president.

Construction of a new factory would take several months, of course, but the plants' management was able to gain the cooperation of some concerns in Wheeling for their immediate needs. One of them might have been the South Side firm H. Northwood Company, where former New Martinsville kingpin George Matheny was foreman of the mould room. Apparently, New Martinsville workers were able to take their company's moulds to other plants and to work glass from the furnaces there. This was reported in the April 19, 1907, issue of *Glass and Pottery World*, along with some other particulars:

*Prompt action on the part of the owners of the New Martinsville Glass Manufacturing Co. started work on orders only a few days after their disastrous fire. Their molds were taken care of by three or four glass factories in Wheeling and vicinity and although these competitive plants were crowded with business they generously* help[ed] in getting many orders filled. Rebuilding will soon begin, now that insurance matters have been adjusted. The concern put out some lines this year even more attractive than usual and the same energy and ingenuity which built up a profitable business on goods not made at other plants will serve to quickly re-establish the business.

The *Wetzel Republican* (October 3, 1907) also mentioned that moulds were placed in other factories and noted that "the business of the company has not suffered in any way, and the orders received for fall business has [sic] been the most gratifying in the history of the company." The newspaper also commented that "the class of workmen employed by this company have been good substantial citizens and they have contributed materially to the prosperity and upbuilding of the city."

Despite attempts to maintain production of their popular patterns, the New Martinville Glass Manufacturing Company was unable to keep up with demands from some customers. For example, the Butler Brothers wholesale catalogue for June, 1907, says "Temporarily Out" in its display ads for the No. 88 Carnation line in crystal and with gold decoration. By mid-summer, however, these assortments were again available through Butler Brothers.

In August, 1907, while the plant was being rebuilt, some managerial changes took place within the New Martinsville Glass Manufacturing Company. The *Wetzel Republican* (August 8, 1907) reported that Robert Combs was appointed as manager and Martin Kavanaugh as glass maker, succeeding "Mr. E. D. Mooney, who was manager and glass maker." This article also took particular note of the association of Kavanaugh with the late Joseph Webb, noting that "this friendship became so strong that Webb intrusted to Mr. Kavanaugh his receipts and formulas for making the different kinds of ware, and probably no other man is so well qualified to make the various kinds of glass produced under Mr. Webb's direction as Mr. Kavanaugh."

By October, 1907, the company had placed ads in trade journals announcing the resumption of production in their new building and soliciting orders. Under the headline "FIRST GLASS MADE," the *Wetzel Republican* (October 17, 1907) revealed that "a small force of men were put to work pressing and blowing glassware." The reporter also noted that a large continuous tank

**From *Glass and Pottery World* (October, 1907).**

would be in operation within a few weeks.

The October 31, 1907, issue of the *Wetzel Republican*, headlined "THE NEW GLASS HOUSE," carried a complete account of the resumption of glassmaking operations:

*Saturday we spent a half hour at the plant of the New Martinsville Glass Mfg. Co. It is a plant to be proud of. Out of the ruins of the old plant has grown the new one and it has been a good growth. The new structure is not only imposing from the outside, but the inside presents the same appearance—solid, substantial and commodious. It is a splendid structure in every respect, and the arrangement of the plant will add materially to the increase in the output of the factory as well as to decrease cost of the manufacturing and the handling of the finished goods.*

*At present there are ten shops working, and at the time of the destruction of the plant there was only eleven shops working. When the continuous tank is completed, the factory will have a capacity of 20 pots, the old factory had a capacity of 14 pots. In other words, the new factory has a capacity 48 per cent greater than the old factory. Everything about the factory has been working smoothly; as an illustration, last week 40 pots of glass was made up into finished goods. In the packing department, compartments have been erected for storing goods*

19

*in and other arrangements made which will decrease the cost of handling goods in this department by the facility of packing and avoiding breakage. The etching department will be above the packing depatment and will be more thoroughly equipped than in the old plant. A new gas engine has been installed, though the old one was not injured by the fire, and is now in operation. The new engine was installed for emergencies, as frequently the old factory had to be shut down on account of the engine.*

*Taking everything into consideration, though it worked hardship upon individuals, the destruction of the plant proved a good thing. A better and larger plant has taken place, with modern improvements and means of decreasing cost of operation.*

An ad in the October, 1907, issue of *Glass and Pottery World* mentioned the No. 705 Klear-Kut line and said that the company took "this method of announcing to the Trade that we are now operating our New Factory and doing business at the same old stand." The firm's advertising listed "pressed and blown table and bar glassware, lamps and novelties" as well as "tea sets, lemonade sets, berry sets, stem ware, beer mugs, [and] tumblers." Despite the twin setbacks of flood and fire, the New Martinsville Glass Manufacturing Company was back on its feet.

# CHAPTER TWO
# THE FISHER YEARS

FOR ABOUT A decade (1908-1917), the New Martinsville Glass Manufacturing Company maintained its prominent place in the glass tableware industry. When general manager David Baird resigned in late 1908 ("because of a difference with the directors of the concern" according to the *American Pottery Gazette* for November, 1908), David I. Fisher assumed the post. A longtime stockholder, Fisher had been actively associated with the company since its inception in 1900, holding such positions as assistant superintendent, manager of the packing room, and western salesman.

On September 26, 1910, Fisher's portrait appeared on the cover of an important glass industry trade journal, *China, Glass and Lamps*. According to an article published in the *Wetzel Democrat* (May 25, 1933) after his death, Fisher was born in 1866, and he learned the glass trade in Bellaire and Martins Ferry "as a youth." He lived on Clark Street in New Martinsville and was president of the First National Bank of New Martinsville at the time of his death.

In addition to some surviving company catalogues and price lists as well as the typical trade journal advertising of the firm's products in this period, there are numerous assortments of New Martinsville glassware in Butler Brothers and G. Sommers & Co. wholesale catalogues. Many of these are included as illustrations in this chapter.

There is also a wealth of evidence about New Martinsville's glassworkers. Letters from the secretary of New Martinsville's AFGWU Local Union No. 16 appeared regularly in the *American Flint*, a monthly publication of the American Flint Glass Workers Union. The local union met in New Martinsville on the first Saturday of each month at 1:30 p.m. in the Jr. OUAM room at the Clark Building.

## PATTERN GLASS LINES

Although the plant discontinued making Muranese ware when it resumed operating after the fire of 1907, its focus upon pattern glass sets was unaltered. The 700-series, which had begun before the fire, was continued in earnest as more than a dozen new lines were added. Two patterns

Gold-decorated No. 705 Klear-Kut items from a Mid-Spring, 1907, Butler Brothers catalogue; at 95 cents per set, these were much more expensive than undecorated ware (see below).

Assortment of No. 705 Klear-Kut from the Mid-Summer, 1907, Butler Brothers catalogue.

developed prior to the fire—No. 702 (Long Leaf Teasel), and No. 704 (Placid Thumbprint)—seem to have been dropped from the firm's line, although No. 702 was revived in the early 1920s. Two other patterns, No. 700 (Pleated Oval) and No. 705 Klear-Kut, remained in production for a few years, and assortments were featured in Butler Brothers catalogues throughout 1907 and 1908. More than a dozen pieces of No. 705 Klear-Kut were in the firm's "Price List" for 1917, and a few pieces even appeared in Butler Brothers catalogues in the 1920s (see Chapter Three). Sixteen pages from the 1917 price list are reproduced later in this chapter (see pp. 48-51), and readers can see lists of items in the many patterns made during this period which remained in production.

VOL. XXX

No. 35.

# CHINA GLASS AND LAMPS

SEPTEMBER 26, 1910.

DAVID FISHER,
New Martinsville Glass Mfg. Co.,
New Martinsville, W. Va.

## PITTSBURG, PA.
### A WEEKLY JOURNAL for the BUYER

From *China, Glass and Lamps* (December 28, 1907).

The two new lines introduced in 1908 were No. 707 and No. 708. A two-piece fruit bowl in pattern No. 707 was shown in the firm's ad in the December 28, 1907, issue of *China, Glass and Lamps*. No. 707 is now known as Horseshoe Medallion, but its original name may have been Mauretania, as reported in the January, 1908, issue of *Glass and Pottery World*, which described it as a "heavy imitation cut" pattern. Berry sets, table sets and water sets were produced, as were some other articles, such as an olive dish [see Fig. 161]. The typical gold/ruby-stain decoration is an attractive combination [see Figs. 169-170 and 209-215]. The pattern bears some resemblance to a later New Martinsville line, No. 717 (Horseshoe Daisy), which was introduced in 1912. The only item from the No. 707 line in the 1917 price list is a 6" nappy, which was available in a crimped version and with gold decoration.

The other new line for 1908, New Martinsville's No. 708, was named Lusitania, and it was probably the company's first venture into etched ware. *Glass and Pottery World* said Lusitania was "massive in its simple elegance." The etching, a simple repetitive geometric motif, was known as No. 2306. In all probability, this etching was also available on other New Martinsville products, such as otherwise plain tumblers and bar ware. The No. 708 line was extensive, as berry sets, table sets and water sets were complemented by a wide variety of occasional pieces—water bottle [see Fig. 282], catsup bottle, sherbets, finger bowls, and several sizes of butter tubs. The firm's 1917 price list mentions about 20 articles, so the line must have been in production for quite some time.

No. 708-2—8 oz. Oil. Etched 2306
12 Doz. to Bbl.

**No. 708 Lusitania cruet (note 2306 etching).**

The namesakes for New Martinsville's Lusitania and the Mauritania patterns were sister ships on the British flag Cunard line at the time. The Mauritania, known as the "Grand Old Lady of the Atlantic," held speed records for the Atlantic crossing until the late 1920s. The ocean liner Lusitania was sunk by German submarines on May 7, 1915, an event generally credited with propelling the United States into World War I.

The new patterns which debuted in 1909 were No. 711, which is now known as Leaf and Star, and No. 712, a plain, colonial-style line which collectors today call simply Placid, perhaps because of its similarity to the earlier No. 704 (Placid Thumbprint). The January, 1909, issue of *Glass and Pottery World* said that No. 711 was "copied from a successful cut glass pattern" but did not elaborate.

No. 711 (Leaf and Star) may be found in crystal glass [see Figs. 143 and 265-269], crystal with gold decoration [see Figs. 133-135] or with the gold/ruby-stain combination [see Figs. 129-131, 141-142, 144-145, and 195]. This was an extensive

Most of the items in this Butler Brothers assortment (Fall, 1908) are from New Martinsville's No. 500 Wetzel line, but there is a No. 88 Carnation celery tray in the upper right and, immediately below it, two pieces of No. 700 (Pleated Oval), a celery holder and a berry bowl.

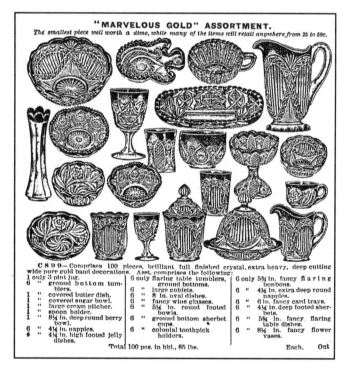

Butler Brothers "Marvelous Gold" assortment (which first appeared in a Fall, 1908, catalogue) included items in several New Martinsville patterns: No. 700 (Pleated Oval); No. 707 (Horseshoe Medallion); No. 500 Wetzel; No. 88 Carnation; and No. 705 Klear-Kut The handled nappy in the top row is pattern No. 800, which is called Heather today. The swung vase at left was probably made from the spooner mould of a colonial line, such as No. 712.

No. 711 items are included in this Spring, 1909 Butler Brothers catalogue, which is otherwise similar to the assortment offered about six months earlier (see below, left).

This Spring, 1909, Butler Brothers assortment contains pieces from the No. 88 Carnation and No. 500 Wetzel lines as well as No. 700 (syrup jug at lower left) and No. 707 (cruet and berry bowl in bottom row).

line, embracing berry sets, table sets and water sets as well as numerous other items—goblets, wines, footed comports in several sizes, salt/pepper shakers, syrup, toothpick holder, etc. The pitcher was produced with a special lip to avoid spilling ice. This pattern remained in production for some time and was revived in the 1920s.

No. 712 (Placid) may have been produced exclusively in crystal, for it has yet to be found in ruby-stain. The No. 712 line was not quite as lengthy as its sister No. 711, but today's collectors can find berry sets, table sets and water sets in addition to a variety of covered bowls and other pieces. Both No. 711 and No. 712 were still in production when the New Martinsville firm issued its 1917 price list.

**No. 711 creamer and covered sugar bowl.**

**No. 712 creamer and covered sugar bowl.**

These No. 711 (Leaf and Star) sets were featured in a Spring, 1909, Butler Brothers catalogue; by December, the price had risen to 85 cents per set. These sets also appeared in catalogues issued by G. Sommers & Co. in 1910.

In January, 1910, two more new patterns were introduced by the New Martinsville firm. These were originally designated by numbers only, but collectors today know No. 713 as Pleated Medallion and No. 714 as Chateau. In keeping with the lines introduced in previous years, No. 713 was somewhat reminiscent of cut glass, while No. 714 was of the colonial order. The January 8, 1910, issue of *China, Glass and Lamps* described the new patterns in considerable detail, including the decorating treatments then available:

*The New Martinsville Glass Mfg. Co., Rooms 541-542, Fort Pitt Hotel, manufacturers of "Klear Cut" glassware, offer two new lines of ware this season, Nos. 713 and 714. The latter is a colonial design made in fancy shapes, and either plain, ruby or gold decorated and it is destined to be one of the most popular sellers, manufactured by the enterprising company. No. 713 is a figured line, also in plain gold and ruby decoration. In addition to these two new lines, they have a nice assortment of etched jugs, tumblers, staples, bar goods, etc. The display is up to the mark in every respect. David Fisher, secretary of the company, is in charge as usual.*

**No. 713 creamer and covered sugar bowl.**

**No. 714 creamer and covered sugar bowl.**

This postcard view of the glass factory was postmarked July 18, 1908.

"OUR LEADER" GOLD BAND DINING SET ASSORTMENT.

*Big, richly decorated sets. A display window and a $1.00 ticket and you'll sell a lot of them.*

1C1667— Extra quality crystal, brilliant finish, massive pattern, large sunburst medallions within prominent framing of intersecting prism bands, all pcs. extra large and with deep burnished gold decorations, on some more than 2 in. wide. Consists of:

2 only 7 pc. water sets—mammoth ½ gal. jug, 6 ground bottom tumblers.
2 " 7 " berry " —8¾ in. extra deep bowl, six 4¼ in. nappies.
2 " 4 " table " —covered butter, covered sugar, spoonholder, creamer.
Total 6 sets in bbl., — lbs. Per set, 69c

These No. 713 (Pleated Medallion) sets appeared in an October, 1909, Butler Brothers catalogue.

"ALL JUMBO" GLASSWARE ASSORTMENT (Crystal)
*Nowhere equaled. You could not show better value on your 10 cent counter.*

1C1571—Big pcs., full finished, majority massive rock crystal design, others deep cut. ½ doz. each:

Mammoth half gal. jug.
8½ in. deep round bowl.
8¼ in. tulip vase.
Ex. large covd. butter.
6 doz. in pkg., — lbs.

Spoonholder.
Creamer.
Covd. sugar.
9¼ in. flared salad.

3 pt. pitcher.
7¼ in. oil bottle.
6 in. nut bowl.
8½ in. deep berry bowl.        Doz. 87c

This assortment (from a June, 1910, Butler Brothers catalogue) included items from these lines: No. 88 Carnation; No. 707 (Horseshoe Medallion); No. 711 (Leaf and Star); and No. 713 (Pleated Medallion).

The No. 713 line [see Figs. 284-286] was relatively modest in size, encompassing berry sets, table sets and water sets, plus a few other items—cruet, celery holder, syrup, toothpick and several sizes of vases. It was made again in the 1920s.

No. 714 (Chateau) must have been among New Martinsville's most ambitious productions, for many different items are to be found in the firm's 1917 price list. Articles are typically crystal, but crystal with ruby-stain does turn up [see Fig. 112]. Of all of New Martinsville's so-called colonial patterns, No. 714 seems to have been the most exten-

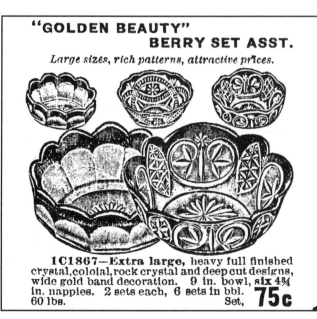

"GOLDEN BEAUTY" BERRY SET ASST.

*Large sizes, rich patterns, attractive prices.*

1C1867—Extra large, heavy full finished crystal, coloial, rock crystal and deep cut designs, wide gold band decoration. 9 in. bowl, six 4¾ in. nappies. 2 sets each, 6 sets in bbl. 60 lbs.        Set, 75c

No. 711 and No. 714 berry sets (Butler Brothers catalogue, June, 1910).

sive and among the most long-lived, for many articles are listed in the firm's 1917 price list. Even a child's set was made [see Figs. 305-306].

The mention of ruby-stain decoration for so many of the above patterns is noteworthy, for the New Martinsville firm was surely one of the most active glass companies in this area. Many New Martinsville motifs were decorated with ruby

These cracker jars in No. 712 (Placid) and No. 30 (Fan in Oval) appeared in an August, 1910, Butler Brothers catalogue.

Three New Martinsville jugs (Butler Brothers catalogue, June, 1910).

No. 711 pitcher with special ice lip (Butler Brothers catalogue, August, 1910).

and/or gold, and the company employed a number of women for this work. Some were listed in the 1910 United States Census of Wetzel County's Magnolia District: Becky Dover, Bertha Fox, Carry List, Inez Long, Rachel Powell, Ivy May Ridge, Emma Smith, Lenora Willson, Ivy Wiltse and Minnie Wiltse. Mary Ridge's occupation was listed as "wiper," and three sisters—Olia, Delia and Callie Chaplin—were selectors at the glass house.

In late July, 1910, the New Martinsville Glass Manufacturing Company was sued by the George G. Garrett Decorating Company (Wetzel County Circuit Court, Rules, case #960). The Garrett firm, which seems to have been composed only of brothers George and Thomas Garrett, sought payment of bills due them as well as $3000 in damages. The case was decided in their favor, but damages were not awarded. Court documents indicate that the Garrett brothers had renovated the glass company's decorating room in 1910 and that they also decorated glassware on a piece work basis. The Garrett brothers apparently did not buy glassware from the company to decorate and resell. Both men were listed as "flint glass workers" in the 1906 *Wetzel County Directory*. Perhaps they later worked as sub-contractors, helping to fill the glass company's orders for decorated ware. Although decorated tumblers are mentioned in the court papers, only one specific pattern, No. 711 (Leaf and Star), was noted.

The New Martinsville company's new pattern lines for 1911 were No. 715 Lenoir and No. 716 Rebecca, although the latter is better known as Japanese Iris to collectors today. Both were featured in full page ads in *Crockery and Glass Journal* (December 29, 1910) and *China, Glass and Lamps* (January 9, 1911). The full-page ad in *Crockery and Glass Journal* made mention of New Martinsville's "come back," an obvious reference to the firm's flood/fire calamity of 1907. The ad in *China, Glass and Lamps* proudly proclaimed "We've Made Good!" Incidentally, the firm's letterhead at this time had the phrase "rebuilt 1907" under a vignette of the plant.

Although No. 715 Lenoir was touted as a "plain or colonial effect line," the motif is certainly regarded as a full-fledged pattern by collectors today. No. 715 Lenoir is usually found with ruby-stain [see Figs. 180-184] or with New Martinsville's characteristic gold/ruby-stain combination [see Figs. 191-194], although pieces do occur in

# We've Made Good!

That's our past record, and we have the ability to "come back." We did a lot of thinking and planning for lines for 1911, and these are two of the results:

**No. 715 "LENOIR."**
Plain or Colonial effect line.

**No. 716 "REBECCA."**
Figured "Iris" floral pattern.

These are only two new propositions we want to tell about here, Mr. Buyer, but as we have reserved three rooms (541-2-3) at the Fort Pitt in January, you can rest assured we have a lot of other good things for you.

Latchstring on the outside—COME IN!

# NEW MARTINSVILLE GLASS MFG. CO.

## New Martinsville, W. Va.

**MR. DAVID FISHER** in charge.

This trade journal ad appeared on December 29, 1910.

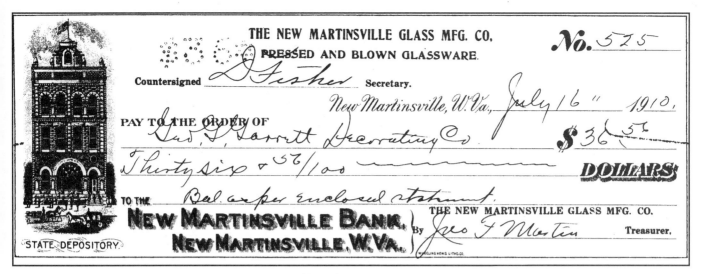

**This check, drawn on the New Martinsville Glass Manufacturing Company's account at the New Martinsville Bank, was for services performed by the George G. Garrett Decorating Co.**

undecorated crystal. The line was apparently short-lived, for only the pitcher and fluted iced tea tumbler are mentioned in the company's 1917 price list.

No. 716 Rebecca was described as a "figured Iris floral pattern," and this has probably given rise to its more popular name, Japanese Iris. The usually found gold/ruby-stain decoration is reminiscent of the earlier No. 88 Carnation, for it virtually covers the article [see Figs. 202-208]. Like No. 715 Lenoir, New Martinsville's No. 716 was probably not a success in terms of sales. The No. 716 puff box was listed in the firm's catalogue of glassware for mounting, but not a single piece of No. 716 appears in the comprehensive 1917 price list.

In early 1912, the New Martinsville Glass Manufacturing Company followed its established practice of introducing yet another pair of new patterns. No. 717, known today as Horseshoe Daisy, is an imitation cut glass motif decorated with ruby and gold, while No. 718 (now called Frontier) is in the colonial style. Both were described in the January 11, 1912, issue of *China, Glass and Lamps*:

"Two lines are being featured this year. No. 717 is a figured pattern, No. 718 possesses a colonial effect. ... The colonial table line is an exceptionally long one. Both lines are to be had in crystal and gold decorated."

No. 717 (Horseshoe Daisy) is reminiscent of the earlier No. 707 (Horseshoe Medallion), although No. 717 is not quite as elaborate. The shapes of

**No. 718 creamer and covered sugar bowl.**

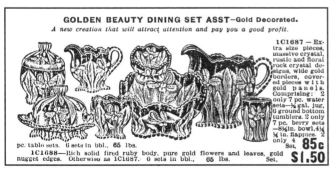

New Martinsville's No. 716 Rebecca was offered in both gold-decorated and the gold/ruby-stain combination in this Mid-Summer, 1911, Butler Brothers catalogue.

**No. 717 creamer and covered sugar bowl.**

handles are, however, nearly identical (compare Figs. 172 and 210). By Mid-Spring, 1912, the No. 717 pitcher was being offered by the Butler Brothers along with pitchers in No. 711 and No. 714 for $2.10 per dozen. As one might suspect, New Martinsville's No. 717 is best known in the gold/ruby-stain combination [see Figs. 125-127 and 171-172]. Berry sets, table sets and water sets are known, but the 1917 price list mentions such items as an ice jug, an olive dish, and a 10" punch bowl with foot.

These three New Martinsviile pitchers—No. 711, No. 712 and No. 717—appeared in the Mid-Spring, 1912, Butler Brothers catalogue.

The 718 (Frontier) line was quite extensive, and many articles are listed in the firm's 1917 price list. Collectors today find items in crystal with ruby-stain [see Figs. 146 and 153-154] or in plain crystal [see Figs. 261-264]. The pitcher appeared alone in a Butler Brothers catalogue for Mid-Spring, 1912, but the No. 718 berry set was combined with sets from the No. 714 line.

The next patterns introduced, probably in late 1912, were No. 719 and No. 720. "Old Glory" was the firm's name to go with the No. 719 line, but some collectors call this pattern Mirror Star today. New Martinsville's No. 720 was originally called Florene. By April, 1913, items from both lines were featured in Butler Brothers catalogues. No.

No. 718 pitcher (Mid-Spring, 1912, Butler Brothers catalogue).

From the Mid-Spring, 1912, Butler Brothers catalogue.

This assortment, from the Mid-Spring, 1912, Butler Brothers catalogue, contains a No. 711 (Leaf and Star) footed comport (center, bottom row) as well as pieces from the No. 713 (Pleated Medallion) and No. 717 (Horseshoe Daisy) lines. The 11" tall swung vase was probably made from the No. 713 spooner mould.

No. 719 creamer and covered sugar bowl.

719 Old Glory was destined to become one of New Martinsville's most popular lines. Assortments appeared regularly in Butler Brothers and G. Sommers & Co. catalogues through 1918, and production was continued in later years as well (see Chapter Three).

No. 719 Old Glory is often found with gold and ruby-stain decoration [see Fig. 115] or with gold decoration [see Figs. 162-165]. The most interesting decoration treatment is a rather crudely-applied green see [Figs. 113-114]. Unfortuately, a production time for this green decoration cannot be ascertained, for it was not featured in any wholesale catalogues. In addition to the berry set, table set and water set in No. 719 Old Glory, several other articles were made, such as the celery holder, a handled custard cup, a handled nappy used for jelly, a jelly comport, a syrup jug or molasses can, a cruet, and salt/pepper shakers.

The No. 720 Florene line occurs in crystal [see Figs. 279-280] as well as gold-decorated crystal [see Figs. 157-158] and crystal with ruby-stain [see Figs 147, and 185-188]. Quite a few pieces appear

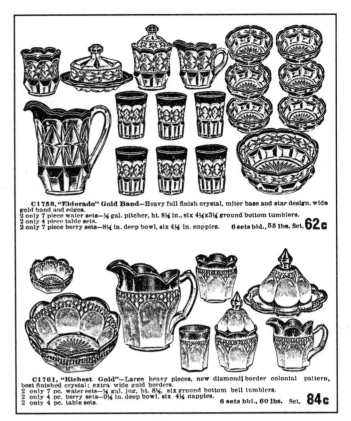

**These No. 719 Old Glory and No. 718 (Frontier) gold-decorated sets are from the Butler Brothers April, 1913, catalogue.**

**New Martinsville's No. 720 Florene was combined with No. 711 (Leaf and Star) in this assortment from an April, 1913, Butler Brothers catalogue. The butterdish on the right is No. 708 Lusitania, but it does not appear to be an etched piece.**

in the New Martinsville company's 1917 price list, so this line must have sold reasonably well and probably remained in production.

The success of these lines was reflected in C. E. Shurtliff's column in the March, 1912, issue of the *American Flint*: "Business is brisk at our plant just now, with expectations for a steady run to the end of the fire. The continuous tank has been in operation some time and is producing better glass than ever." A month later, Shurtliff reported that many glassworkers from Local Union 16 had joined the Loyal Order of Moose, a fraternal lodge which had recently been instituted in New Martinsville. Another member of the family, Howard Shurtliff,

**New Martinsville's No. 720 Florene creamer was shown in this full-page ad in a December, 1912, trade journal.**

This group of men is Howard Shurtliff's cup foot press shop at New Martinsville, c. 1912-13. Shurtliff is seated in the right center; identities of the others are not known. Courtesy of Mr. O. O. Brown.

Only two men have been identified in this photo of glassworkers taken outside the New Martinsville plant. "Polly" Long is standing third from the left, and Howard Shurtliff (in light shirt) is seventh from the left. Courtesy of Mr. O. O. Brown.

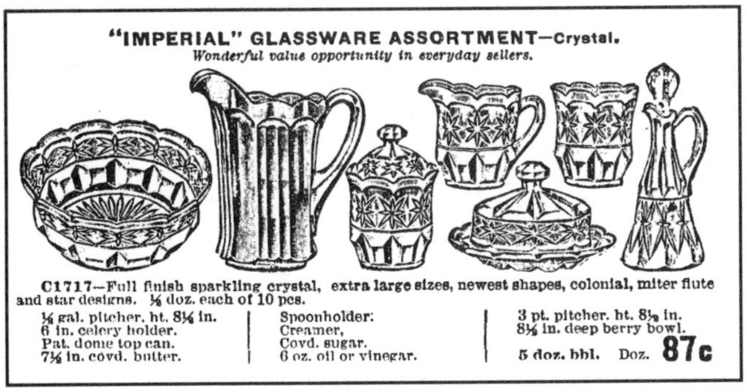
"IMPERIAL" GLASSWARE ASSORTMENT—Crystal.
Wonderful value opportunity in everyday sellers.
C1717—Full finish sparkling crystal, extra large sizes, newest shapes, colonial, miter flute and star designs. 1/6 doz. each of 10 pcs.
1/2 gal. pitcher, ht. 8 1/4 in.
6 in. celery holder.
Pat. dome top can.
7 1/4 in. covd. butter.
Spoonholder:
Creamer,
Covd. sugar.
6 oz. oil or vinegar.
3 pt. pitcher, ht. 8 1/8 in.
8 1/4 in. deep berry bowl.
5 doz. bbl. Doz. 87c

**One of New Martinsville's No. 715 Lenoir pitchers is included with an assortment of No. 719 Old Glory in the April, 1913, Butler Brothers catalogue.**

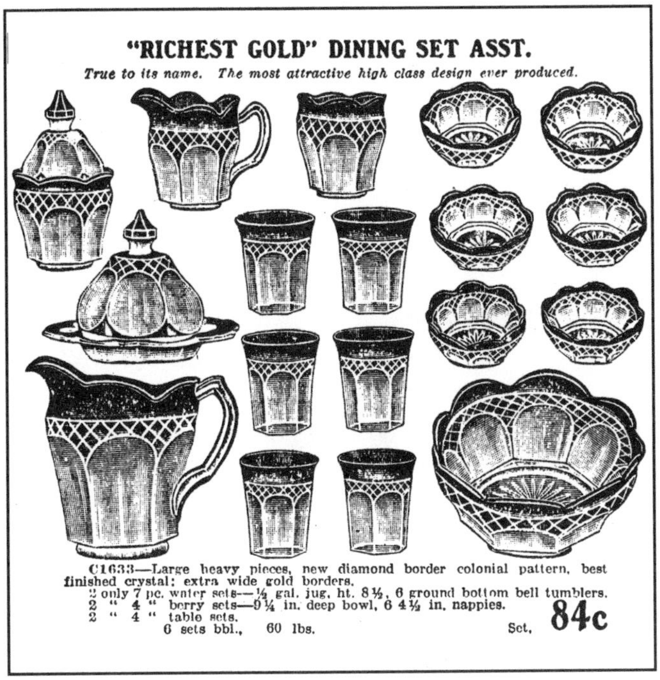
"RICHEST GOLD" DINING SET ASST.
True to its name. The most attractive high class design ever produced.
C1633—Large heavy pieces, new diamond border colonial pattern, best finished crystal; extra wide gold borders.
2 only 7 pc. water sets—1/2 gal. jug, ht. 8 1/2, 6 ground bottom bell tumblers.
2 " 4 " berry sets—9 1/4 in. deep bowl, 6 4 1/2 in. nappies.
2 " 4 " table sets.
6 sets bbl., 60 lbs.
Set, 84c

**Gold-decorated No. 718 (Frontier) articles were featured in this assortment from a Butler Brothers catalogue.**

was a presser at the New Martinsville plant for some years. A skilled glassworker known as a "cup foot" presser, he is pictured in several photographs taken in and around the plant about 1912-13.

The financial success of the New Martinsville Glass Manufacturing Company was also reflected in this article from the July 14, 1913, issue of *China, Glass and Lamps*:

*That the New Martinsville Glass Co., New Martinsville, W. Va., is in a prosperous condition was evidenced recently when the stockholders received notice that a dividend of 7 per cent had been declared and that dividend checks would be mailed out promptly. The company's stock has been advancing by leaps and bounds until now it is considerably above par, and is much in demand in the market. The factory is one of the*

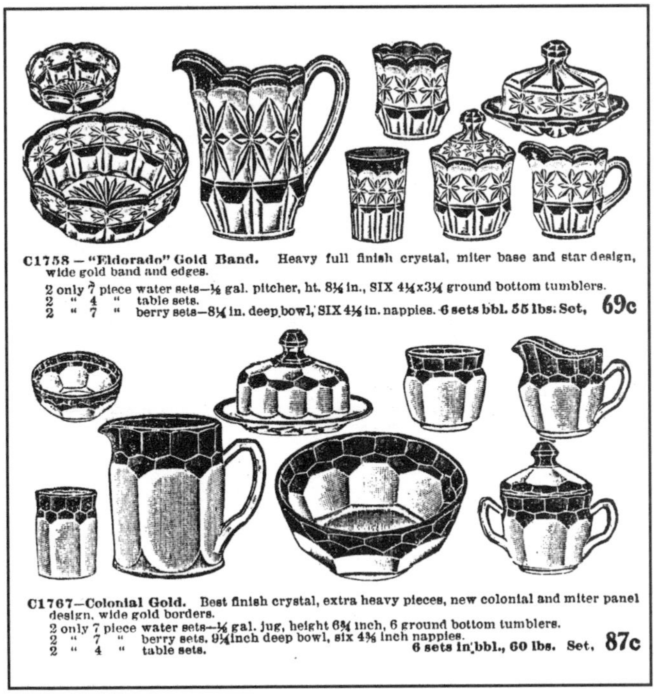
C1758 — "Eldorado" Gold Band. Heavy full finish crystal, miter base and star design, wide gold band and edges.
2 only 7 piece water sets—1/2 gal. pitcher, ht. 8 1/4 in., SIX 4 1/4x3 1/4 ground bottom tumblers.
2 " 4 " table sets.
2 " 7 " berry sets—8 1/4 in. deep bowl, SIX 4 1/2 in. nappies. 6 sets bbl. 55 lbs. Set, 69c
C1767—Colonial Gold. Best finish crystal, extra heavy pieces, new colonial and miter panel design, wide gold borders.
2 only 7 piece water sets—1/2 gal. jug, height 6 3/4 inch, 6 ground bottom tumblers.
2 " 7 " berry sets, 9 1/4 inch deep bowl, six 4 3/8 inch nappies.
2 " 4 " table sets.
6 sets in bbl., 60 lbs. Set, 87c

**These No. 719 Old Glory and No. 720 Florene gold-decorated sets are from the Butler Brothers April, 1913, catalogue.**

*most complete and best equipped flint plants in the country and has been the chief industry of New Martinsville for several years. The company's ware now finds a market in almost every large city in the United States.*

Apparently, the plant was damaged by early summer flooding on the Ohio River in 1913. New Martinsville glassworker Frank Edmonds reported in the August, 1913, issue of the *American Flint* that the factory had been closed for ten days: "... The last flood gave things here quite a setback for a while, owing to putting out the fires in the entire plant and breaking all the pots in the furnaces. The water got so deep on the factory floor, it was necessary to use gum boots inside the place."

Under the headline "Sending Glass to England," the November 9, 1913, issue of *China,*

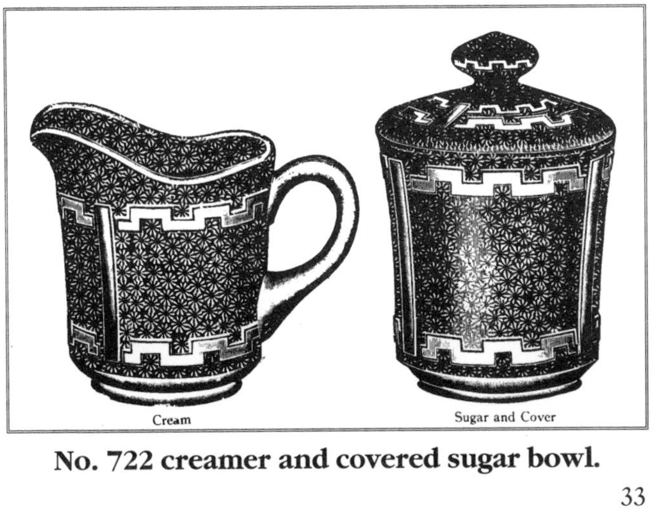
Cream
Sugar and Cover

**No. 722 creamer and covered sugar bowl.**

# We Drive a Nail and Hang a Fact on It.

We are full of CONFIDENCE—it is an effect. We've BEEN PUT TO THE TEST. We've SUCCEEDED BETTER THIS SEASON THAN EVER BEFORE. In fact, we've STOOD THE ACID TEST OF TIME.

No. "722" Line.

*Fort Pitt Hotel, Pittsburgh, Pa., month of January. Room 716.*

No. "721" Line.

Both lines illustrated herewith are made in plain and gold decorated, and each line is an extensive one, containing table sets, berry sets, water sets, goblets, wines, sherbets, and includes a complete assortment of vases.

Samples and illustrations are ready and will be sent on request.

# New Martinsville Glass Mfg. Co.,

## NEW MARTINSVILLE, W. VA.

*Glass and Lamps* carried this account of the New Martinsville plant's fortunes:

*Among the American glass companies now sending glass to England is the New Martinsville Glass Co., of New Martinsville, W. Va. The plant has been going full time for months, and since the war broke out its shipments of glassware to England have been larger than during the whole of last year. Orders from the other side are still being booked in sufficient quantitiy to assure continued good business from that direction. The company's ware is getting to be pretty well known over there, and the orders being booked are most satisfactory. The company has engaged its usual quarters at the Ft. Pitt Hotel for the annual glass show, and Mr. David Fisher, secretary of the company, will be there as usual to look after the business.*

About January, 1914, two more lines were added to the New Martinsville plant's lengthy and ever-growing 700-series. These were No. 721 (now called Studio), which bears some resemblance to No. 719 Old Glory, and No. 722, a beautifully decorated line now called Lorraine. No. 721 (Studio) occurs in the gold/ruby-stain combination [see Fig. 128] as well as ruby-stain only [see Fig. 200] and plain crystal.

New Martinsville's No. 722 (Lorraine) features a finely-mottled background that makes the crystal glass nearly opaque; this provides an excellent contrast for the ruby-stain decoration [see Figs. 173-179 and 229]. Although No. 721 consisted of the typical berry set, table set and water set plus additional items, it was apparently out of produc-

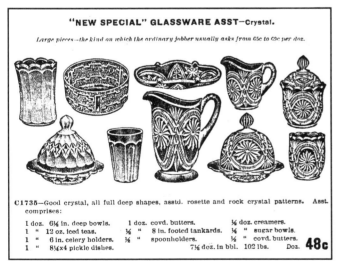

This interesting assortment of New Martinsville glassware appeared in the Spring, 1915, Butler Brothers catalogue. The berry bowl (top row, second from left) is surely No. 722 (Lorraine), but the butterdish at lower left has yet to be identified; it could be No. 726.

No. 719 Old Glory and No. 722 (Lorraine) water sets; from a Butler Brothers catalogue issued for Spring, 1915.

tion by 1917, for there is no entry for it in the firm's price list. No. 722 is well-represented in the 1917 price list, and the articles mentioned include a 9" scalloped fruit bowl and a 10" plate.

In December, 1914, the company began an advertising campaign for its next new patterns. These were No. 723, a plain motif called Express today, and No. 724, a decorated line popularly called Heart in Sand. They were described in the January 14, 1915, issue of *Pottery, Glass and Brass Salesman*:

*Two complete new lines of tableware greet the buyer in this firm's large and attractive showing. A double-panel Colonial design, which is called No. 723 is a departure from the conventional without loss of distinction. It is shown in crystal, gold decorated and in deep plate etch-*

From the December 17, 1914, issue of *Pottery, Glass and Brass Salesman.*

## NEW MARTINSVILLE, W. VA.

### By Frank Edmonds.

As there has been no news in The Flint from our locality for the last couple of months, I will send a few items:

As Labor Day is past and gone and a matter of history, the celebration, we are glad to say, will be well remembered by all the old and young of this place as it was well observed by all here. The Loyal Order of Moose gave a demonstration on that day, of which one-half of the members of Local Union No. 16 are members, and took great interest in it. Dock Mosser, president of Local Union No. 16, and delegate to the last convention. was chief marshal of the parade, in which the Flints turned out in a body, as did a number of members of the G. B. B. A. of Padden City, a few miles below here, also members of the Moose. Jos. Newmyer, prominent member of both the Moose and the G. B. B. A., took a very active part.  The Sistersville Lodge of Moose also turned out in a body, having special cars to bring them and their band to the city, and helped to make the affair one grand success; also a number from up the river from various points. Bellaire, Wheeling, Moundsville, Martins Ferry, also were here with the A. F. and M. band from Moundsville, and joined in the successful day.  Most every business house in the city was well represented by floats in the parade, either by wagon or automobile.  The men on foot marched three abreast, so the readers who have visited this city will know Labor Day was well remembered when they hear the parade reached from the Elk Hotel on Maple avenue to beyond the bridge in Brooklyn. After the parade the workers held a picnic in Martin's orchard, where they had contests of various kinds, such as foot racing for the women, men, fat men, boys and girls, the three-legged race, the throwing match for the ladies, for which Alma Hicks took first prize, and one of our members', Joe Brogan's, best girl. A Mrs. Herrigan took first prize for the nail driving contest, which Polly Long says was nat fair as he says there were to be no professionals in it, and he claims the winner built three shanty boats in her time.  Addresses were were delivered by the mayor, J. H. Jackson, Clarence Bennett and Jackson Glenn, of Pittsburg, officials of the order, and Deputy Supreme Dictator Harris, of Parkersburg. Rev. G. W. Twynham, of St. John's M. E. church of this city, delivered an interesting and instructive address on "Labor." Mostly every person who took an active part in the affair was well pleased with the way everything was conducted and say this should not be the last Labor Day celebration. Harry Marshall, a glass worker of Bellaire, and Wm. Van Horn, of Follansbee, were here and turned out with the Flints. We are a little inclined to believe there is some attraction here for the latter. He states he comes quite often to see Ellra Stagger, but we believe Bill has a best girl in this neck of the woods.  Never mind, boys, come again.  Some of the latest arrivals here are Joe Brogan, Harry Edmonds and Geo. Shipley.  Last meeting we initiated Ellem Hoskins.  The following officers were elected: Dock Mosser, president; Fred Hassner, corresponding secretary; Joe Vickers, financial secretary; John Edmonds, treasurer; A. Charlton, inspector; C. Noland, inner guard; A. Noland, outer guard; W. Deighton, W. Brooner, W. Hassner, trustees—the three Bills; Tom Martin, press secretary.

**Press secretary Frank Edmonds penned this column for the October, 1914, issue of the *American Flint*, a union publication.**

No. 723. SUGAR.

One piece of a long, complete line, to give you an idea of what will be on display during the month of January, Room 716, Fort Pitt Hotel, Pittsburgh.

The No. 723 covered sugar bowl was shown in this December, 1914, ad in a glass trade publication.

"CHALLENGE" GOLD DECORATED TABLE SET ASSTM'T.
Stunning new shapes, popular Colonial pattern.

3K227X—A strictly high grade assortment; heavy fired gold bands with narrow gold verge lines; gold edges, highly polished crystal glass; Colonial panels; extra heavy weight; all full size pieces; an assortment for your best trade.
2 only 7 Pc. Water Sets; ½ gal. jugs and six tumblers.
2 only 7 Pc. Berry Sets; deep 8 in. bowl and six nappies.
2 only 4 Pc. Table Sets; full size.
Total 6 sets in a bbl.  (No pkg. chg.)
Per set ................................................................ .95

Gold-decorated items in New Martinsville's No. 723 (Express) line, as shown in a 1915 G. Sommers & Co. catalogue.

*ings. The other is a "frosted" ground line with heart-shaped sections left perfectly plain. This is designated as No. 724 and may be had in crystal, in gold decorated and in fired enamel floral decorations. They are both popular price lines of unusually classy appearance.*

No. 723 is designated "Colonial Pattern" in the 1917 price list, but articles are relatively hard to find today [see Fig. 292]. The nature of the "deep plate etchings" mentioned in the trade publication quoted above remains a mystery; these may be similar to the etching No. 2306 which was used on the No. 708 Lusitania line. On the other hand, New Martinsville's No. 724 (Heart in Sand) motif is well-known among today's collectors. The No.

New Martinsville's No. 724 (Heart in Sand) appeared in G. Sommers & Co. catalogues during 1917; note the reference to "hand painted design."

No. 712 (Placid) and No. 713 (Pleated Medallion) pitchers from the August, 1915, Butler Brothers catalogue.

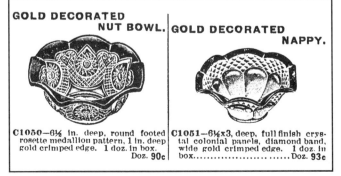

The January, 1916, Butler Brothers catalogue showed these gold-decorated bowls in New Martinsville's No. 707 (Horseshoe Medallion) and No. 718 (Frontier).

This Butler Brothers assortment (January, 1916) contains a celery tray and footed comport from the No. 500 Wetzel line as well as a No. 713 (Pleated Medallion) pitcher, a colonial-style butterdish and five pieces of No. 719 Old Glory. The imitation cut glass berry bowl (top row, second from left) is No. 557, which is called Salem by collectors today.

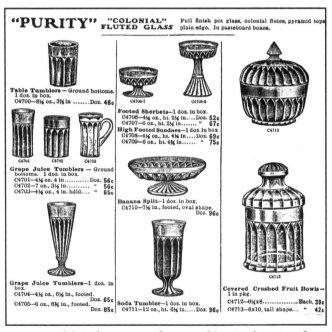

No. 97 Old Colony was featured in Butler Brother catalogues during March and April, 1916; the "Footed Sherbets" and the "High Footed Sundaes" were shown in the December 27, 1915, issue of China, Glass and Lamps when the line made its debut.

724 line was made in crystal, but articles with the hand-painted floral decoration (see p.110) or in ruby-stain [see Figs. 216-225] are decidedly more popular. Crystal pieces with gold decoration are difficult to find. Both No. 723 and No. 724 are listed in the company's 1917 price list.

The new patterns for 1916 apparently broke with the 700-series which had been used for a number of years. The December 27, 1915, issue of *China, Glass and Lamps* showed articles from the new line, No. 97 Old Colony. A week later, this same publication showed a fruit bowl and foot in the No. 558 pattern; this heavy, imitation cut glass motif, called Elite today, was probably not a full pattern line, for only two sizes of footed bowls and a jelly compote are known.

The No. 97 Old Colony line was made in crystal, of course, but articles in ruby-stain [see Figs. 159-160] or the gold/ruby-stain combination [see Figs. 136-140 and 189-190] are of much more interest to collectors today. The 1917 price list mentions "Gold Dec. 6", so this line may also have been made with gold decoration alone. At any rate, the line was a lengthy one, and many articles appear in the 1917 price list.

Several other patterns are known to exist in New Martinsville's 700-series, and these were probably introduced during the latter part of the 1908-1917 period, perhaps around the time of the 1913 flood/fire when both production and advertising were curtailed. No. 725 also carried the name Plain Colonial, and No. 728 was called Colonial Line. No. 726 is now called Embassy by collectors. A long listing of items in No. 725 appears in the 1917 price list, but neither No. 726 nor No. 728 is to be found there. Items from the No. 726 line, however, were in G. Sommers & Co. catalogues as late as 1924-25.

As 1916 drew to a close, John Forbes' letter to the *American Flint* (November, 1916) struck an optimistic note while recounting improvements in the plant: "... we are all working steady and doing well. We got started up in full after our summer vacation. ... The management informs me that they could use another furnace and then not get caught up with their orders this year." Forbes also reported there were "five men employed in the cutting shop turning out a line of inks and toilet ware such as talcum, tooth powder, smelling salts etc."

Forbes' letter in the January, 1917, issue of *American Flint* recounted conditions as of December 18, 1916:

*... we all got a cool reception at the factory this morning. There is plenty of gas, but not for us. ... The firm here has plenty of orders and plenty of boys, and we surely would get good time if we could get the gas. ... We were off a week on account of the delay of a car of soda, so I think Christmas money will be kind of scarce here.*

Cream
10 Doz. to Bbl.

Sugar and Cover
8 Doz. to Bbl.

**No. 726 creamer and covered sugar bowl.**

Cream
9 Doz. to Bbl.

Sugar and Cover
8 Doz. to Bbl.

**No. 728 creamer and covered sugar bowl.**

About a year later, the *Wetzel Democrat* (December 28, 1917) reported that the local gas company, the Manufacturers Light and Heat Co., sought approval from the West Virginia Public Service Commission to discontinue gas service to the glass factory. The newspaper said that "the plant ... would be compelled to close down indefinitely, many men would be thrown out of work, and like conditions would prevail in other cities." The glass company soon installed producers which generated natural gas from coal, thus averting a fuel shortage (*Wetzel Democrat*, May 24, 1918).

A 1917 "Price List" issued by the New Martinsville Glass Manufacturing Co. provides an excellent summary of the pattern lines that were being made at the close of David I. Fisher's tenure at the plant. These listings are useful information for today's collectors. The following pattern numbers and original names appear in the company's price list from 1917: No. 10 Plain Pattern; No. 88 Carnation; No. 97 Old Colony; No. 146; No. 147; No. 148; No. 310; No. 500; No. 556 Royal; No. 557; No. 705; No. 708 Lusitania; No. 711; No. 712; No. 713; No. 714; No. 717; No. 718; No. 719 Old Glory; No. 720 Florene; No. 722; No. 723 Colonial; No.

1C812, Cream Pitcher—Ht. 3½ in., diam. top 3½ in., fancy colonial fluted design, footed, purest brilliant crystal with deep pure burnt in gold band edge, in some places 1½ in. wide. 1 doz. in box..Doz. **82c**

1C813, Open Sugar—Ht. 3½ in., diam. top 3½ in., pattern and decoration to match 1C812. 1 doz. in box.........................Doz. **82c**

1C812    1C813

These No. 146 (Plain Arches) pieces appeared in an April, 1909, Butler Brothers catalogue.

Slipper Match Holder

New Martinsville's slipper remained in production from the early 1900s through the mid-1930s.

724; No. 725 Plain Colonial; and No. 900. Some of these pattern lines were quite extensive. For example, the No. 97 Old Colony line amounted to over 40 different articles, although some items sold separately were actually made from the same moulds and finished into different shapes. Others were confined to just a few items, such as No. 146 (now called Plain Arches) and No. 147 (now called Star in Bullseye), each of which consisted of sugar and creamer.

Because of material shortages caused by World War I, the New Martinsville firm was compelled to curtail production of many of the patterns in its 1917 price list. The copy of the price list reproduced in this chapter reflects many deletions anticipated by the company in its correspondence with the War Trades Board. The firm proposed to reduce its total count of items manufactured from 1266 to 611. Many anticipated deletions can be seen where individual items have lines drawn through them or where a large "X" shows the elimination of an entire pattern. The moulds for these patterns were apparently well-maintained, however, and some patterns were revived and reissued in the 1920s after Ira M. Clarke became general manager of the plant (see Chapter Three).

## OTHER PRODUCTS

The New Martinsville Glass Manufacturing Company was not just a producer of pattern glass lines between 1908 and 1917. Like virtually all other glass plants, the firm made any number of staple articles and specialized goods. Fortunately, the correspondence between the New Martinsville plant and the National Association of Manufacturers of Pressed and Blown Glassware makes it possible to ascertain at least a few of these items.

In April, 1908, the firm was making items as diverse as "percolator tops" and novelty slippers.

## PRESSED CRYSTAL TOOTHPICK AND MATCH HOLDERS

1C750—2¼ in., ribbed crystal, barrel shape. 1 doz. in box. Doz. **42c**

This toothpick holder (from a May, 1919, Butler Brothers catalogue) also appears in original New Martinsville catalogues.

The percolator tops may be hard to identify, but the slipper was a lady's shoe with daisy/button motif. This article must have remained in the line for some time, as it appears in the 1917 price list. Another novelty item is the Hat Match Holder (sometimes called Lincoln Hat) which is known in opal and turquoise [see Fig. 59].

The 700-series used for pattern glass lines was also employed for an extensive product line of kerosene lamps. These ranged from an array of relatively plain hand lamps to the impressive assortment of No. 702 lamps in decorated opal glass. The No. 702 lamps were, in all likelihood, decorated at New Martinsville, but the firm probably purchased the chimneys from another concern. Another lengthy assortment consisted of lamps called No. 705; these were prominent in the lighting goods sections of Butler Brothers catalogues for several years. At least three "Library Lamps" were also available complete with fixtures, and these featured massive bases and elaborate chimneys.

Footed Hand. 6 doz. in. bbl.
**No. 700 Lamp**

Footed Hand
**No. 706 Lamp**

O Footed Hand
**No. 701 Lamp**

Footed Hand. No. 1 and 2 Collar
**No. 709 Lamp**

O—Footed Hand
**No. 702 Lamp**

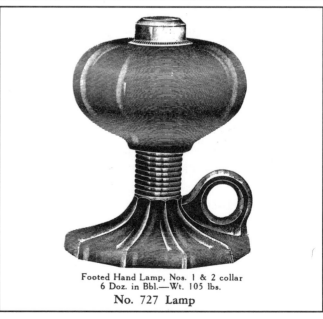

Footed Hand Lamp, Nos. 1 & 2 collar
6 Doz. in Bbl.—Wt. 105 lbs.
**No. 727 Lamp**

**From an original catalogue.**    **From an original catalogue.**

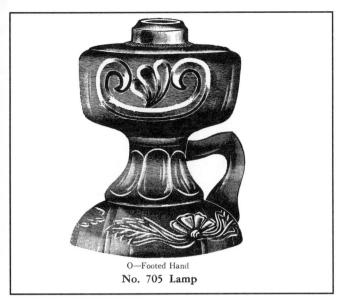

O—Footed Hand
No. 705 Lamp

New Martinsville's No. 705 lamp bears a design similar to that of the No. 711 (Leaf and Star) pattern line.

No. 36—Jeff Refrigerator Jug
2 Doz. to Bbl.

No. 46—Mutt Jug
2½ Doz. to Bbl.

**Mutt and Jeff pitchers.**

**New Martinsville lamps (from a February, 1910 Butler Brothers catalogue).**

41

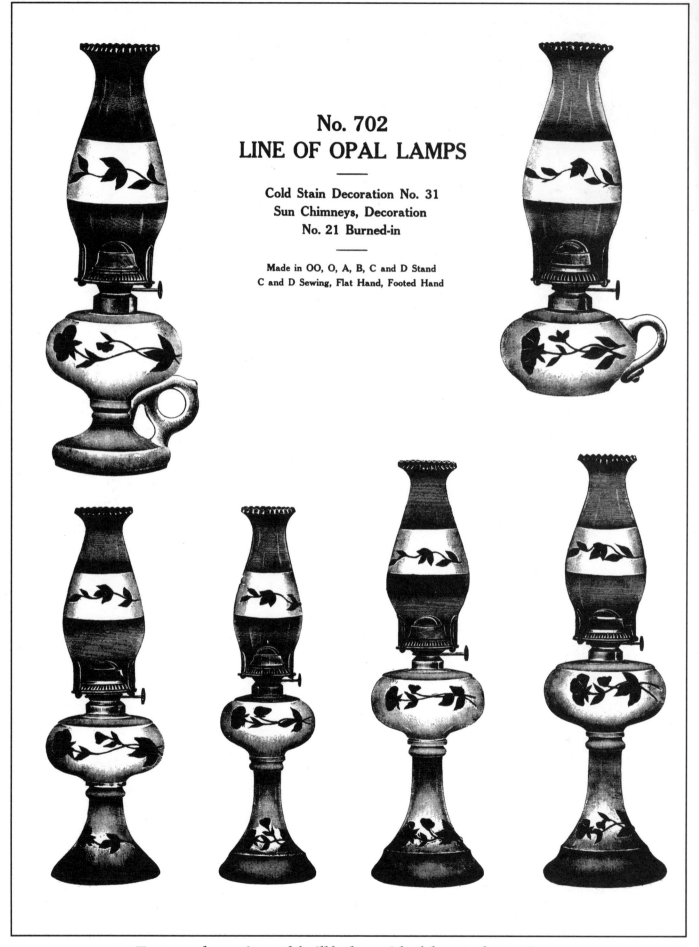

# No. 702
# LINE OF OPAL LAMPS

---

**Cold Stain Decoration No. 31
Sun Chimneys, Decoration
No. 21 Burned-in**

---

Made in OO, O, A, B, C and D Stand
C and D Sewing, Flat Hand, Footed Hand

**Kerosene lamps in opal (milk) glass with elaborate decorations.**

No. 708—Library Lamp Complete
1 Doz. to Bbl.
Lamp only 1½ Doz. to Bbl.

No. 900—Library Lamp Complete
1 Doz. to Bbl.
Lamp only 1½ Doz. to Bbl.

No. 1000—Library Lamp Complete
1 Doz. to Bbl.
Lamp only 1½ Doz. to Bbl.

**Three impressive "library" lamps; from an original catalogue.**

The 1917 "Price List" issued by the New Martinsville Glass Manufacturing Co. affords a good view of the other glassware that was made at the plant at this time. The forty-page list bills the firm as "Manufacturers of Crystal and Decorated Glassware" on its front cover and mentions "Tableware, Tumblers, Goblets, Mugs, Lamps, Candle Sticks, Vases (and) Soda Supplies." The first ten pages are given over to common ware—pressed tumblers, bar tumblers, ice teas, beer mugs and steins, stemware, and sherbets and sundaes—and several pages are devoted to molasses cans as well as to pressed and blown salt and pepper shakers. A number of individual salt dips are present, and there is even a celery dip!

One page lists "miscellaneous opal [milk glass]

ware," including tumblers, sherbets, and sundaes as well as comports, banana splits and novelties such as child's mugs, a baby plate and match holders. Both the No. 708 creamer and the No. 714 sundae were made in this hue.

A careful analysis of the 1917 Price List reveals other interesting articles made by the New Martinsville Glass Company. A pressed pitcher called No. 46 was also known as "Mutt," and a pitcher named "Jeff" carried the designation No. 36. The inspiration for these names probably came from a popular newspaper comic strip, "Mutt & Jeff." Other pressed pitchers are more staid, such as No. 34 (Statesman) and No. 43 (Icicle and Window).

The New Martinsville Glass Manufacturing Co.

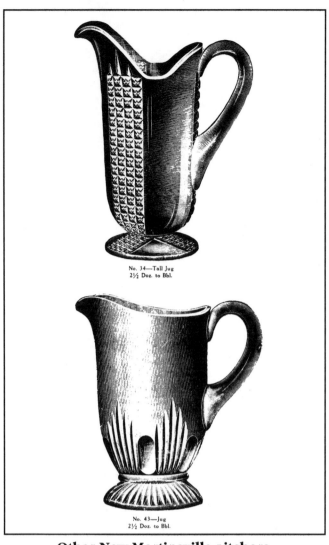

No. 34—Tall Jug
2½ Doz. to Bbl.

No. 43—Jug
2½ Doz. to Bbl.

**Other New Martinsville pitchers.**

also issued 1917 price lists for "Stationers' Glassware" and for "Glassware for Mounting." Stationers' glassware generally consisted of office supplies—inkwells, sponge cups, pen trays, stamp plates and paperweights—although ashtrays and match holders were also included in this classification [see pp. 45-46].

The mounting glassware consisted of toilet articles—soap boxes, talcum jars, salve jars, pomade jars, puff boxes and hair receivers—as well as a few smoker's accessories such as cigar jars and tobacco jars. All of these could be fitted with silver-plated or other metal lids [see Figs. 263, 266-267, 276 and 292-294]. Many items in New Martinsville's list of glassware for mounting were actually adaptations or extensions of its tableware lines. Some of the various jars were identified by numbers associated with the earlier tableware patterns in the firm's 700-series.

### FISHER GOES TO PADEN CITY

On April 28, 1916, the *Wetzel Democrat* reported that David Fisher had signed a contract with a committee seeking to build a new glass tableware plant at Paden City, a small town which straddles the border of Wetzel and Tyler counties about five miles south of New Martinsville. The newspaper gave credit to Fisher for the New Martinsville plant's "remarkable success," and predicted that the Paden City plant would "insure a building

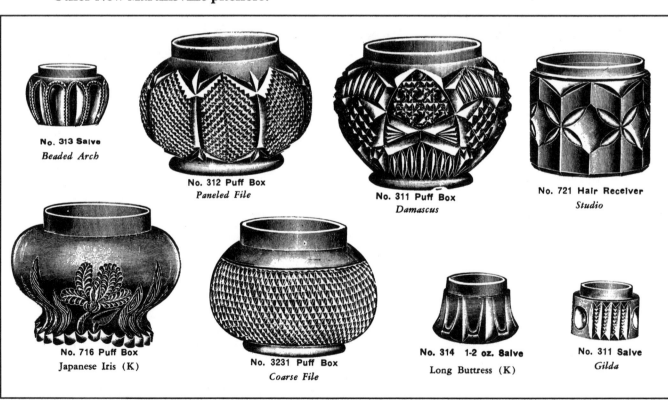

No. 313 Salve
*Beaded Arch*

No. 312 Puff Box
*Paneled File*

No. 311 Puff Box
*Damascus*

No. 721 Hair Receiver
*Studio*

No. 716 Puff Box
*Japanese Iris (K)*

No. 3231 Puff Box
*Coarse File*

No. 314 1-2 oz. Salve
*Long Buttress (K)*

No. 311 Salve
*Gilda*

**These articles from New Martinsville's extensive line of "Glassware for Mounting" were designed to go with standard-sized lids.**

44

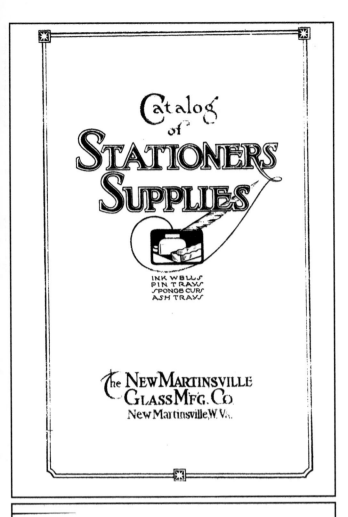

Catalog
of
STATIONERS
SUPPLIES

INK WELLS
PIN TRAYS
SPONGE CUPS
ASH TRAYS

The NewMartinsville
Glass Mfg. Co
New Martinsville, W. Va.

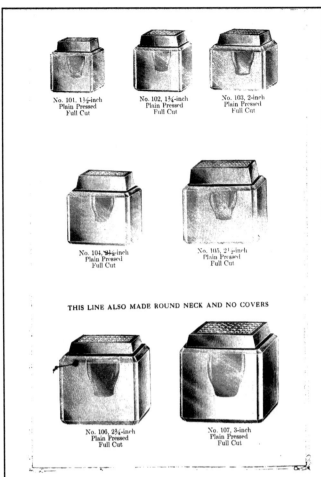

No. 101, 1½-inch
Plain Pressed
Full Cut

No. 102, 1¾-inch
Plain Pressed
Full Cut

No. 103, 2-inch
Plain Pressed
Full Cut

No. 104, 2½-inch
Plain Pressed
Full Cut

No. 105, 2½-inch
Plain Pressed
Full Cut

THIS LINE ALSO MADE ROUND NECK AND NO COVERS

No. 106, 2¾-inch
Plain Pressed
Full Cut

No. 107, 3-inch
Plain Pressed
Full Cut

A Catalog
of
STATIONERS
SUPPLIES

The NewMartinsville Glass Mfg. Co.
New Martinsville, W. Va.

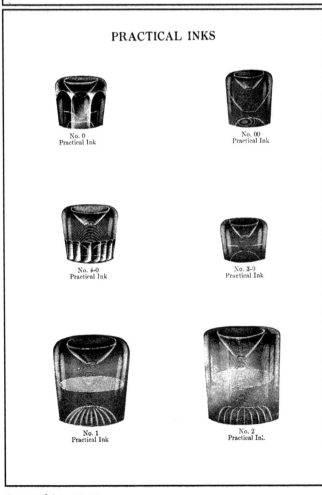

PRACTICAL INKS

No. 0
Practical Ink

No. 00
Practical Ink

No. 4-0
Practical Ink

No. 3-0
Practical Ink

No. 1
Practical Ink

No. 2
Practical Ink

**This catalogue was issued in 1917**

# INKS

No. 60 2½-inch
Bankers' Ink

No. 1 Safety Ink

No. 2 Safety Ink

# PAPER WEIGHT

No. 21

No. 22

No. 23

Star Photo Frame

No. 10 Pen Tray, 8-inch

# STAMP PLATES

No. 15 Stamp Plate
Sizes:
4, 5, 6, 7, 8, 9, 10-inch

# SPONGE CUPS

3-inch

3½-inch

4-inch

# MATCH HOLDERS

No. 4 Match Holder

# ASH TRAYS

No. 1 Ash Tray

No. 2 Ash Tray

No. 3 Ash Tray

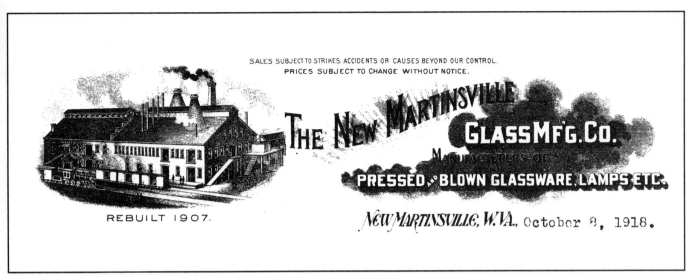

SALES SUBJECT TO STRIKES, ACCIDENTS OR CAUSES BEYOND OUR CONTROL.
PRICES SUBJECT TO CHANGE WITHOUT NOTICE.

THE NEW MARTINSVILLE GLASS MFG. CO.

MANUFACTURERS OF

PRESSED & BLOWN GLASSWARE, LAMPS, ETC.

REBUILT 1907.

New Martinsville, W. Va., October 8, 1918.

**This letterhead was used throughout the Fisher years.**

boom" and make Paden City "one of the most thriving towns in the Ohio Valley."

Some of New Martinsville's skilled glass workers followed Fisher to Paden City when the plant opened; among them was mould room foreman John Creighton, who became head of Paden City's mould shop (*American Flint*, November, 1916). Al Charlton became foreman of the mould shop at New Martinsville. Ida Tisher, who had been New Martinsville's bookkeeper, also went to Paden City. Over the next several decades, many glass-workers, especially those who were particularly adept pressers or finishers, found employment at Paden City when work was slack in New Martinsville or vice-versa.

It is difficult to determine who succeeded Fisher as general manager at New Martinsville. The *American Flint* (November, 1916) called Robert Thomas "our good old factory manager" and said that Julius Braun ("who has been at the head of this firm for several months") had resigned. The *Flint* also stated that "D. J. McGrail is to be factory manager."

On December 18, 1916, the *Wetzel Democrat* reported that Charles S. Rockhill had "accepted a position with the New Martinsville Glass Manufacturing Company" and that he "has leased the residence of Rev. J. H. Jackson on Clark Street." Glassworker John Forbes, writing on December 18, 1916, called Rockhill "a man who needs no introduction to the glass trade" and

noted that he had been at the Monongah Glass Co. in Fairmont (*American Flint*, January, 1917).

Rockhill remained until M. J. Conroy took over. Conroy was, in turn, succeeded by Ira M. Clarke about mid-1919. Clarke came to New Martinsville shortly after the death of long-time company officer Samuel R. Martin, 89, who had passed away on May 15, 1919. In a front-page obituary in the *Wetzel Democrat* (May 16, 1919), Martin was remembered as being "instrumental in establishing ... the New Martinsville Glass Manufacturing Company." Martin was the first president of the company when officers were elected in December, 1900.

David Fisher remained with the Paden City Glass Manufacturing Company until his death on May 21, 1933. Fisher's son Samuel, who had also been active in the Paden City firm, succeeded his father as president of the Paden City Glass Manufacturing Company and was associated with this firm until it closed in the early 1950s.

As one might suspect, many of the Paden City firm's products bear strong resemblances to glass-ware made at New Martinsville. This is due to the influence of Fisher as well as that of Robert McEldowney, a later general manager of the New Martinsville Glass Manufacturing Company who also left New Martinsville to join this concern (see Chapter Four). Readers interested in the products of the Paden City firm should consult Jerry Barnett's *Paden City: The Color Company*, which was published in 1978.

## No. 10 PLAIN PATTERN

| | Fin. | Unfin. | Dozens in Bbls. | Weight of Bbl. Lbs. |
|---|---|---|---|---|
| 7 Inch Candy Tray | $1.32 | | 8½ | 160 |
| 8 inch Candy Tray | 1.50 | | 6¾ | 160 |
| 10 inch Candy Tray | 1.70 | | 3¾ | 160 |
| 5 inch Square Olive | .70 | | 20 | 160 |
| 2 Bottle Caster Boxed | 1.80 | | 5 | 100 |
| 2 Bottle Caster Bulk | 1.70 | | 6 | 125 |
| 6 inch Open Bowl | 1.90 | | 3 | 125 |
| 7 inch Open Bowl | 2.60 | | 2½ | 125 |
| 8 inch Open Bowl | 3.20 | | 2 | 125 |
| 6 inch Covered Bowl | 2.70 | | 2½ | 135 |
| 7 inch Coverd Bowl | 3.50 | | 2¼ | 135 |
| 8 inch Covered Bowl | 4.40 | | 1½ | 135 |
| 5 inch Open Bowl | | $1.20 | 3 | 125 |
| 6 inch Open Bowl | | 1.80 | 3 | 125 |
| 7 inch Open Bowl | | 2.50 | 3 | 125 |
| 5 inch Covered Bowl | | 2.10 | 2½ | 130 |
| 6 inch Covered Bowl | | 2.80 | 2¼ | 130 |
| 7 inch Covered Bowl | | 3.90 | 1½ | 130 |
| 9½ inch Salver | 2.70 | | 1¾ | 125 |
| 4 inch Stamp Plate | .90 | .56 | 48 | 150 |
| 5 inch Stamp Plate | 1.10 | .64 | 38 | 150 |
| 6 inch Stamp Plate | 1.60 | .80 | 20 | 150 |
| 7 inch Stamp Plate | 2.00 | 1.04 | 18 | 150 |
| 8 inch Stamp Plate | 2.50 | 1.36 | 15 | 150 |
| 9 inch Stamp Plate | 3.30 | 1.90 | 12 | 150 |
| 10 inch Stamp Plate | 4.50 | | 10 | 150 |
| 7 inch Berry Full Flat | 2.40 | | | |

## No. 88 CARNATION PATTERN

| | Plain | Dec. 6 | | |
|---|---|---|---|---|
| Spoon | $1.30 | $2.40 | 10 | 160 |
| Cream | 1.50 | 3.00 | 10 | 160 |
| Hotel Sugar | 1.50 | 2.90 | 13 | 160 |
| Sugar and Cover | 2.20 | 4.10 | 8 | 180 |
| Butter and Cover | 2.80 | 5.00 | 4½ | 150 |
| Set (with Covered Sugar) | 7.70 | 14.50 | 1½ | 150 |
| Tumbler | .86 | 1.70 | 21 | 160 |
| Pitcher | 3.60 | 7.50 | 2 | 150 |
| Lemonade Set | 8.76 | 17.70 | 1¼ | 150 |
| 4½ Inch Berry | .70 | 1.70 | 22 | 175 |
| 8 inch Berry | 3.30 | 7.00 | 3½ | 150 |
| Berry Set | 7.50 | 17.20 | 1¾ | 150 |
| Handled Custard | .84 | 1.70 | 30 | 150 |
| 14 inch Punch Bowl and Ft | 24.00 | 60.00 | ½ | 125 |
| Tooth Pick | .50 | 1.10 | 30 | 125 |
| 8 inch Flat Dish | 2.50 | 6.50 | 4½ | 150 |
| 11 inch Celery Tray | 1.80 | 3.50 | 9 | 175 |

## No. 97 OLD COLONY PATTERN

| | Plain per Dozen | Gold Dec. 6 | Dozens in Bbl. | Weight of Bbl. Lbs. |
|---|---|---|---|---|
| Butter and Cover | $3.00 | $5.50 | 4½ | 140 |
| Sugar and Cover | 2.00 | 4.70 | 8 | 140 |
| Cream | 1.60 | 3.00 | 9 | 140 |
| Spoon | 1.40 | 2.80 | 9½ | 140 |
| Tea Set | 8.00 | 16.00 | 1¾ | 140 |
| 4½ inch Berry | .70 | 1.60 | 26 | 150 |
| 8 inch Berry | 3.00 | 7.60 | 4½ | 150 |
| 9 inch Berry | 4.00 | 7.80 | 3½ | 150 |
| Berry Set, 8 inch | 7.20 | 16.60 | 2½ | 150 |
| Tumbler | .96 | 1.60 | 20 | 160 |
| Jug | 5.20 | 9.50 | 2 | 140 |
| Water Set | 10.60 | 19.10 | 1⅓ | 140 |
| Tall Celery | 2.40 | 3.50 | 5 | 135 |
| 8 in. Ftd. Banana Split | 2.40 | | 11 | 135 |
| 8¾ inch Flat Banana Split or Pickle | 1.80 | | 18 | 135 |
| 4½ ounce Grape Juice Hi Ball | .90 | | 30 | 160 |
| 4½ ounce Grape Juice Hi Ball, Hld. | 1.70 | | 25 | 150 |
| 4½ ounce Grape Juice Ftd | 1.10 | | 15 | 125 |
| 6 ounce Grape Juice, Ftd | 1.30 | | 12 | 125 |
| 9 ounce Goblet | 1.20 | 2.00 | 9 | 125 |
| Oil Bottle | 1.70 | 3.40 | 10 | 170 |
| Low Crushed Fruit, 2 quart | 8.00 | | 2 | 145 |
| Hi Crushed Fruit, 2 quart | 9.00 | | 2 | 165 |
| 8 ounce Bell Soda | .80 | 1.60 | 20 | 140 |
| 10 ounce Bell Soda | .94 | 1.80 | 18 | 140 |
| 12 ounce Bell Soda | 1.04 | 2.20 | 14 | 140 |
| Footed Soda | 1.60 | | 9½ | 135 |
| Footed Soda Hld | 2.60 | | 7½ | 125 |
| 4½ ounce Shallow Ftd. Sundae | 1.00 | 2.00 | 24 | 140 |
| 6 ounce Shallow Ftd. Sundae | 1.10 | 2.10 | 20 | 130 |
| Handled Custard | .90 | 1.80 | 28 | 150 |
| 4½ ounce Cone Ft. Sundae | 1.10 | 2.20 | 12 | 135 |
| 6 ounce Cone Ft. Sundae | 1.30 | | 11 | 130 |
| 7 ounce Water Tumbler | .84 | | 28 | 150 |
| 12 ounce Ice Tea, Straight | 1.10 | | 14 | 150 |
| 12 ounce Ice Tea, Fld. Top | 1.10 | | 13 | 150 |
| Straw Jar | 8.50 | | 2½ | 140 |
| 10 ounce Hld. Lemonade | 1.40 | | 10 | 135 |
| Shaker Nickel Top, Gross | 11.00 | | 30 | 160 |
| Shaker Cast Nickel Top, Gross | 15.00 | | 30 | 160 |
| Shaker Silver Plated Top, Gross | 17.00 | | 30 | 160 |
| Shaker Combination Top, Gross | 21.00 | | 30 | 160 |
| 10 inch Plate | 3.20 | | 3½ | 125 |
| 12 inch Plate | 4.20 | | 3 | 125 |
| No. 1 8 ounce Paper Cup Holder | .72 | | 19 | 165 |
| No. 2 12 ounce Paper Cup Holder | .84 | | 15 | 165 |
| 9 inch Shallow Berry | 3.00 | | 3⅓ | 150 |
| 10 inch Shallow Berry | 4.00 | | 3 | 150 |
| 9 inch Flared Berry | 3.00 | | 4½ | 150 |
| 10 inch Flared Berry | 4.00 | | 3⅓ | 150 |

## No. 310 LINE

| | Plain | Price per Dozen | Dozens in Bbl. | Weight of Bbl. Lbs. |
|---|---|---|---|---|
| 7 ounce Tumbler Grd | | $.84 | 25 | 160 |
| 4 ounce Grape Juice Hi Ball | | .90 | 27 | 160 |
| 4 ounce Grape Juice Hi Ball, Hld | | 1.70 | 22 | 150 |
| 4½ ounce Grape Juice Ftd | | 1.10 | 15 | 135 |
| 6 ounce Grape Juice Ftd | | 1.30 | 12 | 135 |
| 4 ounce Sherbet | | 1.00 | 24 | 140 |
| 6 ounce Sherbet | | 1.10 | 15 | 140 |
| 2 quart Low Crushed Fruit Bowl | | 8.00 | 2 | 145 |
| 2 quart Hi Crushed Fruit Bowl | | 9.00 | 2 | 165 |
| Childs Hld. Mug | | .75 | 20 | 150 |
| Footed Soda, 12 ounce | | 1.60 | 9½ | 135 |
| Footed Soda Hld | | 2.60 | 7½ | 130 |
| Soda Holder | | 1.20 | 18 | 150 |
| Banana Split, 8 inch | | 2.40 | 10 | 135 |
| 8 inch Tulip Vase | | 1.60 | 6 | 115 |
| 12 inch Vase | | 1.60 | 5 | 115 |
| 16 inch Vase | | 1.80 | 4 | 115 |
| 18 inch Vase | | 2.60 | 2 | 115 |
| 9 inch Bud Vase, Grd. Top | | 1.44 | 8 | 100 |
| 10 to 12 inch Bud Vase, Grd Top | | 1.50 | 8 | 100 |
| 13 inch Bud Vase, Grd Top | | 1.80 | 8 | 100 |
| 10 to 12 inch Bud Vase, Crpt Top | | 1.56 | 8 | 100 |
| Jug, 64 ounce | | 5.00 | 2 | 150 |
| Ice Jug, 64 ounce | | 5.50 | 2 | 150 |

## No. 500 PATTERN UNFINISHED

| | Plain | Dec. 6 | Dozens in Bbl. | Weight of Bbl. Lbs. |
|---|---|---|---|---|
| Cream | $1.20 | $2.60 | 8 | 165 |
| Butter and Cover | 1.60 | 3.50 | 4 | 160 |
| Sugar and Cover | 1.30 | 3.30 | 7 | 160 |
| Spoon | 1.10 | 2.20 | 11 | 160 |
| Set | 5.20 | 11.60 | 1¼ | 150 |
| 4 inch Berry | .34 | 1.20 | 20 | 160 |
| 7 inch Berry | 1.50 | 4.60 | 4½ | 150 |
| 8 inch Berry | 2.00 | 5.60 | 3 | 150 |
| Berry Set, 7 inch | 3.54 | 11.80 | 1¾ | 150 |
| Berry Set, 8 inch | 4.04 | 12.80 | 1¾ | 150 |
| Pickle Tray | .70 | 1.60 | 18 | 175 |
| Celery Tray | 1.40 | 3.60 | 9 | 175 |
| Tumbler, Grd. Fin | .80 | 1.50 | 19 | 150 |
| Goblet, Fin | .80 | 1.60 | 9 | 125 |
| Jug, Fin | 3.60 | 6.80 | 2 | 150 |
| Water Set, Grd Tumb | 7.80 | 16.80 | 1¼ | 150 |
| Hotel Sugar | 1.00 | 2.20 | 7 | 160 |
| Hotel Cream, Fin | 1.00 | 2.20 | 8 | 160 |
| 5 inch Ftd. Jelly | 1.40 | 2.40 | 7 | 140 |
| Oil | 1.60 | 2.40 | 12 | 170 |
| Wine | .50 | 1.30 | 30 | 150 |
| Custard | .80 | 1.60 | 28 | 150 |

## No. 556 ROYAL PATTERN

| | Price per Dozen | Dozens in Bbl. | Weight of Bbl. Lbs. |
|---|---|---|---|
| 8 inch Berry | $4.50 | 2½ | 150 |
| 4½ inch Berry | .90 | 13 | 150 |
| 6 inch One Hld, Nappy | 1.60 | 5 | 150 |
| 7 inch Two Hld. Nappy | 2.50 | 4½ | 150 |
| 12 inch Footed Vase | 8.00 | 1¼ | 135 |

## No. 557 PATTERN

| | Fin. | Unfin. | Dec. 6 | Dozens in Bbl. | Weight of Bbl. Lbs. |
|---|---|---|---|---|---|
| 4 inch Berry | | $ .33 | | 40 | 160 |
| 4½ inch Berry | $ .55 | | $1.15 | 40 | 160 |
| 7 inch Berry | | 1.20 | | 4 | 140 |
| 8 inch Berry | 1.70 | | 4.20 | 5 | 140 |
| 9 inch Berry | 1.70 | | | 6 | 140 |
| 9 inch Berry, Crimpt | 1.70 | | | 6 | 140 |
| 9 inch Berry, Bell | 1.70 | | | 6 | 140 |

## No. 558 PATTERN

| | Price per Dozen | Dozens in Bbl. | Weight of Bbl. Lbs. |
|---|---|---|---|
| 9 inch Bowl and Foot | $8.20 | 1½ | 140 |
| 10 inch Bowl and Foot | 8.20 | 1½ | 140 |
| 9 inch Bowl only | 6.50 | 2½ | 150 |
| 10 inch Bowl only | 6.50 | 2½ | 150 |
| 6 inch Footed Jelly | 1.70 | 6 | 150 |

## No. 705 PATTERN

| | Plain | Dec. 6 | | |
|---|---|---|---|---|
| Butter and Cover | $2.40 | $4.80 | 4½ | 150 |
| Sugar and Cover | 1.90 | 3.90 | 5½ | 160 |
| Cream | 1.30 | 2.60 | 9 | 150 |
| Spoon | 1.10 | 2.40 | 9 | 150 |
| Tea Set | 6.70 | 13.70 | 1¼ | 150 |
| Tumbler Straight | .80 | 1.40 | 21 | 140 |
| Tumbler, Belled | .80 | 1.40 | 21 | 140 |
| Jug | 3.60 | 7.60 | 2 | 140 |
| Water Set | 8.40 | 16.00 | 1⅓ | 140 |
| 4½ inch Berry | .55 | 1.30 | 21 | 150 |
| 7 inch Berry | 1.70 | 4.80 | 4½ | 140 |
| 8 inch Berry | 2.50 | 5.50 | 4 | 140 |
| Berry Set, 8 inch | 5.80 | 13.30 | 2 | 160 |
| 5 inch Berry, Crimpt | .70 | 1.50 | 21 | 140 |
| 5 inch Berry, Shallow | .70 | 1.50 | 21 | 140 |
| 5 inch Berry, Bell | .70 | 1.50 | 21 | 140 |
| 8 inch Berry, Fld | 1.70 | 4.80 | 4 | 150 |
| 7 inch Berry, Cupt | 1.70 | 4.80 | 4 | 150 |
| 9 inch Berry, Bell | 1.70 | 4.80 | 5 | 150 |
| 9 inch Berry, Crimpt | 1.70 | 5.00 | 5 | 150 |
| 9 inch Berry, Shallow | 1.70 | 5.00 | 5 | 150 |
| 8 inch Berry, Cupt | 2.50 | 6.00 | 5 | 150 |
| 9 inch Berry, Fld | 2.50 | 6.00 | 4 | 150 |
| 10 inch Berry, Bell | 2.50 | 6.00 | 4 | 150 |
| 10 inch Berry, Crimpt | 2.50 | 6.00 | 4 | 150 |

## No. 708 LUSITANIA PATTERN

| | Plain | Dec. 39 or 47 | Etched 2306 | Dozens in Bbl. | Weight of Bbl. Lbs, |
|---|---|---|---|---|---|
| Butter and Cover | $2.80 | $4.80 | $4.00 | 4½ | 160 |
| Cream | 1.50 | 2.50 | 2.50 | 10 | 160 |
| Spoon | 1.30 | 2.20 | 2.10 | 10 | 160 |
| Sugar and Cover | 1.90 | 3.60 | 3.40 | 8 | 160 |
| Set | 7.50 | 13.10 | 12.00 | 1½ | 160 |
| 4 inch Nappy | .70 | 1.50 | 1.40 | 22 | 150 |
| 8 inch Berry | 2.80 | 6.80 | 6.00 | 3½ | 150 |
| Berry Set | 7.00 | 15.20 | 14.40 | 1¾ | 150 |
| Pitcher, Half Gallon | 5.00 | 9.00 | 8.00 | 2¼ | 140 |
| Tumbler | .80 | 1.30 | 1.10 | 21 | 140 |
| Lemonade Set | 9.80 | 16.80 | 14.60 | 1½ | 140 |
| Molasses Can., N. T. | 2.40 | 3.20 | ........ | 8 | 125 |
| Molasses Can, C. N. T. | 3.20 | 3.60 | ........ | 8 | 125 |
| Sugar Sifter, N. T. | 1.50 | 1.90 | ........ | 8 | 100 |
| Sugar Sifter, B. T. | 1.90 | ........ | ........ | 8 | 100 |
| Shaker, N. T. | 5.20 gro. | 1.00 doz | ........ | 30 | 100 |
| Shaker, C. N. T. | 9.00 gro. | 1.30 doz | ........ | 30 | 100 |
| Water Bottle | 6.00 | ........ | 9.00 | 2¾ | 160 |
| Water Bottle, Optic | 6.50 | ........ | ........ | 2¾ | 160 |
| Catsup Bottle | 4.00 | ........ | ........ | 7 | 180 |
| Handled Custard | .84 | 1.60 | ........ | 30 | 150 |
| 10 inch Ftd. Sherbert Bowl | 12.00 | 22.00 | ........ | ⅝ | 125 |
| Sherbet Set, 13 pcs | 22.80 | 41.20 | ........ | ½ | 125 |
| Finger Bowl | 1.60 | 2.50 | ........ | 20 | 150 |
| Goblet | 1.20 | 1.90 | ........ | 9 | 125 |
| Footed Sherbet | .90 | 1.60 | ........ | 24 | 150 |
| Oil | 1.70 | 3.00 | ........ | 12 | 180 |
| Cracker Jar and Cover | 4.00 | 7.20 | ........ | 2½ | 150 |
| Individual Cream | .65 | 1.24 | ........ | 50 | 200 |
| 9 inch Berry Crimpt | 2.80 | 6.80 | ........ | 2½ | 150 |
| 4½ inch Butter Tub, Flat | 1.75 | ........ | ........ | 20 | 150 |
| 4½ inch Butter Tub, Full, Flat | 2.00 | ........ | ........ | 20 | 150 |

## No. 712 PATTERN

| | Plain | Dec. No. 6 | Dozens in Bbl. | Weight of Bbl. Lbs. |
|---|---|---|---|---|
| Butter and Cover | $3.10 | $4.70 | 4 | 160 |
| Cream | 1.70 | 3.00 | 8 | 160 |
| Spoon | 1.70 | 3.00 | 8 | 160 |
| Sugar and Cover | 2.40 | 4.00 | 6 | 160 |
| Set | 8.90 | 14.70 | 1¼ | 160 |
| Tumbler | .90 | 1.50 | 20 | 160 |
| Ice Tea Tumbler | 1.20 | 1.90 | 11 | 150 |
| Pitcher, one-half gallon | 5.00 | 8.00 | 1¾ | 165 |
| Goblet | 1.20 | 2.10 | 8 | 125 |
| Wine | .66 | 1.30 | 30 | 125 |
| Oil, 5 oz | 1.70 | 2.70 | 12 | 180 |
| Oil, 6 oz | 1.90 | 3.00 | 10 | 180 |
| Molasses Can Blown T. T. | 1.80 | 2.50 | 6 | 115 |
| Molasses Can Blown N. T. | 2.50 | 3.20 | 6 | 115 |
| Tall Celery | 2.20 | 3.30 | 6 | 175 |
| Boquet Holder | 3.30 | 4.30 | 4 | 180 |
| Tulip Vase | 1.44 | 2.30 | 6½ | 100 |
| Shaker, small, N. T. | 5.20 gro. | 1.50 doz. | 30 | 100 |
| Shaker, small, C. N. T. | 9.00 gro. | 1.80 doz. | 30 | 100 |
| Shaker, large, N. T. | 7.00 gro. | 1.80 doz. | 23 | 100 |
| Shaker, large, C. N. T. | 11.00 gro. | 2.00 doz. | 23 | 100 |
| Sugar Sifter, N. T. | 1.40 | 2.80 | 14 | 100 |
| 4½ inch Berry | .70 | 1.60 | 26 | 150 |
| 5 inch Berry | 1.00 | 1.80 | 26 | 150 |
| 6 inch Berry | 1.30 | 3.50 | 6½ | 150 |
| 7 inch Berry | 1.80 | 4.50 | 5½ | 150 |
| 8 inch Berry | 3.50 | 7.40 | 4 | 150 |
| 5 inch Ftd. Jelly | 1.60 | 3.00 | 6 | 150 |
| Tooth Pick | .60 | 1.30 | 30 | 125 |
| Hotel Sugar | 1.50 | 3.00 | 10 | 165 |
| Soda Spoon Holder | 3.30 | .... | 5¼ | 175 |
| Hotel Cream | 1.40 | 2.90 | 14 | 165 |
| 6 inch Open Bowl | 3.60 | .... | 3 | 125 |
| 7 inch Open Bowl | 4.10 | 9.00 | 2 | 125 |
| 8 inch Open Bowl | 5.50 | .... | 1½ | 125 |
| 6 inch Covered Bowl | 5.00 | .... | 2½ | 140 |
| 7 inch Covered Bowl | 6.10 | .... | 2 | 140 |
| 8 inch Covered Bowl | 7.70 | .... | 1¼ | 140 |
| Cracker Jar and Cover | 4.50 | 7.70 | 3 | 145 |
| Lemonade Set, 7 pce | 10.40 | 17.00 | 1 | 150 |
| Berry Set, 7inch, 7 pce | 6.12 | 14.20 | 1¾ | 150 |
| Berry Set, 8 inch, 7 pce | 7.82 | 17.00 | 1¾ | 150 |
| Hld. Custard | .84 | 1.60 | 26 | 150 |

## No. 711 PATTERN

| | Plain | Dec. No. 6 | Dozens in Bbl. | Weight of Bbl. Lbs. |
|---|---|---|---|---|
| Spoon | $1.30 | $2.50 | 8 | 150 |
| Cream | 1.50 | 3.00 | 8 | 150 |
| Sugar and Cover | 2.20 | 4.40 | 7 | 150 |
| Butter and Cover | 3.00 | 5.10 | 4½ | 150 |
| Tea Set | 8.00 | 15.00 | 1½ | 150 |
| Pitcher | 4.00 | 7.80 | 2 | 150 |
| Tumbler | .86 | 1.60 | 24 | 160 |
| Lemonade Set | 9.16 | 17.40 | 1¼ | 150 |
| 4½ inch Berry, reg | .70 | 1.60 | 22 | 160 |
| 4½ inch Berry, fld | .70 | 1.60 | 22 | 160 |
| 5 inch Bon Bon | .70 | 1.60 | 22 | 160 |
| 6 inch Plate | .70 | 1.70 | 22 | 160 |
| 6 inch Ice Cream | .70 | .... | 22 | 160 |
| 7 inch Berry, reg | 2.40 | 6.40 | 4 | 150 |
| 7 inch Berry, fld | 2.40 | 6.40 | 4 | 150 |
| 7 inch Berry, cupt | 2.40 | 6.40 | 4 | 150 |
| 7 inch Berry, crimpt | 2.40 | 6.90 | 4 | 150 |
| 8 inch Berry, reg | 3.30 | 7.60 | 3 | 150 |
| 8 inch Berry, fld | 3.30 | 7.60 | 3 | 150 |
| 8 inch Berry, cupped | 3.30 | 7.60 | 3 | 150 |
| 10 inch Berry, crimpt | 3.30 | 8.00 | 3 | 150 |
| Berry Set (4½ and 8 inch) | 7.50 | 17.20 | 1½ | 150 |
| Ice Jug | 4.50 | 9.50 | 2 | 150 |
| Tumbler, bell | .86 | 1.70 | 24 | 145 |
| 6 inch Ftd. Berry | 1.50 | 2.70 | 5½ | 140 |
| 6½ inch Ftd. Fruit, crimpt | 1.50 | 2.70 | 1½ | 125 |
| 7 inch Cake Stand | 1.50 | 2.70 | 2 | 125 |
| Celery, Tall | 1.70 | 3.30 | 6 | 150 |
| Celery Tray | 1.80 | 3.80 | 9 | 150 |
| Ftd. Sherbet, hld | .84 | 1.60 | 23 | 160 |
| Oil | 1.70 | 2.50 | 12 | 175 |
| Shaker, N. T. | .75 | 1.50 | 30 | 150 |
| Shaker, C. N. T. | 1.00 | 1.80 | 30 | 150 |
| Tooth Pick | .50 | 1.10 | 30 | 125 |
| 8 inch Pickle | .90 | 1.70 | 18 | 150 |
| Goblet | 1.00 | 1.70 | 9 | 125 |
| Wine | .56 | 1.20 | 30 | 125 |
| Boquet Holder | 1.70 | 3.10 | 5 | 150 |
| 4½ inch Ftd. Comport, crimpt. | .80 | 1.80 | 18 | 150 |
| 4½ inch Ftd. Comport, fld. | .80 | 1.80 | 18 | 150 |
| 6½ inch Ftd. Comport, Oblong | 3.60 | 8.50 | 2 | 125 |
| 4½ inch Ftd. Comport, cupt. | .80 | 1.80 | 18 | 150 |
| 7 inch Ftd. Comport, reg. | 3.60 | 8.50 | 2 | 125 |
| 7 inch Ftd. Comport, fld. | 3.60 | 8.50 | 2 | 125 |
| 8 inch Ftd. Comport, crimpt. | 3.60 | 8.50 | 2 | 125 |
| 8 inch Ftd. Comport, reg. | 4.50 | 9.50 | 1½ | 125 |
| 8 inch Ftd. Comport, fld. | 4.50 | 9.50 | 1½ | 125 |
| 10 inch Ftd. Comport, crimpt. | 4.50 | 10.00 | 1½ | 125 |

## No. 713 PATTERN

FINISHED AND UNFINISHED

| | Plain | Dec. No. 6 | Dozens in Bbl. | Weight of Bbl. Lbs. |
|---|---|---|---|---|
| Sugar and Cover | $1.24 | $3.30 | 8 | 140 |
| Butter and Cover | 1.36 | 3.60 | 4½ | 140 |
| Spoon | .60 | 1.90 | 10 | 140 |
| Cream, fin | .86 | 2.40 | 10 | 140 |
| Set, 4 pce | 4.00 | 11.20 | 1½ | 135 |
| Pitcher No. 1, fin | 2.30 | 5.20 | 2½ | 140 |
| Pitcher No. 2, fin | 3.60 | 7.00 | 2 | 150 |
| Tumbler, fin | .66 | 1.40 | 24 | 150 |
| Water Set (No. 2 Jug) | 7.56 | 15.40 | 1½ | 150 |
| Water Set (No. 1 Jug) | 6.26 | 13.60 | 1½ | 150 |
| 4 inch Berry | .30 | 1.10 | 24 | 150 |
| 7 inch Berry | 1.14 | 4.70 | 5 | 150 |
| 8 inch Berry | 1.58 | 5.40 | 4 | 150 |
| Berry Set, 8 inch | 3.38 | 12.00 | 2 | 150 |
| Berry Set, 7 inch | 2.94 | 11.30 | 2¼ | 150 |
| Shaker, N. T. | 7.00 gro. | 1.50 doz. | 30 | 100 |
| Tall Celery, fin | 1.60 | 3.00 | 6 | 135 |
| Tooth Pick | .50 | 1.00 | 30 | 100 |
| Molasses Can, T. T. | 1.60 | 2.70 | 8 | 100 |
| Molasses Can, N. T. | 2.30 | 3.10 | 8 | 100 |
| Oil Bottle | 1.50 | 2.70 | 12 | 165 |
| 12 inch Vase | 1.30 | .... | 5 | 125 |
| 18 inch Vase | 1.70 | .... | 2¼ | 125 |

## No. 714 PATTERN

| | Plain | Dec. No. 6 | Dozens in Bbl. | Weight of Bbl. Lbs. |
|---|---|---|---|---|
| Butter and Cover | $3.00 | $ 5.60 | 4 | 150 |
| Sugar and Cover | 2.20 | 4.60 | 8 | 150 |
| Cream | 1.50 | 2.90 | 9 | 150 |
| Spoon | 1.40 | 2.60 | 9 | 150 |
| Set | 8.00 | 15.60 | 1½ | 150 |
| 9 inch Berry | 3.60 | 7.50 | 3 | 160 |
| 8 inch Berry | 3.20 | 7.20 | 4 | 160 |
| 7 inch Berry | 2.50 | 6.50 | 4½ | 160 |
| 4½ inch Berry | .72 | 1.60 | 20 | 180 |
| Berry Set, 8 inch | 7.52 | 16.80 | 1½ | 160 |
| 6 inch Plate | .80 | 1.90 | 13 | 150 |
| 6 inch Ice Cream | .80 | 1.90 | 21 | 150 |
| Tumbler | .80 | 1.60 | 20 | 150 |
| Tumbler,–I cupped | .90 | 1.80 | 20 | 150 |
| No. 0 Jug, Hall Boy | 3.10 | .... | 3½ | 145 |
| No. 1 Jug, small | 4.00 | 7.70 | 2 | 140 |
| No. 2 Jug, large | 7.00 | 11.60 | 1½ | 140 |
| Water Set No. 1 | 8.80 | 17.30 | 1½ | 150 |
| Water Set, N. E., 3770 | 14.00 | .... | 1½ | 150 |
| Goblet | 1.20 | 1.70 | 9 | 135 |
| Low Ft. Goblet | 1.20 | 1.70 | 11 | 125 |
| Wine | .66 | 1.40 | 30 | 125 |
| Wine Tumbler, 2 oz | .56 | 1.00 | 50 | 175 |
| Handled Custard | .84 | 1.50 | 30 | 150 |
| Tulip Sundae | 1.40 | .... | 6½ | 100 |
| Hi Ft. Sundae or Champagne | 1.40 | 1.80 | 12 | 100 |
| Low Ftd. Sherbet | 1.10 | 1.60 | 15 | 135 |
| Egg Cup or Ice | .90 | 1.50 | 20 | 135 |

**No. 714 PATTERN—Continued**

| | Plain | Dec. No. 6 | Dozens in Bbl. | Weight of Bbl. Lbs. |
|---|---|---|---|---|
| Ice Tea | $1.30 | $2.50 | 16 | 150 |
| No. 1 Shaker, N. T. | 8.00 gro. | 1.60 doz. | 30 | 175 |
| No. 1 Shaker, C. N. T. | 11.50 gro. | 1.80 doz. | 30 | 175 |
| No. 1 Shaker, glass top, nic. bd. | 9.00 gro. | .... | 30 | 175 |
| No. 1 Shaker, glass top, cast nic. bd | 12.00 gro. | .... | 30 | 175 |
| No. 1 Shaker, glass top, silver bd | 14.00 gro. | .... | 30 | 175 |
| No. 2 Shaker, N. T. | 12.00 gro. | 1.70 doz. | 30 | 175 |
| No. 2 Shaker, C. N. T. | 15.00 gro. | 2.00 doz. | 30 | 175 |
| No. 2 Shaker, glass top, nic. bd. | 14.00 gro. | .... | 30 | 175 |
| No. 2 Shaker, glass top, cast nic. bd | 15.50 gro. | .... | 30 | 175 |
| No. 2 Shaker, glass top, silver bd | 17.00 gro. | .... | 30 | 175 |
| Sugar Sifter | 1.50 | 2.80 | 14 | 100 |
| Sugar Sifter, B. Top | 1.90 | .... | 14 | 100 |
| Tooth Pick | .50 | 1.20 | 32 | 125 |
| Pickle Tray | 1.30 | 2.50 | 18 | 150 |
| Celery Tray | 2.20 | 3.40 | 9 | 150 |
| Cracker Jar and Cover | 4.80 | 9.60 | 2¾ | 150 |
| Oil Bottle | 1.70 | 3.10 | 10 | 190 |
| Catsup Bottle | 2.60 | 4.20 | 7 | 190 |
| Molasses Can, N. T. | 2.50 | 3.40 | 9 | 160 |
| Molasses Can, C. N. T. | 3.40 | 3.80 | 9 | 160 |
| Straw Jar | 7.50 | .... | 2½ | 150 |
| 14 inch Punch Bowl and Ft. | 24.00 | 60.00 | ½ | 125 |
| Footed Jelly | 1.50 | 3.00 | 7 | 150 |
| 5 inch Vase | .56 | 1.40 | 32 | 125 |
| 12 inch Vase | 1.50 | 3.30 | 5 | 125 |
| 16 inch Vase | 1.70 | 3.70 | 4 | 125 |
| 18 inch Vase | 4.00 | 9.00 | 1¾ | 125 |
| Claret Jug | 5.00 | 9.20 | 2½ | 150 |
| Water Bottle | 5.00 | 8.70 | 2¾ | 140 |
| Decanter | 5.00 | 9.20 | 2½ | 140 |
| Toy Punch Cup | .20 | .50 | 50 | 175 |
| Toy Punch Bowl | .76 | 1.60 | 20 | 150 |
| Candlestick | 2.50 | .... | 6½ | 145 |
| Cigar Jar and Cover | 2.34 | .... | 8 | 160 |
| Tobacco Jar and Cover | 3.75 | .... | 4 | 160 |

**No. 717 LINE**

| | Finished | Unfinished | Dec. No. 6 | Dozens in Bbl. | Weight of Bbl. Lbs. |
|---|---|---|---|---|---|
| Butter and Cover | $2.60 | $1.60 | $4.90 | 4½ | 160 |
| Sugar and Cover | 1.90 | 1.36 | 3.90 | 8 | 160 |
| Cream | 1.30 | 1.10 | 2.60 | 11 | 160 |
| Spoon | 1.10 | .90 | 2.40 | 11 | 160 |
| Set | 6.90 | 4.90 | 12.90 | 1½ | 160 |
| 4½ inch Berry | .50 | .40 | 1.30 | 26 | 165 |
| 7 inch Berry | 1.70 | 1.50 | 4.70 | 5 | 160 |
| 8 inch Berry | 2.40 | 1.90 | 6.50 | 3 | 160 |
| Berry Set, 8 inch | 5.40 | 4.30 | 14.30 | 2 | 160 |
| Jug | 3.50 | .... | 7.40 | 2 | 150 |
| Tumbler | .64 | .... | 1.36 | 24 | 150 |
| Water Set | 7.34 | .... | 15.50 | 1¼ | 150 |
| Ice Jug | 4.00 | .... | 8.00 | 2 | 150 |
| Shaker.................Gross | 7.00 | .... | 14.60 | 30 | 175 |
| Oil | 1.50 | .... | 2.40 | 12 | 175 |
| Olive | .90 | .... | 1.60 | 14 | 150 |
| 4 inch Ftd. Sherbet | .60 | .... | 1.34 | 28 | 135 |
| 10 inch Bowl and Foot | 10.50 | .... | 22.00 | 1 | 125 |

**No. 718 LINE**

| | Plain | Dec. 6 | Dozens in Bbl. | Weight of Bbl. Lbs. |
|---|---|---|---|---|
| Butter and Cover | $3.10 | $5.70 | 4½ | 150 |
| Sugar and Cover | 2.20 | 4.70 | 8 | 150 |
| Cream | 1.50 | 3.10 | 10 | 150 |
| Spoon | 1.30 | 2.80 | 12 | 150 |
| Set | 8.00 | 16.20 | 1½ | 150 |
| 4½ inch Berry | .72 | 1.60 | 25 | 180 |
| 8 inch Berry | 3.20 | 7.60 | 3½ | 160 |
| 9 inch Berry | 3.70 | 8.50 | 3½ | 160 |
| Berry Set, 8 inch | 7.52 | 17.20 | 2 | 160 |
| Berry Set, 9 inch | 8.02 | 18.10 | 2 | 160 |
| No. 1 Jug, ½ gal | 4.00 | 8.40 | 2 | 140 |
| No. 2 Jug, extra large | 6.50 | 11.20 | 1⅔ | 145 |
| Tumbler, bell | .80 | 1.60 | 18 | 150 |
| Tumbler, straight | .80 | 1.60 | 21 | 160 |
| Water Set No. 1 | 8.80 | 18.00 | 1½ | 150 |
| Water Set No. 2 | 11.30 | 20.80 | 1 | 160 |
| 5 inch Ice Cream | .72 | 1.70 | 25 | 160 |
| 9½ inch Shallow Fruit | 3.30 | 7.90 | 4 | 160 |
| 12 inch Cake Plate | 3.50 | 8.20 | 1⅔ | 140 |
| Wine | .66 | 1.40 | 30 | 125 |
| Goblet | 1.00 | 1.80 | 9 | 150 |
| Ice Tea, straight | 1.20 | 2.20 | 13 | 155 |
| Ice Tea, bell | 1.20 | 2.20 | 11 | 150 |
| Champ. or Hi Ft. Sundae | 1.40 | 2.30 | 12 | 100 |
| Low Ft. Sundae | 1.10 | 1.60 | 18 | 135 |
| Hld. Custard | .84 | 1.50 | 30 | 150 |
| 7 inch Open Ftd. Bowl | 3.50 | .... | 2 | 125 |
| 7 inch Cov'd ftd. Bowl | 6.00 | .... | 1½ | 125 |
| 7 inch Crushed Fruit Bowl and Cover | 6.00 | .... | 2 | 125 |

**No. 718 LINE—Continued**

| | Plain | Dec. 6 | Dozens in Bbl. | Weight of Bbl. Lbs. |
|---|---|---|---|---|
| 10 inch Salver | $ 3.60 | .... | 1⅔ | 135 |
| Cracker Jar and Cover | 4.50 | $9.20 | 1⅔ | 150 |
| Oil | 1.70 | 3.20 | 12 | 180 |
| Tall Celery | 2.40 | 3.70 | 4½ | 160 |
| Celery Tray, 11 inch | 2.00 | 3.60 | 8½ | 150 |
| Pickle Tray, 8 inch | 1.40 | 2.80 | 18 | 150 |
| Tooth Pick | .50 | 1.20 | 30 | 125 |
| 14 inch Ftd. Sherbet Bowl | 23.00 | 60.00 | 1½ | 140 |
| No. 1 Salt and Pepper, N. T. | 8.00 gro. | 1.50 doz. | 30 | 160 |
| No. 1 Salt and Pepper, G. T. N. Bd | 9.00 gro. | 1.60 doz. | 30 | 160 |
| No. 1 Salt and Pepper, C. N. T. | 11.50 gro. | 1.70 doz. | 30 | 160 |
| No. 2 Salt and Pepper, N. T., large Rest | 14.00 gro. | 1.90 doz. | 23 | 160 |
| No. 2 Salt and Pepper, C. N. T., large Rest | 18.00 gro. | 2.10 doz. | 23 | 160 |
| 10 inch Cemetery Vase | 2.60 | .... | 7¾ | 135 |
| 10 inch Vase | 1.40 | .... | 5 | 130 |
| 12 inch Vase | 1.40 | .... | 5 | 130 |
| 14 inch Vase | 1.70 | .... | 4½ | 130 |
| 18 inch Vase, No. 1 | 2.50 | .... | 2¾ | 130 |
| 18 inch Vase, No. 2 | 4.60 | .... | 2¾ | 130 |
| Violet or Tulip Vase | 1.40 | 3.70 | 6 | 130 |
| Individual Cream | .90 | 1.70 | 30 | 160 |
| Individual Sugar | .90 | 1.70 | 20 | 160 |
| 7 inch Rd. Condiment Tray | 1.30 | .... | 15 | 150 |
| Condiment Set (Oil, S. & P.) | 4.60 | .... | 4 | 150 |
| Mustard Jar and Cover | 1.20 | .... | 16 | 150 |
| 5 inch Footed Jelly | 1.60 | 3.20 | 6 | 150 |

**No. 719—OLD GLORY PATTERN**

| | Finished | Unfinished | Dec. 6 | Dozens in Bbl. | Weight of Bbl. Lbs. |
|---|---|---|---|---|---|
| Butter and Cover | $2.40 | $1.60 | $4.20 | 5 | 140 |
| Sugar and Cover | 1.70 | 1.24 | 3.60 | 8 | 140 |
| Cream | 1.20 | .86 | 2.50 | 9 | 140 |
| Spoon | .80 | .70 | 1.90 | 10 | 140 |
| Tea Set | 6.00 | 4.20 | 12.20 | 1⅝ | 140 |
| 4½ inch Berry | .50 | .40 | 1.34 | 22 | 150 |
| 7 inch Berry | 1.40 | 1.12 | 5.00 | 4 | 150 |
| 8 inch Berry | 1.90 | 1.50 | 5.70 | 4 | 150 |
| 7 inch Berry Set | 4.40 | 3.50 | 13.50 | 2¼ | 160 |
| 8 inch Berry Set | 4.90 | 3.90 | 13.70 | 2 | 160 |
| Tumbler | .66 | .... | 1.40 | 19 | 150 |
| Jug, ½ gal | 3.20 | .... | 6.60 | 2¼ | 140 |
| Water Set | 7.16 | .... | 15.00 | 1⅓ | 140 |
| Tall Celery | 1.60 | 1.50 | 2.70 | 6 | 125 |
| Handled Custard | .60 | .40 | 1.30 | 30 | 155 |
| Handled Jelly | .64 | .52 | 1.60 | 18 | 150 |
| 5 inch Footed Jelly | 1.20 | 1.00 | 2.40 | 6 | 125 |
| Molasses Can, T. T. | 1.70 | .... | 2.50 | 8 | 100 |
| Molasses Can, N. T. | 2.40 | .... | 3.00 | 8 | 100 |
| Salt and Pepper, N. T. | 7.00 gro. | .... | 1.50 doz. | 36 | 125 |
| Oil | 1.50 | .... | 2.70 | 10 | 160 |
| 9 inch Shallow Berry | 1.90 | .... | 5.70 | 5 | 125 |

**No. 720—FLORENE PATTERN**

| | Plain | Dec. 6 | Dozens in Bbl. | Weight of Bbl. Lbs. |
|---|---|---|---|---|
| Butter and Cover | $3.00 | $5.70 | 5 | 160 |
| Sugar and Cover | 2.30 | 4.70 | 6 | 160 |
| Cream | 1.50 | 3.10 | 9½ | 160 |
| Spoon | 1.30 | 2.80 | 12 | 160 |
| Tea Set, 4 pce | 8.00 | 16.20 | 1⅓ | 160 |
| 4½ inch Berry | .72 | 1.60 | 25 | 170 |
| 7 inch Berry, reg | 2.70 | 7.20 | 4½ | 160 |
| 7 inch Berry, fld. to 8 inch | 2.80 | 7.30 | 5 | 165 |
| 8 inch Berry, reg | 3.60 | 8.00 | 3½ | 160 |
| 8 inch Berry, fld. to 9 inch | 3.70 | 8.10 | 4 | 165 |
| 7 inch Berry Set, 7 pce | 7.02 | 16.80 | 2⅓ | 160 |
| 8 inch Berry Set, 7 pce | 7.92 | 17.60 | 2 | 160 |
| Tumbler | .80 | 1.60 | 20 | 170 |
| Jug, ½ gallon | 4.20 | 8.40 | 2⅓ | 150 |
| Water Set, 7 pce | 9.00 | 18.00 | 1 5/12 | 150 |
| Handled Custard | .84 | 1.50 | 20 | 160 |
| Footed Sherbet, Low | 1.10 | 1.60 | 19 | 150 |
| Saucer Handled Sherbet | 1.50 | 2.20 | 14 | 140 |
| Champ. or Hi Ft. Sundae | 1.40 | 2.30 | 12 | 125 |
| 5 inch Handled Jelly | 1.50 | 2.80 | 10 | 150 |
| 5 inch Footed Jelly | 1.60 | 3.20 | 5¾ | 150 |
| 5 inch Footed Jelly and Cover | 2.20 | 4.00 | 5⅓ | 150 |
| Ice Tea Tumbler | 1.20 | 2.30 | 12 | 140 |
| Oil | 1.70 | 3.20 | 10 | 180 |
| Tall Celery | 2.40 | 3.70 | 5 | 160 |
| Tooth Pick | .50 | 1.20 | 30 | 125 |
| Wine | .66 | 1.40 | 30 | 140 |
| Ice Cream, 6 inch | .80 | 1.70 | 25 | 160 |
| Spoon Tray | 1.20 | 2.70 | 20 | 150 |
| Pickle Tray | 1.20 | 2.70 | 15 | 150 |
| Bon Bon | 1.20 | 2.70 | 17 | 150 |
| Open Sugar | 1.20 | 2.60 | 7 | 150 |
| 9½ inch Ftd. Vase, plain | 2.90 | .... | 3½ | 135 |
| 9½ inch Ftd. Vase, scol | 2.90 | .... | 3½ | 135 |
| Water Bottle | 6.00 | .... | 2¾ | 140 |
| Individual Salts | 4.00 gro. | .... | 100 | 250 |
| Molasses Can, San., 13½ oz., glass top | 4.00 | .... | 8 | 125 |
| No. 1 Shaker, N. T. | 7.00 gro. | 1.60 doz. | 30 | 120 |
| No. 1 Shaker, C. N. T. | 11.00 gro. | 1.90 doz. | 30 | 120 |
| No. 2 Shaker, N. T. | 9.00 gro. | 1.80 doz. | 23 | 120 |
| No. 2 Shaker, C. N. T. | 12.00 gro. | 2.10 doz. | 23 | 120 |
| 4 inch Honey Bowl and Cover | 1.70 | 4.10 | 10 | 160 |

## No. 722 PATTERN

| | Finished | Unfinished | Dec. 6 | Dozens in Bbl. | Weight of Bbl. Lbs. |
|---|---|---|---|---|---|
| Butter and Cover | $2.40 | $1.64 | $4.20 | 5½ | 140 |
| Sugar and Cover | 1.70 | 1.30 | 3.50 | 8 | 140 |
| Cream | 1.20 | .90 | 2.30 | 9 | 140 |
| Spoon | .84 | .76 | 1.70 | 9 | 140 |
| Set | 6.20 | 4.60 | 11.70 | 1¾ | 140 |
| 4½ inch Berry | .54 | .44 | 1.36 | 30 | 140 |
| 7 inch Berry | 1.50 | 1.20 | 4.30 | 6 | 140 |
| 8 inch Berry | 2.00 | 1.60 | 5.00 | 5 | 140 |
| Berry Set, 7 inch | 4.74 | 3.84 | 12.50 | 2½ | 150 |
| Berry Set, 8 inch | 5.24 | 4.24 | 13.20 | 2½ | 150 |
| Jug | 3.40 | 3.00 | 6.20 | 2 | 135 |
| Tumbler | .70 | .70 | 1.40 | 16 | 135 |
| Water Set | 7.60 | 7.20 | 14.60 | 1⅓ | 135 |
| 9 inch Scolloped Fruit | 2.20 | .... | .... | 4½ | 125 |
| 10 inch Plate | 2.20 | .... | .... | 5 | 125 |

## No. 723—COLONIAL PATTERN

| | Plain | Dec. No. 39 | Dozens in Bbl. | Weight of Bbl. Lbs, |
|---|---|---|---|---|
| Butter and Cover | $3.20 | $5.30 | 4½ | 160 |
| Sugar and Cover | 2.60 | 4.50 | 7 | 160 |
| Cream | 1.70 | 2.80 | 10 | 160 |
| Spoon | 1.50 | 2.40 | 9 | 160 |
| Table Set, 4 pce | 9.00 | 15.00 | 1¾ | 160 |
| 4½ inch Berry | .90 | 1.50 | 20 | 175 |
| 8 inch Berry | 3.50 | 6.20 | 4½ | 160 |
| 9 inch Berry | 4.20 | 7.20 | 3 | 160 |
| Berry Set, 8 inch | 8.90 | 15.20 | 2 | 160 |
| Berry Set, 9 inch | 9.60 | 16.20 | 1⅝ | 160 |
| Tumbler | 1.00 | 1.50 | 20 | 150 |
| Jug | 5.00 | 7.90 | 2⅔ | 150 |
| Jug, 3 qt., S. H. | 9.00 | | 1½ | 150 |
| Water Set | 11.00 | 16.90 | 1½ | 150 |
| 11½ inch Tray | 4.60 | .... | 3½ | 140 |
| Footed Soda | 1.30 | .... | 10 | 125 |
| 4½ oz. Low Sundae | 1.00 | .... | 25 | 135 |
| 4½ oz. Hi Sundae | 1.40 | .... | 13 | 125 |
| 6½ oz. Low Sundae | 1.10 | .... | 15 | 135 |
| 6½ oz. Hi Sundae | 1.40 | .... | 10 | 125 |
| Ice Tea | 1.20 | .... | 12 | 150 |
| Tooth Pick | .60 | 1.20 | 30 | 125 |
| Goblet | 1.10 | 1.60 | 9 | 125 |
| Wine | .66 | 1.30 | 30 | 125 |
| Oil Bottle | 1.70 | 2.90 | 10 | 170 |
| Handled Custard | .84 | 1.50 | 28 | 150 |
| Hotel Sugar | .90 | 1.70 | 18 | 160 |
| Hotel Cream | .90 | 1.70 | 20 | 160 |
| Molasses Can, N. T. | 3.00 | 4.40 | 6½ | 160 |
| Molasses Can, C. N. T. | 4.00 | 5.20 | 6½ | 160 |
| Shaker, N. T. | 8.50 gro. | 1.00 doz. | 36 | 175 |
| Shaker, C. N. T. | 12.00 gro. | 1.30 doz. | 36 | 175 |
| Shaker, G. T. N. R. | 9.50 gro. | .... | 36 | 175 |
| No. 2, 20 inch Vase | 8.00 | .... | ½ | 100 |

## No. 723—COLONIAL PATTERN—Continued

| | Plain | Dec. No. 39 | Dozens in Bbl. | Weight in Bbl. Lbs. |
|---|---|---|---|---|
| No. 2, 14 inch Vase | 8.00 | .... | ¾ | 100 |
| Horse Radish Jar and Cover | 1.40 | .... | 16 | 160 |
| No. 2, 8 oz. Schoppen | 1.00 | .... | 16 | 160 |
| No. 1, 6 oz. Schoppen | .86 | .... | 20 | 180 |

## No. 724—PATTERN

| | Fin. Plain | Dec. No. 6 | Unfin. Plain | Dozens in Bbl. | Weight of Bbl. Lbs. |
|---|---|---|---|---|---|
| Butter and Cover | $1.90 | $3.70 | $1.56 | 4½ | 150 |
| Sugar and Cover | 1.60 | 3.40 | 1.30 | 8 | 150 |
| Cream | 1.00 | 2.50 | .90 | 10 | 150 |
| Spoon | .80 | 2.00 | .70 | 10 | 150 |
| Tabel Set, 4 pce | 5.20 | 11.60 | 4.40 | 1⅔ | 150 |
| 4½ inch Berry | .50 | 1.36 | .36 | 25 | 150 |
| 7 inch Berry | 1.30 | 4.50 | .... | 6 | 150 |
| 8 inch Berry | 1.90 | 5.00 | .... | 4½ | 150 |
| 6 inch Berry | .... | .... | 1.20 | 5 | 150 |
| 7 inch Berry | .... | .... | 1.40 | 4 | 150 |
| Berry Set, 8 inch | 4.90 | 13.16 | .... | 2 | 150 |
| Berry Set, 7 inch | .... | .... | 3.56 | 2¼ | 150 |
| Tumbler | .66 | 1.30 | .... | 20 | 160 |
| Jug No. 2, Large | 3.60 | 6.90 | 3.60 | 2¼ | 140 |
| Jug No. 1, Small | 2.30 | 5.00 | 2.20 | 2½ | 140 |
| Water Set No. 2 | 7.56 | 14.70 | .... | 1⅓ | 150 |
| Water Set No. 1 | 6.26 | 12.80 | .... | 1¾ | 150 |
| Tall Celery | 1.50 | 2.60 | 1.30 | 6 | 125 |
| 5 inch Ftd. Jelly | 1.20 | 2.40 | 1.00 | 6 | 140 |
| Tooth Pick | .50 | 1.10 | .... | 30 | 125 |
| Shaker, N. T. | 5.20 gro. | 1.00 doz. | .... | 36 | 125 |
| Goblet | .74 | 1.50 | .... | 9 | 135 |
| Wine | .50 | 1.00 | .... | 30 | 125 |
| ~~Molasses~~ Can, T. T | 1.70 | 2.50 | .... | 8 | 100 |
| ~~Molasses~~ Can, N. T | 2.40 | 3.00 | .... | 8 | 100 |
| Oil Bottle | 1.50 | 2.70 | .... | 12 | 160 |
| ~~Handled Cust~~ard | .60 | 1.20 | .... | 30 | 150 |
| ~~10 inch Vase~~ | .95 | .... | .... | 6 | 100 |

Decorated No. 36 on No. 724 Line,
10% advance over decorated No. 6.

## No. 725—PLAIN COLONIAL

| | Plain | Dozens in Bbl. | Weight of Bbl Lbs. |
|---|---|---|---|
| Butter and Cover | $3.00 | 4½ | 150 |
| Sugar and Cover | 2.00 | 7 | 150 |
| Cream | 1.35 | 9 | 150 |
| Spoon | 1.10 | 10 | 150 |
| Set | 7.45 | 1¾ | 150 |
| 4½ inch Berry | .60 | 30 | 160 |
| 8 inch Berry | 2.70 | 4 | 160 |
| 9 inch Berry | 3.60 | 3½ | 160 |
| Berry Set, 8 inch | 6.30 | 2¼ | 150 |
| Berry Set, 9 inch | 7.20 | 2 | 150 |
| Tumbler | .80 | 20 | 150 |
| Jug No. 2 | 4.50 | 2⅓ | 140 |
| Jug No. 1 | 3.00 | 3½ | 140 |
| Water Set No. 2 | 9.30 | 1⅓ | 150 |
| Water Set No. 1 | 7.80 | 1⅔ | 150 |
| Goblet | 1.10 | 9 | 125 |
| Wine | .60 | 30 | 125 |
| Low Footed Sherbet | 1.00 | 18 | 140 |
| Hi Ftd. Sundae or Champagne | 1.20 | 12 | 125 |
| Handled Custard | .84 | 30 | 150 |
| 5 inch Footed Jelly | 1.75 | 6½ | 135 |
| 5 inch Footed Jelly and Cover | 2.40 | 5½ | 135 |
| Oil Bottle | 1.70 | 12 | 160 |
| Cracker Jar and Cover | 4.80 | 2½ | 140 |
| Hotel Sugar | 1.20 | 13 | 150 |
| Hotel Cream | .90 | 23 | 150 |
| Molasses Can, N. T. | 2.50 | 8 | 150 |
| Molasses Can, C. N. T. | 3.40 | 8 | 150 |
| Shaker, N. T. | 8.50 | 30 | 135 |
| Shaker, C. N. T. | 12.00 | 30 | 135 |
| Shaker, Glass Top | 9.50 | 30 | 135 |
| Tooth Pick | .50 | 30 | 100 |
| Tall Celery | 2.10 | 5 | 150 |
| Ice Tea | 1.20 | 12 | 140 |
| 6 inch Ftd. Flower Vase | 1.50 | 9 | 125 |
| 8 inch Ftd. Flower Vase | 2.50 | 5½ | 125 |
| 11 inch Ftd. Flower Vase | 4.50 | 3⅛ | 125 |
| 5½ inch Ice Cream | .70 | 20 | 140 |
| 6 inch Plate | .70 | 14 | 140 |
| 10 inch Shallow Berry | 3.60 | 5 | 140 |
| 14 inch Ftd. Punch Bowl | 23.00 | ½ | 125 |

## No. 900 PATTERN

| | | | |
|---|---|---|---|
| 4½ inch Nappy | $0.70 | 25 | 140 |
| 4½ inch Nappy, all shapes | .70 | 21 | 140 |
| 8 inch Berry, reg | 2.00 | 4 | 140 |
| 9 inch Berry, bell | 2.00 | 4½ | 140 |
| 7 inch Berry, cupt | 2.00 | 4 | 140 |
| 9 inch Berry, shallow | 2.00 | 5 | 140 |
| 9 inch Berry, crimpt | 2.00 | 4 | 140 |

## Nos. 700, ~~702~~, ~~705~~, ~~706~~, 708 and 709 PATTERNS CRYSTAL LAMPS

Lamps Only

| | Price per Doz. | Dozens in Bbl. | Weight of Bbl. Lbs. |
|---|---|---|---|
| 00 Stand Lamps, No. 1 Collar | $1.40 | 5 | 115 |
| 0 Stand Lamps, No. 1 Collar | 1.60 | 4½ | 115 |
| A Stand Lamps, No. 1 Collar | 2.00 | 3½ | 115 |
| A Stand Lamps, No. 2 Collar | 2.10 | 3½ | 115 |
| B Stand Lamps, No. 2 Collar | 2.50 | 2¾ | 115 |
| C Stand Lamps, No. 2 Collar | 3.00 | 2¼ | 115 |
| D Stand Lamps, No. 2 Collar | 3.70 | 1¾ | 115 |
| C Sewing Lamps, No. 2 Collar | 3.00 | 2½ | 115 |
| D Sewing Lamps, No. 2 Collar | 3.70 | 2 | 115 |
| O Flat Hand Lamps, No. 1 Collar | 1.20 | 9 | 115 |
| O Footed Hand Lamps, No. 1 Collar | 1.60 | 5½ | 115 |
| No. 100 Flat Hand, No. 1 Collar | 1.20 | 9 | 115 |
| No. 250 Flat Hand, No. 2 Collar | 1.70 | 9 | 115 |
| No. 250 Footed Hand, No. 2 Collar | 2.50 | 5½ | 115 |
| Handled Fount, No. 2 Collar | 2.00 | 4½ | 100 |
| Unhandled Fount, No. 2 Collar | 1.50 | 4½ | 100 |

Opal Lamps, 20 per cent advance over Crystal.

## No. 707—GIANT LIBRARY LAMPS

| | | | |
|---|---|---|---|
| Lamps Only | $3.60 | 1½ | 135 |
| Lamps, plain complete | 5.40 | 1 | 100 |
| Lamps, decorated complete | 7.70 | 1 | 100 |

## No. 708—JUMBO LIBRARY LAMP

| | | | |
|---|---|---|---|
| Lamp only | $3.70 | 1½ | 135 |
| Lamp only, Dec. No. 35 | 4.50 | 1½ | 135 |
| Lamp, plain complete | 5.70 | 1 | 100 |
| Lamp, Dec. 35, complete, plain chimney | 6.50 | 1 | 100 |
| Lamp, Dec. 35, complete, Dec. chimney | 7.70 | 1 | 100 |

## No. 709—LIBRARY LAMP

| | | | |
|---|---|---|---|
| Lamp Only, plain | $3.80 | 1½ | 135 |
| Lamp Only, decorated | 4.50 | 1½ | 135 |
| Lamp, plain complete | 6.00 | 1 | 100 |
| Lamp, Dec., complete, plain chimney | 6.70 | 1 | 100 |
| Lamp, Dec., complete, Dec. chimney | 7.80 | 1 | 100 |

## No. 900—LIBRARY LAMP AND MAMMOTH LIBRARY LAMP

| | | | |
|---|---|---|---|
| Lamp Only, plain | $3.60 | 1½ | 135 |
| Lamp with Burner and Chimney, plain | 5.80 | 1 | 100 |
| Lamp Only, decorated | 5.20 | 1½ | 135 |
| Lamp with Burner and Chimney, Dec. | 7.90 | 1 | 100 |

## No. 1000—LIBRARY LAMPS

| | | | |
|---|---|---|---|
| Lamps Only, plain | $3.30 | 1½ | 135 |
| Lamps Only, decorated | 4.00 | 1½ | 135 |
| Plain complete | 5.50 | 1 | 100 |
| Decorated, complete, chimney fired | 7.00 | 1 | 100 |
| Decorated, complete, plain chimney | 6.30 | 1 | 100 |

# CHAPTER THREE
# THE CLARKE YEARS

FROM 1919 TO September, 1926, the New Martinsville Glass Manufacturing Company was guided by Ira M. Clarke, who came to the firm from Bridgeville, Pa., shortly after his previous employer, the J. B. Higbee Glass Company, was closed. While at Higbee, Clarke obtained design patents for a candy container/bank featuring a sitting cat (#48,667 granted March 7, 1916) and a combined match-box holder and ash tray (#52,840 granted January 7, 1919). Clarke was listed as secretary or secretary/general manager on the New Martinsville firm's stationery, but letterheads from 1925-26 listed Clarke as treasurer and general manager, while Robert E. McEldowney, who had been assistant sales manager under Clarke, assumed the position of secretary. As Clarke's tenure began, Charles Schulte was head shipping clerk, and Paul Kirrig was packing room boss. The mould shop foreman was George Crimmel. Miss Mary Glenn and Miss Smith were the office employees (*American Flint*, July, 1919).

THE NEW MARTINSVILLE GLASS MFG. CO.
MANUFACTURERS OF
PRESSED AND BLOWN GLASSWARE, LAMPS, ETC.
NEW MARTINSVILLE, W. VA.

**This plain letterhead was in use from about 1919 through 1921.**

Clarke secured a number of design patents during his time at New Martinsville, and he seems to deserve the credit for restoring the company to a position in the glass trade close to that which it had occupied when David I. Fisher was in charge. The company advertised regularly in the glass trade publications, and these ads offer excellent documentation for a wide variety of New Martinsville products. A series of ads with the theme "The Refinement of Pot Glass" appeared in *Pottery,*

*Glass and Brass Salesman* in 1923-24, and many different items were featured, including the various colored wares being made at that time.

Colored glass was much in vogue during the 1920s, and the New Martinsville firm kept pace with the times. Staple goods and blanks for decorating were made primarily in crystal, of course, although console sets were made in color and then decorated. In addition to crystal, these colors were the main ones used from 1922 to 1926 for console sets, vanity sets, smokers' articles and other items: amber, blue, green, and amethyst (other colors were introduced later; see Chapter Four). There are just one or two mentions of canary glass in the 1920s, such as the debut of the No. 149-3 candy jar in April, 1925. A few articles which originated in this time period were also made in black glass, but they could be part of later production when black glass was popular (see Chapter Four). In May, 1926, a color called "Peach Melba" was introduced; this was probably a pale pink hue, and it may have been satin-finished by acid [see Figs. 344-345].

About a year before Clarke came to New Martinsville, glassworker John Forbes summarized the local conditions in this rather plaintive column in the April, 1918, issue of the *American Flint*:

*It has been some time since there has been a letter in the Flint from New Martinsville because it has been so dull here for some months and all I could send in would be a hard luck story, and I guess nearly every one else has had their share of that and would not care to hear it. But the once prosperous New Martinsville works is down now to eight or nine shops at present. When we were running full we had about 15 or 16 shops, but since the weather has warmed up we hope to get more gas.*

A few months later, longtime New Martinsville glassworker Elzie Miller said that "Our factory is doing pretty good at present" and predicted the firm would be "running full blast the coming fall and winter" (*American Flint*, June, 1918). Eight months, later even Forbes was optimistic about matters—both local and worldwide:

*Just a few lines to let you know that New Martinsville is still on the map. We now have a six-ring tank in oper-*

*Letterhead stationery from 1922.*

*ation, and it is a dandy too. We are running 12 shops and the glass is just fine, but when we have a chance to work, the weather man brings along a cold wave, and then the gas man shuts off the gas, Producers are about ready to light up. Expect to be in operation about March 1st. By another month or two, I hope to be able to say that the New Martinsville glass factory is going along better than ever. We all hope by that time the Peace Conference will be over, and the world will be at peace again (American Flint, February, 1919).*

In June, 1919, *Crockery and Glass Journal* noted that "Ira M. Clarke ... is now in charge of the factory" and said that he was making "a number of additions ...to the lines [which] ... will be ready to show to the trade early in the fall." Not long after Clarke joined the firm, the New Martinsville Glass Manufacturing Co. purchased a number of Higbee moulds. A copy of the original list (furnished to Everett and Addie Miller by Viking Glass Company president Eugene Miller in 1972) shows 89 moulds and records a purchase price of $2000, "payable in stock at par if it can be bought

in as per agreement of Jan. 13/[19]20." Some undated pencil notes on this same list reveal sales in excess of $43,000 including $24,000 to the Woolworth chain and $12,000 to the Butler Brothers wholesale house.

Perhaps the Higbee moulds provided some diversification for New Martinsville's product line, but there seems little doubt that Ira Clarke was both an able manager and an effective sales promoter. John Forbes had this to say about him in the September, 1919, issue of the *American Flint*:

*Just about three months ago the old New Martinsville plant was just about ready to take the count for down and out, but along came a man by the name of Ira M. Clarke and took hold of the old plant. Although slightly disfigured, she is still in the ring. When Mr. Clarke came here the place was stocked full from cellar to attic, and we had to wait until the mail would come in to see if any orders came in, but now the stock is all sold and orders are piling up so that their intentions are to run her now to its fullest capacity.*

Under Clarke's guidance, the New Martinsville

*Letterhead stationery from 1926.*

## New Martinsville Glass Manufacturing Co.

Date .... *1/24* ............. 19*25*

| Day Turn No. *11* | | Night Turn No. |
|---|---|---|

WARE MADE  *149 - 3 Cand. Jar + Blue*   *Crystal*

MOVE ........................................... *2.36*

| 1 Hr | 1½ Hrs | 2 Hrs | 2½ Hrs | 3 Hrs | 3½ Hrs | 4 Hrs | ~~4½ Hrs~~ |
|---|---|---|---|---|---|---|---|

Do Not Mark In Space Below

| | | |
|---|---|---|
| Presser | *Geo. Ellson* | 4.38 |
| Foot Presser | | |
| Finisher | | 3.94 |
| Pat. Tool Fins | | |
| Cutter Down | | |
| Handler | | |
| Foot Setter | *J. Berr* | 3.94 |
| Blower | | |
| Blower | | |
| Caser | | |
| Core Gatherer | | |
| Core Gatherer | | |
| Gatherer | *J. Keslar* | 3.50 |
| Gatherer | | |
| Foot Gatherer | | |
| Spot Mould Blower | | |
| | | |
| Pay for | *Crystal* | 1.53 |
| | *Blue* | 3.19 |
| Selected Good at Lehr | | |
| Selected Bad at Lehr | *Crystal* | .23 |
| | *Blue* | .27 |

## New Martinsville Glass Manufacturing Co.

| 1 Hr | 1½ Hrs | 2 Hrs | 2½ Hrs | 3 Hrs | 3½ Hrs | 4 Hrs | ~~4½ Hrs~~ |
|---|---|---|---|---|---|---|---|

| | | |
|---|---|---|
| Carrying in | *Julia Bruhey* | 1.25 |
| Carrying in | | |
| Sticker up | | |
| Sticker up | | |
| Sticker up | | |
| Sticker up | | |
| Snapper | | 1.50 |
| Snapper | | 1.50 |
| Snapper | | 1.50 |
| Snapper | | 1.50 |
| Handle Maker | | |
| Handle Maker | | |
| Cleaner Off | | |
| Cleaner Off | | |
| Carrying Over | | 1.00 |
| Carrying Over | | |
| Mould Holder | | |
| Mould Holder | | |
| Lever Boy | | |
| Turner Out | | |
| Straightener | | |

*This original shop card records the performance of George Ellson's press shop on January 24, 1925, when the group of ten workers was making the No. 149-3 candy jar in crystal and blue glass. At the completion of a 4 hour-15 minute turn, the shop had made 472 candy jars. Note the range of scheduled wages, from $4.38 for the presser to $1.25 for those who carried-over or carried-in. The carrying-in "boy" on this shop was a woman, Julia Bruhey.*

firm moved away from the production of pattern lines or sets which had been so prevalent during the Fisher years. Clarke patented a wide variety of glassware items, ranging from ashtrays and other smoking accessories to powder boxes and vanity sets. Clarke also patented a bowl with integral flower frog and a floor lamp. In the mid-1920s, the company began to make liquor and other kinds of specialty beverage sets, including some novelties such as decanters in the likenesses of animals.

During this time period, the New Martinsville Glass Manufacturing Company marked some pieces with a distinctive trademark—a block M with a vertical line in its middle which creates the

TRADE **M** MARK

**QUALITY**
**AND**
**SERVICE**

*This New Martinsville trademark is typically found on items made in the mid-1920s, such as console bowls, trays for vanity sets and perfume bottles.*

appearance of an N superimposed upon the M. This mark was frequently used in the firm's advertising along with a slogan ("New Martinsville Quality and Service"). Interestingly, relatively few pieces of glass seem to bear the mark, and it was not officially registered as a trademark with the U. S. Patent Office.

The strength of Clarke's leadership should not be underestimated, but he certainly had able help. Robert E. McEldowney was listed as Assistant Sales Manager in the firm's ad in the December 16, 1920, issue of *Pottery, Glass and Brass Salesman*. The son of a pioneer New Martinsville settler, McEldowney had been to business school and was an insurance agent prior to joining the glass plant. About 1925, he became secretary of the company, probably in addition to other duties in sales. Another young man who joined the firm about 1920 was Harry Barth; he later became assistant general manager and, ultimately, was himself in charge of the plant.

Unfortunately, the last several years of Clarke's tenure at New Martinsville were marked by considerable animosity between members of the local glassworkers' union and two factory managers, brothers Theodore and Ross Schwing. Some account of these difficulties is given later in this chapter.

In the early fall of 1925, the popular actress Gloria Swanson was in New Martinsville with a movie crew to film a feature called "Stage Struck." Employee Arch Hill, writing in the *American Flint* (October, 1925), noted that the crew "took pictures of the glass company employees here, leaving the factory at noon and returning after dinner ...." According to *Pottery, Glass and Brass Salesman* (October 8, 1925), Miss Swanson "was greatly struck by the second son of Robert McEldowney, assistant sales manager of the New Martinsville Glass Manufacturing Company." Swanson "told the father that if he films well there is a big future ahead for him. The lad may turn out to be another Jackie Coogan."

## STAPLE GOODS

Although the items mentioned in this section may have little allure for today's glass collectors, they were important, perhaps even vital, to the economic stability of the New Martinsville Glass Manufacturing Company during this period. They were advertised in the major glass trade journals, particularly during the early 1920s, and this under-

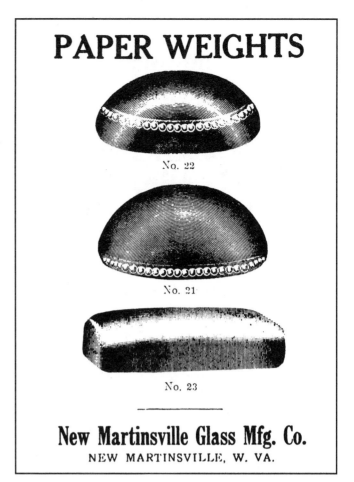

# PAPER WEIGHTS

No. 22

No. 21

No. 23

## New Martinsville Glass Mfg. Co.
### NEW MARTINSVILLE, W. VA.

*These standard paperweights sold for about $1.50 per dozen when purchased by the gross; from* **Pottery, Glass and Brass Salesman** *(September 4, 1919).*

*Paperweight/photo frame.*

scores their significance to the New Martinsville firm.

Items of stationer's glassware—inkwells, sponge cups, pen trays, etc.—were made regularly. The line of inkwells was essentially the same as those illustrated in the previous chapter (see p. 45-46), and the No. 10 pen tray [see Fig. 298] was also

55

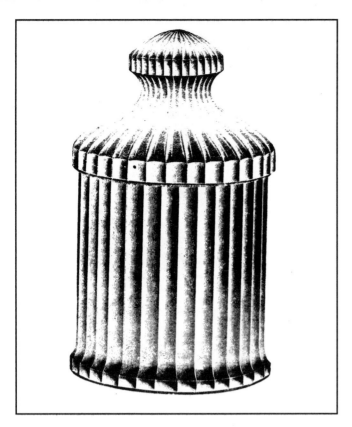

*This No. 310 (Mansion) crushed fruit bowl, shown in an original catalogue, was for soda fountain use.*

No. 541 — Measuring Cup.
No. 544½ — Measuring Cup, Front Lip
No. 545 — Measuring Cup, Side Lip
18 Doz. to bbl.

*This illustration from a New Martinsville catalogue details the three varieties of measuring cups then available.*

a holdover from previous years. Three plain paperweights were advertised in the fall of 1919, and the company also produced a star-shaped paperweight which was marketed as a photo frame.

Soda fountain glassware was also made. Sherbets and banana split dishes were advertised in July, 1920. Items from the No. 97 Old Colony line were continued, for this colonial-style glassware was intended for this market. A long-lived line called only No. 310 (now known as Mansion)

*From an original catalogue.*

was probably intended for soda fountain use also, for a company catalogue lists such articles as large fruit bowls, sherbets, parfaits, grape juice glasses and child's mugs. Measuring cups were made in several styles.

Two plain punch bowls, known only as No. 38 and No. 39, were also being made in 1920, based upon correspondence between the company and the National Association of Manufacturers of Pressed and Blown Glassware. The soda fountain line also included such articles as tall straw jars as well as a delightful device for an ice cream cone. This was designated as the No. 1000 cone holder in a company catalogue [see Fig. 307]; these sold for fifty cents per dozen wholesale and were packed 36 dozen to a barrel!

56

# Soda Fountain Glassware

*(In Crystal and Opal)*

## Full Line of Desirable Shapes

No. 31  Sherbet          No. 310  8-in. Banana Split

### Pot Glass Only

---

## New Martinsville Glass Mfg. Co.

NEW MARTINSVILLE, W. VA.

New York Rep.: Malone & Nicholson, 50 Park Place

Pottery, Glass and Brass Salesman *(July 1, 1920)*.

---

# SANITARY-SUGAR-POUR

*Opens and Closes Automatically*

## NO FLIES—NO DIRT—NO DUST

14 Dez.
to
Barrel

No. 708

### No. 714—Polished Aluminum Top
### Does Not Corrode

## New Martinsville Glass Mfg. Co.
### New Martinsville, W. Va.

Pottery, Glass and Brass Salesman *(July 28, 1921)*.

---

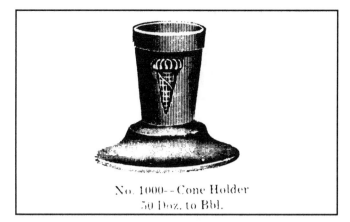

No. 1000—Cone Holder
50 Doz. to Bbl.

*The little ice cream cone on the No. 1000 cone holder shows up better on this original catalogue illustration than it does on the real thing!*

---

### COLONIAL RIBBED

1C2296—3¼ in., colonial ribbed fluted sides, clear crystal, aluminum top, equal number salt and peppers. 3 doz. in carton. ..............Doz. **39c**
(Total $1.17)

---

### TALL COLONIAL

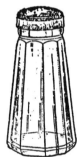

An old time favorite returned to the 10c counter class.

1C2301—4¼ in. high, taper shape, wide base, colonial panel pattern, heavy cast nickel plated top. Asstd. salts and peppers. 2 doz. in case.
(Total $1.44)  Doz. **72c**

---

### SQUARE PANELED

This is a staple on every variety counter.

1C502—3 in., square paneled shape, full finished pressed crystal, aluminum dome tops, equal number salts and peppers. Asstd. 1 doz. in box.  Doz. **89c**

---

### GENUINE CUT

The always popular household utility in a rich cut pattern.

1C507—Ht. 3¼ in., aluminum dome top, 2 floral and leaf cuttings on clear crystal blanks, ½ doz. salts and ½ doz. peppers. Asstd. 1 doz. in pkg.

Doz. **92c**

*New Martinsville salt/pepper shakers from a January, 1924, Butler Brothers catalogue.*

57

No. 64 — Shaker

No. 65 — Shaker

No. 66 — Shaker

*From an original catalogue.*

## A Revolution in Glass Making

Just a year ago we secured the patent rights (U. S. Patent No. 1,057,899) for a little item that is going to revolutionize the footed bowl, salver and display vase business in this country. This permits of these items being knocked down and packed to save at least 50 per cent package charge. Beyond this the display vases can be made absolutely true, while certain items such as the footed bowl can be separated and the bowl part used as a berry bowl. We know this is a winner and want to tell you more about it. Just note these figures on package contents of barrels when items are knocked down:

Display Vases—4″, 15 doz.; 6″, 13 doz.; 8″, 12 doz.; 10″ 9 doz.; 12″, 8 doz.; 14″, 6 doz.; 16″, 5 doz.
Footed Bowls—8″, 4 doz.; 9″, 3 doz.
Cake Salvers—9″, 4 doz.; 11″, 3 doz.

## New Martinsville Glass Mfg. Company
### New Martinsville, W. Va.

Malone & Nicholson, 125 Fifth Avenue, New York representatives

*From* Pottery, Glass and Brass Salesman *(March 1, 1923).*

A sanitary sugar container fitted with a special metal top for pouring was on the market in 1921. In 1924, these "Sugar Pours," as they were called, were being advertised with special rubber protectors on the base to forestall breakage and to prevent the marring of soda fountain counters and restaurant tabletops.

Many common salt/pepper shakers were listed in the firm's 1917 price list, and production of these certainly continued in the 1920s. Among those seen in company catalogues are No. 64 (Palm Tendril); No. 65 (Plume Band); No. 66 (Footed Four Petal); and No. 150 (Oriole).

The New Martinsville firm made a special small cream pitcher with a thick base for use on railroad dining cars. This article was called the No. 708 Pullman creamer. It was not part of the earlier No. 708 (Lusitania) line, which had been discontinued by this time.

In 1922, the New Martinsville concern obtained a patent (U. S. Patent #1,057,899) on a threaded connector which could be used to join two otherwise separate pieces of glass. This connector made

# WINDOW TRIM VASES

Both practical and ornamental. These vases will improve the looks of your window displays and at the same time make the work of decorating easier if used as shelf supports.

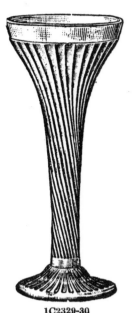
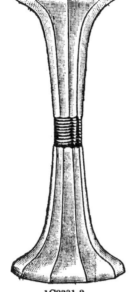

1C2329-30          1C2331-2

Spiral Futed Design—Tapered clear crystal.
1C2329—9 in. high, diam. at top 3½ in. 3 doz. in bbl., 52 lbs.
Doz **$2.35**

1C2330—12 in. high, diam. at top 5 in. 2 doz. in case, 75 lbs.
Doz **$4.25**

Colonial Design—Clear crystal, patented 2 pc. construction, joined in center by nickel plated brass ferrule. Top and bottom ground and polished so that stand sets true and level.

1C2331—8 in. high, diam. 5 in., top and bottom. 3 doz. in bbl.
Doz **$3.25**

1C2332—12½ in. high, diam. 5 in., top and bottom. 2½ doz. in bbl., 55 lbs.
Doz **$4.25**

*These store fixtures were made at New Martinsville; the patented display vase came in several sizes (Butler Brothers catalogue, July, 1924).*

it possible to market seven sizes of display vases plus footed bowls and large cake salvers. These were widely advertised in March, 1923. All items made with the threaded connector carried the factory designation No. 727. Some of them appeared in Butler Brothers catalogues later in the 1920s. The patented connector was also used for lamps about a year later, and these are discussed elsewhere in this chapter.

In 1925, a dispute arose between New Martinsville's workers and the plant management regarding the wages and moves for an item called the No. 534 relay cover. This was probably a plain crystal glass cover for a meter, and it would be somewhat similar to those seen today on outdoor electric meters. There is evidence that the New Martinsville plant also made containers to be used for perfume atomizers, but only perfunctory sketches of rather bulbous small bottles remain today.

## CUT AND DECORATED WARE

Among the product innovations which may be credited to Ira Clarke is the introduction of substantial lines of cut glassware from the New Martinsville plant. This ware, produced primarily by using copper wheels, was known as "light cut" or "gray cutting" in the trade. This should not be confused with the deep, intricate mitres of the earlier, heavyweight cut glass from such factories as Libbey and Hawkes. A few cutters were probably working in New Martinsville when Clarke came to the plant, but their ranks were soon increased.

A full-page ad in *Pottery, Glass and Brass Salesman* showed the firm's new array of cut ware

(continued on p. 64)

## Something New!

OUR new cut line is a humdinger — the illustration shows that. Our entire range of products, including our new lines of pressed, blown, etched and decorated glassware, will be on display at

*Room 714, Fort Pitt Hotel, Pittsburgh, Jan. 9-28*
*Balcony B4, Hotel Morrison, Chicago, Feb. 6-18*

### New Martinsville Glass Mfg. Co.
#### New Martinsville, W. Va.

*From Pottery, Glass and Brass Salesman (December 15, 1921).*

"THE REFINEMENT
OF POT GLASS —

### NEW MARTINSVILLE
*No. 190-0 Molasses Jug, Cover and Plate*

A NEW ITEM and one of the largest sellers. Supplied in numerous attractive cuttings. Can be used as a sanitary molasses or cream jug. Easily washed. Suitable for the finest table.

THE NEW MARTINSVILLE GLASS MFG. CO.

NEW MARTINSVILLE, W. VA.

AT THE PRICE
OF TANK GLASS"

*This full-page ad in* **Pottery, Glass and Brass Salesman** *(May 31, 1923) shows a piece of cut ware.*

No. 140-1

## Cut Guest Jug and Tumbler

*A* pressed glass jug and tumbler with a cutting of unusual beauty. A fast selling item that will enable you to clean up a good profit.

Packs 3 doz. per bbl.
Gross weight 110 lbs.

### THE NEW MARTINSVILLE GLASS MFG. CO.

NEW MARTINSVILLE, W. VA.

---

## NEW MARTINSVILLE

### No. 10—Sandwich Tray

ONE of the newest and most improved patterns with full finished blanks. *A* ready seller everywhere.

¶ Supplied in a variety of cuttings at prices that permit retailing at one to ten dollars each.

### THE NEW MARTINSVILLE GLASS MFG. CO.

NEW MARTINSVILLE, W. VA.

---

## NEW MARTINSVILLE

### No. 727—Hotel Water Tray and No. 10 Hall Boy Jug

ONE of the newest and handsomest items of this kind shown this year. Made from the finest clear pot glass and available at prices that for the quality have never before been approached.

### THE NEW MARTINSVILLE GLASS MFG. CO.

NEW MARTINSVILLE, W. VA.

---

## No. 149-3 Candy Jar

A NEW cone shaped half pound candy jar that meets a popular demand. Useful and very attractive. A high class piece of glassware with finished cover and foot. Made in crystal, blue, canary, amber and amethyst.

### THE NEW MARTINSVILLE GLASS MFG. CO.

NEW MARTINSVILLE, W. VA.

## No. 10 Candy Box

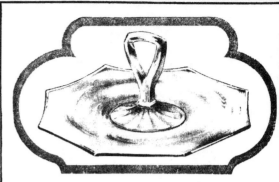

A VERY popular item at the Pittsburgh Show and a big seller this year. Holds about 1 1-2 pounds of candy. Made from good quality pot glass, finely finished and very attractive in blue, green, amber and amethyst.

### The New Martinsville Glass Mfg. Co.
#### New Martinsville, W. Va.

---

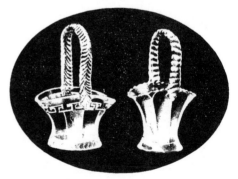

## No. 10-2 Octagon
## SANDWICH TRAY

A new item of more than usual beauty made from fine clear pot glass. It has been admired wherever it has been shown and nice sales have resulted.

Furnished in crystal and blue, green, amber and the new peach melba; a beautiful rose color. Packs 2 dozen to the barrel and is worthy of a trial. Write today for prices; or better yet, order a barrel and watch them sell.

### The New Martinsville Glass Mfg. Co.
#### New Martinsville, W. Va.

---

## NEW MARTINSVILLE

### No. 10—Ten Inch Plate and Cheese Compote

SUPPLIED plain or in a variety of handsome cuttings at prices that encourage you to order and make it easy to sell at a profit.

¶ A new style that is making a big hit with the trade.

### The New Martinsville Glass Mfg. Co.
#### New Martinsville, W. Va.

---

## New Martinsville Flower Baskets

FURNISHED in two sizes— Nos. 1 and 2. Fine items for a fast Spring and Summer turnover. Plain or attractively cut and finished all over in a workmanlike manner.

Packs 12 doz. to the barrel.
Gross weight 90 lbs.

### The New Martinsville Glass Mfg. Co.
#### New Martinsville, W. Va.

# *Meet Us at the Chicago Show*

## JULY 9th to 21st

### SHERMAN HOUSE

Rooms 906 and 907

No. 10 - 10" Sandwich Tray, Cut 147
No. 10—10" Cake Plate, Cut 147

We will exhibit our extensive and interesting line of

### Cut Glass and Novelties

with new special items for the large Premium Buyers.

### Cutter's Blanks Hotel Supplies ——and—— Tableware Lines

Will also be represented in the display.

## DON'T MISS IT !

# The New Martinsville Glass Mfg. Co.
## NEW MARTINSVILLE, W. VA.

*From* Crockery and Glass Journal *(July 5, 1923).*

which was to be introduced at shows in Pittsburgh and Chicago in January and February, 1922. By late April of that year, iced tea sets and water sets were featured, and the company boasted in its advertising that "any style of cutting desired" could be furnished.

The success of New Martinsville's venture into cut decorations for its glassware is captured in this column from the February, 1923, issue of the *American Flint*.

*We are still running in full with eleven turns a week. Mould shop is working overtime to get out some new moulds, and the cutting shop is running full time, with nine cutters working hard to keep up with the orders. We have had a very mild winter here, so far, and have been using natural gas most all winter. We are well fixed for cold weather as we have plenty of coal and oil ready when they turn off the gas. Our firm has a fine display of glassware at the show in Pittsburgh and we hope they will get orders to keep us going in full all winter. ... We were only off one day for Christmas and one for New Years as they are behind in their orders.*

Four months later, the *American Flint* reported that New Martinsville had "eleven cutters working full time and cannot keep up with the orders." Quite a few pieces of New Martinsville cut ware were illustrated in advertisements in trade journals, especially in the full-page "Refinement of Pot Glass" series which ran in *Pottery, Glass and Brass Salesman* during 1923 and 1924. Many of the items featured in these ads were also used as quarter-page ads in *Crockery and Glass Journal* during this same period.

Among the cut articles shown in one or more of these ads were the following: No. 10 molasses can; No. 190-0 molasses can; No. 10 sandwich tray; No. 160-6 iced tea jug and cover; No. 727 hotel water tray and No. 10 Hall Boy jug; No. 140-1 guest jug and tumbler (also available plain); flower baskets; No. 723 and No. 511 bud vases; and No. 10 ten-inch plate and cheese compote. The No.10 sandwich tray and No. 10 cake plate were shown with an elaborate cutting (designated Cut 147) in a full-page ad in *Crockery and Glass Journal*.

A full-page ad in *Pottery, Glass and Brass Salesman* (June 21, 1923) showed Clarke's sweetmeat or candy boxes with a special "June Bug" cutting motif. The ad copy predicted these would "get across the feminine mind like a streak." The design for these sectional containers was registered by Clarke in 1924 (#63,995).

In December, 1923, *Crockery and Glass Journal*

No. 10 Double, Cut 137     No. 10 Triple, Cut 137     No. 10 Single, Cut 137
Each compartment is 1½ in. in diameter and 1½ in. deep

**"Multum in Parvo" Sweatmeats Boxes With "June Bug" Cutting**

*The No. 10 Sweetmeat Boxes could be stacked to create different kinds of containers (Pottery, Glass and Brass Salesman, June 21, 1923).*

showed three different sets of New Martinsville's candlesticks, each with a distinctive cut decoration. The ad noted that these were particularly appropriate for holiday buying, probably because of the association of candles with Christmas. The company likely had a variety of candlesticks in its line by this time, of course, and some lent themselves to cut decorations more easily than others [see Fig. 303]. Such candlesticks were also available plain [see Figs. 302 and 304].

In September, 1924, Clarke reported to the National Association of Manufacturers of Pressed and Blown Glassware that the firm's cutting business was "pretty much on the bum" during the past few months with only four or five men employed part-time. Times were so trying for the men, Clarke wrote, that "we have allowed them to go out and sell goods from house to house in the surrounding towns." In contrast, Clarke noted, a dozen men had worked full-time as cutters at the plant throughout most of 1923. After 1925, there is little mention of cut ware in reports from New Martinsville or in the company's advertising.

Decoration in the form of hand-painting was also done at the New Martinsville glass house. These items were not well-advertised in glass trade publications, although many are shown in the 1926 catalogue. The No. 149-3 candy jar—which was made in amber, blue, canary, green and amethyst—may have been available with hand-

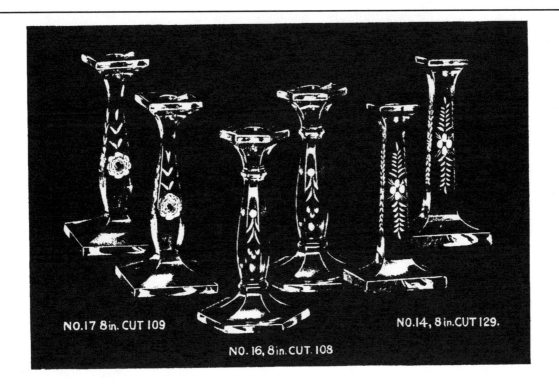

NO.17 8in. CUT 109

NO. 16, 8 in. CUT 108

NO.14, 8 in. CUT 129.

# Candlesticks Are Always Big Sellers

We have a line of attractively cut and decorated numbers, in
the accepted good styles, in full finished pot glass, on which
we can make immediate delivery. Their attractiveness and
excellent value will at once be appreciated by the wide-
awake merchant.

*From* Crockery and Glass Journal *(December 13, 1923).*

painted decoration as early as April, 1925, and it is
shown in the 1926 catalogue [see p. 116]. Other
jars with hand-painted decoration include the No.
9 mint jar and the No. 728 half-pound candy jar
[see p. 126]. Another attractive decorated article is
the No. 150 sweet pea vase with decoration 3010
[see p. 124].

Hand-painted decorations may also be found on
some smoking sets and vanity sets. The No. 2001
vanity set was available "in an eye catching combination of brilliant colors" according to *Crockery
and Glass Journal* (October 21, 1926), and these are
displayed in the 1926 catalogue [see p. 125].

Each hand-painted decorating motif was identified by its own number. The best source for these
numbers is surely the firm's 1926 catalogue.
Numbers for decorations typically follow the
numerical designation of the item; see p. 125 for
decoration 3001 on the No. 1926 vanity set and decoration 3006 on the No. 728 guest set. Sometimes
the decoration number would simply stand alone;
see pp. 121 and 124 for decoration 2003.

## PATTERN GLASS AND RELATED ITEMS

When Clarke came to New Martinsville, the
firm had a long history of introducing two new pattern lines each year. Such ventures must have
been quite costly, for the expense of making new
moulds for a full set is considerable. If a pattern
line proved unpopular, the costs of launching it
might never be recovered. Clarke revived several
New Martinsville patterns made earlier, and he
was, no doubt, instrumental in the purchase of
moulds from the then-closed Higbee firm. In
addition, he pioneered the development of console sets at New Martinsville.

Popular patterns which had been developed
during the Fisher years remained in production
under Clarke. No. 719 Old Glory appeared in
Butler Brothers or G. Sommers & Co. catalogues
regularly from 1919 through 1924-25. In February,
1920, the Butler Brothers called it "a universally
popular pattern that is in constant demand." The
No. 726 (Embassy) line, which was probably introduced late in the Fisher years or slightly there-

## DOUBLE GOLD BAND GLASS WARE ASSORTMENT.
**Newest design in gold decorated glassware.**

**K242X**—Fine grade finished pot glass; wide optic flutes; heavy fired gold edge; band around center; star bottom. Assortment as follows:
2 only 7 pc. Water Sets.
2 only 4 pc. Table Sets.
2 only 7 pc. Berry Sets.
6 sets in bbl. (No less sold.)
Per set ..................... **1.69**

## "SUNBURST GOLD" DECORATED TABLE SET ASSTM'T.
**Attractive looking pattern. Be the first in your town to get this assortment.**

**K241X**—Best finished crystal glass; large showy pieces; diamond and sunburst pattern; extra wide gold border; a neat assortment at a very low price. Assortment consists of the following:
2 only 7-pc. Water Sets, ½ gal. jugs, and six ground bottom tumblers to match.
2 only 7-pc. Berry Sets, 9½ in. deep bowl
and six 4½-in. nappies to match.
2 only 4-pc. Table Sets.
Total six sets in a bbl. No package charge.
No less sold. Set ..................... **1.65**

*No. 726 (Embassy) and No. 719 Old Glory assortments from a 1922 G. Sommers & Co. catalogue.*

after, also remained in production for several years. It can be found in G. Sommers & Co. catalogues during 1922, and this line also appears there as late as 1925. Likewise, the No. 725 Plain Colonial line was in production for much of the 1920s.

The No. 97 Old Colony line from 1915 (intended primarily for soda fountains) was sold as

## GOLD DECORATED CRYSTAL
## 7 PIECE WATER OR LEMONADE SETS

**These sets will make a striking display in your window. Attractive summer leader value.**

**1C1819**—2 styles, ½ gal. squat and colonial tankard jugs, SIX 9 oz. tumblers to match. clear heavy crystal, deep pressed design. **wide gold border**, 3 sets each. Asstd. 6 sets in bbl.. 66 lbs.
(Total $9.60)     SET (7 pcs.)     **$1.60**

*From the Butler Brothers Mid-Summer, 1921 catalogue.*

# DINING SET ASSORTMENTS
**Gold decorated glassware** is more popular than ever before. We are showing the big selling popular priced patterns that will bring you good sales with generous profits. **NO PACKAGE CHARGE.**

### "GOLDEN BEAUTY" DINING SET ASSORTMENT—Gold Decorated
*Always a big seller that is universally popular.*

**f1762**—Heavy full finished crystal, deep cut pattern, wide gold edges. Asst. comprises 6 sets as follows, all pcs. to match.
Two 7 pc. Water Sets:
2 only ½ gal. pitchers.
12 " 8 oz. tumblers.
(Total for asst. $9.90)

Two 7 pc. Berry Sets:
2 only 8 in. bowls.
12 " 4½ in. nappies.
6 sets in bbl., 75 lbs.

Two 4 pc. Table Sets:
2 only creamers.
2 " sugars.
2 " spoon holders.
2 " butters.
Set, $1.65

### "ELDORADO" DINING SET ASSORTMENT—Gold Decorated
*A universally popular pattern that is in constant demand.*

**C1759**—Heavy full finished crystal, miter base and star design, wide gold band and edges. Asst. comprises 6 sets as follows, all pieces to match:
Two 7 pc. Water Sets:
2 only ½ gal. pitchers.
12 " 4¼ tumblers.

Two 7 pc. Berry Sets:
2 only 8½ in. bowls.
12 " 4½ in. nappies.
Asstd. 6 sets in bbl., 60 lbs.

Two 4 pc. Table Sets.
2 creamers, 2 sugars.
2 spoonholders, 2 butters.
Set, Out

### "TREASURY" DINING SET ASSORTMENT—Gold Decorated

*A design of unusual beauty that will sell readily.*

**C1896**—Brilliant finish crystal, colonial panels, diagonal optic pattern, wide gold border. Asst. comprises 6 sets as follows, all pcs. to match:
Two 7 pc. Water Sets.
2 only ½ gal. jugs.
12 only 9 oz. tumblers.
Two 7 pc. Berry Sets.
2 only 8½ in. bowls.
12 only 4½ in. nappies.

Two 4 pc. Table Sets.
2 only creamers, ht. 4¼ in.
2 only covd. sugars, ht. 6½ in.
2 only spoonholders, ht. 4¼ in.

2 covd. butters, diam. 8 in.
Asstd. 6 sets in bbl., about 75 lbs.
(Total for asst. |

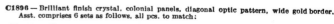

*Three important New Martinsville sets—No. 711 (Leaf and Star), No. 719 Old Glory and No. 97 Old Colony—appear together in this January, 1920, Butler Brothers catalogue.*

66

a regular set. Gold-decorated assortments were offered by the Butler Brothers in their May, 1919, catalogue, and water sets were available in conjunction with patterns revived by Clarke. For instance, in their Mid-Summer, 1921, catalogue, the Butler Brothers showed the No. 97 Old Colony set along with No. 711 (Leaf and Star), which had first been introduced in 1909. No. 97 Old Colony also appeared in a January, 1922, Butler Brothers catalogue with No. 702 (Long Leaf Teasel), which had debuted in August, 1906.

A few months later, Clarke had re-introduced the berry set, table set and water set in No. 711 and convinced the Butler Brothers concern to market it. An assortment of New Martinsville pitchers—including No. 500 Wetzel, No. 713 (Pleated Medallion) and the colonial-style No. 712 (Placid)—was also in the January, 1922, Butler

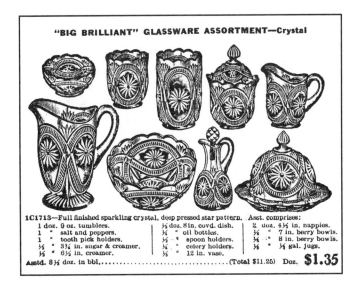

*An assortment of No. 713 (Pleated Medallion) from the May, 1922, Butler Brothers catalogue.*

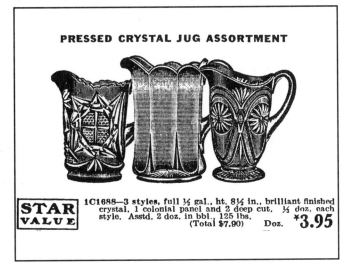

*New Martinsville's No. 500 Wetzel, No. 712 (Placid) and No. 713 (Pleated Medallion) appear together in this January, 1922, Butler Brothers catalogue.*

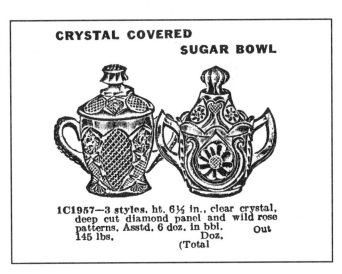

*No. 705 Klear-Kut and No. 717 (Horseshoe Daisy) covered sugar bowls (Butler Brothers catalogue, January, 1922).*

*Butler Brothers catalogue (January, 1922).*

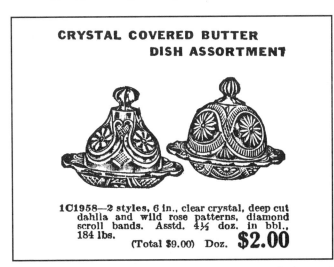

*No. 717 (Horseshoe Daisy and No. 713 (Pleated Medallion) butterdishes from a January, 1922, Butler Brothers catalogue.*

*These No. 705 Klear-Kut items appeared in a May, 1922, Butler Brothers catalogue.*

Brothers catalogue; when they appeared again in May, 1922, the price had dropped from $3.95 to $3.65 per dozen. No. 500, of course, dated all the way back to early 1905. A few items from the No. 705 Klear-Kut and No. 717 (Horseshoe Daisy) lines also appeared.

By May, 1922, New Martinsville's No. 713 (Pleated Medallion) was almost completely resurrected, as the Butler Brothers offered the traditional sets (berry, table and water) as well as salt/pepper shakers, a tall celery holder and a cruet for $1.35 per dozen wholesale. Two pieces (butterdish and covered sugar bowl) from the No. 705 Klear-Kut line also made their way into this catalogue.

As mentioned at the outset of this chapter, the New Martinsville firm acquired a large number of moulds from the defunct Higbee enterprise. Many of these moulds were put into service in the early 1920s. It may be difficult to ascertain whether a given item found today was made at the Higbee firm or at New Martinsville. Many, but not all, of the earlier Higbee pieces carried the com-

pany's distinctive trademark, a small but accurate rendition of a honeybee which may have the letters HIG on it. Presumably, this mark would have been removed by the machinists in New Martinsville's mould room, but some items may have been overlooked.

Identifying those Higbee moulds which were used at New Martinsville is quite a challenge. The notes in pencil on the original list of moulds is helpful, as is a photocopy of a New Martinsville catalogue from the 1920s which was annotated by the Millers during their research as they talked with former glassworkers.

Quite a few of the articles made at New Martinsville from original Higbee moulds were imitation cut glass motifs marketed in the early years of the twentieth century. Moulds for the No. 21 pattern (called Alpha by Higbee) were used to

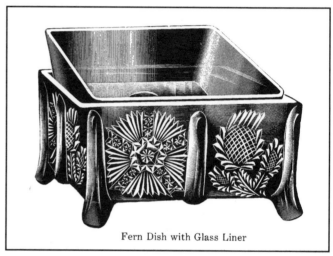

Fern Dish with Glass Liner

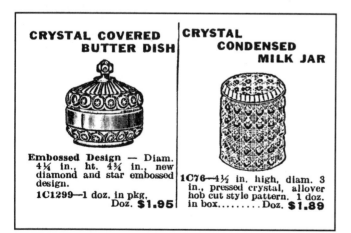

*These two articles were made at New Martinsville with moulds acquired from Higbee (Butler Brothers catalogue, May, 1922).*

*These items were originally called Delta at Higbee; New Martinsville marketed them as their No. 557 line.*

make the open and covered comports now known as Romona and Rexford [see Fig. 241], respectively. Several other items occur in the Rexford series [see Figs. 237-240 and 245-247], including a four-piece child's table set [see Figs. 248-251].

Other imitation cut glass articles can be found in Floral Oval [Figs. 230-235] and Perkins [see Fig. 236]. Perkins had been called Fortuna at Higbee, and the original name for Floral Oval may have been Banner, although this name was also used for some moulds which are now called Lacy Daisy. A pickle jar in the Lacy Daisy motif was marketed as a condensed milk container in Butler Brothers catalogues along with the No. 524 Landberg covered dish.

Among the other pattern items made at New Martinsville from Higbee moulds are these: No. 501 ice tub and No. 502 sugar sifter (both called Paris today); No. 517 (originally called Highland, but now known as Coarse Zig Zag) celery holder;

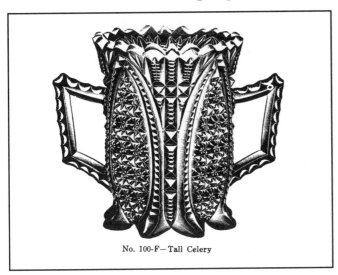

No. 100-F—Tall Celery

*Called Fortuna by Higbee, this New Martinsville piece is known as Perkins today.*

No. 601—Cream

*Diamond Point Disc creamer.*

*New Martinsville's No. 608 shaving mug was available plain or with gold decoration.*

No. 523 Melrose water tray; No. 601 creamer (originally called Crescent, but now known as Diamond Point Disc); No. 553 (now called Helio) covered nappy; and the No. 608 and No. 610 shaving mugs.

In addition to making glass with the Higbee moulds and reviving some of its own old patterns, the New Martinsville firm introduced a few new patterns in the 1920s. The pace fell far, far short of the Fisher years, however, when at least two patterns were readied for the annual January glass exhibits in Pittsburgh.

In December, 1924, the New Martinsville firm unveiled its new pattern with a full-page ad in

### Our New 728 Colonial Line

IS one of our stars for the New Year. It includes a full range of tableware made of good grade pot glass. Nicely finished and attractive in design and priced to make a general appeal.

It is only one of our new and attractive things we have been keeping up our sleeve for the New Year.

*This ad for New Martinsville's No. 728 Colonial Line appeared in the December 11, 1924, issue of* **Pottery, Glass and Brass Salesman.**

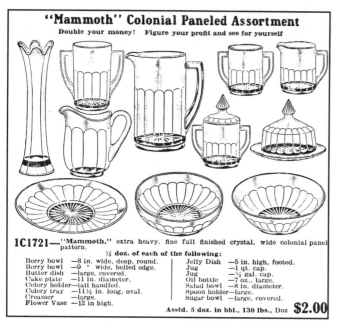

No. 728 Colonial assortment (Butler Brothers catalogue, June, 1925).

Octagon Sandwich Tray No. 10/2

Pottery, Glass and Brass Salesman (May 20, 1926).

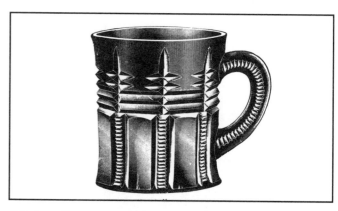

Zipper Cross mug, from an original catalogue.

No. 149 (Monitor) covered sugar bowl, from an original catalogue.

*Pottery, Glass and Brass Salesman.* The new line was dubbed No. 728 Colonial, and it bore a strong resemblance to the No. 97 Old Colony line. No. 728 included table set pieces, but it was probably intended primarily for soda fountain use. No. 97 Old Colony had been introduced in 1915 and sold successfully through at least 1922 (the No. 97 water set was advertised with its counterpart in No. 711 as late as the winter of 1927). By June, 1925, No. 728 had made its way into Butler Brothers catalogues, too. Merchants who purchased 5 dozen pieces at $2.00 per dozen could, claimed the Butler Brothers, "Double your money!"

Another new line from New Martinsville may have been called Victoria. An ad for the "Octagon Sandwich Tray No. 10/2" (*Pottery, Glass and Brass Salesman*, May 20, 1926) was followed by an ad for the "Octagon Bowl, Princess, 12-inch" (*Pottery, Glass and Brass Salesman*, August 12, 1926). The latter ad referred to the company's Victoria line, and said the firm "expects to have the line rounded out by the end of this month by the introduction of several other popular items." Clarke had a registered design for an octagonal "sandwich plate or similar article (#71,514; granted November 23, 1926).

If other items were indeed added, they were not well-advertised, so this line may have been short-lived at best. The octagonal shape seems to have been the defining characteristic of the line, but the No. 10-12 console set (see p. 120) was also

called Princess (although a round console bowl is labeled "Princes" in the 1926 catalogue; see p. 126).

Other motifs were made by New Martinsville in the 1920s, but their dates of origin have yet to be determined: No. 116 (Zipper Cross) and No. 149 (Monitor), a line which ranged from table set pieces to handled pickle dishes.

Several of New Martinsville's competitors (such as Diamond, Fenton and Northwood) made console sets in the 1920s. These consisted of a rather large bowl flanked by two candlesticks, and they were intended for display on furniture in a home's entry hall area or on a dining room table or sideboard. New Martinville's first effort in this area was probably its No. 160-10 console set, which was illustrated in *Pottery, Glass and Brass Salesman*. According to the ad, the set was available in crystal, blue, green, amber and amethyst, the colors then in production at New Martinsville. Unlike most of the console sets made by its competitors, New Martinsville's No. 160-10 was a four-piece set with a separate 13" plate under the bowl.

Other console sets followed shortly thereafter. The No. 2015E was illustrated in *Pottery, Glass and Brass Salesman*, and No. 10/2 was in *Crockery and Glass Journal* (for a color illustration of this set, see p. 72). The decoration on No. 2051E was

Console Set No. 2051E

**Pottery, Glass and Brass Salesman** *(May 6, 1926).*

*From an original catalogue.*

described as a mixture of etching and hand-painted enameling: "the festoon of grapes has green foliage and purple fruit and the centaur and dancing nymphs ... are in black and white." By the time the firm issued its 1926 catalogue, several other console sets—designated No. 10-10, No. 10-12, No. 10-21—were on the market (see pp. 117 and 131).

Some of New Martinsville's candlesticks were probably not part of console sets, however. Some plain candlesticks were intended for cut decorations, as discussed earlier in this chapter, but others simply exist on their own. Among these are the plain No. 10 [see Fig. 295], the No. 18 Saucer Candlestick, and the No. 21-9. others were designated with numbers between 11 and 19 in an original catalogue. In the company's 1926 catalogue, an interesting round candlestick designated No. 10-3 can be found along with others labelled No. 10/2 and No. 10/4, both of which are decorated with hand-painting (see p. 126).

As accents to home furnishings, console sets were primarily decorative, but New Martinsville

## No. 160-10 Console Set

A NEW CONSOLE SET that lends itself to several uses. Consists of two No. 10 10-inch candlesticks, new style 10-inch bowl and 13-inch plate. Bowl can rest on plate or, if desired, can remain on the buffet holding fruit while the plate is being used for some other purpose.

Furnished in crystal and colors—blue, green, amber and amethyst.

### THE NEW MARTINSVILLE GLASS MFG. CO.
#### NEW MARTINSVILLE, W. VA.

***From* Pottery, Glass and Brass Salesman *(April 16, 1925); Weatherman named this set "Patti."***

*(continued on p. 74)*

No. 10/2
Console
Set

# Brighten Up Your Stock!
# Jazz Up Your Sales!

Here is an entirely new idea: Glass Comport candlesticks for the Large Whip Candles. Made in the beautiful colors of the vogue:

*Amber, Green, Blue or*
*Amethyst and Crystal*

They can also be had in Most Attractive Black Decorations

Packed 1½ dozen to a barrel

## THE NEW MARTINSVILLE GLASS CO.
### New Martinsville, W. Va.

———

Ira M. Clark, Gen. Mgr.

*From* Crockery and Glass Journal *(August 6, 1925).*

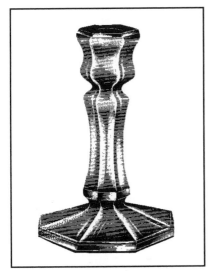

*From an original catalogue.*

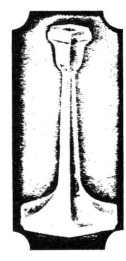

*From* **Pottery, Glass and Brass Salesman** *(June 4, 1925).*

67,011. RELISH PLATE. IRA M. CLARKE, New Martinsville, W. Va. Filed Dec. 4, 1924. Serial No. 11,589. Term of patent 7 years.

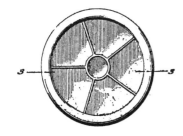

*Design drawing for the No. 10 relish dish.*

**Crockery and Glass Journal** *(November 10, 1925)*

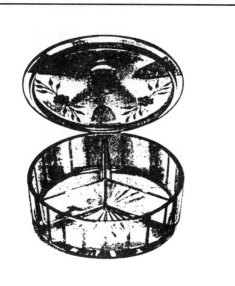

No. 107 Three-Compartment Candy Box

*From* **Pottery, Glass and Brass Salesman**
*(December 31, 1925).*

also made utilitarian products in the form of salad sets and relish dishes. Two salad sets, No. 160-12 and No. 728-12, are in the 1928 catalogue [see p. 117].

The design for a sectional relish dish was registered by Ira Clarke (#67,011) on April 14, 1925, and this item was featured in ads in the glass trade publications less than a month later. A removable glass liner for cocktail sauce in the center section made this article "less expensive than the old style seven piece relish dishes and much more convenient and easy to clean." These are shown in the 1926 catalogue, and the liner is clearly visible [see p. 117].

**3 Piece Novelty Sugar and Creamer Set**

Excellent item for your gift glassware section. Attractively colored in amber, green, blue or amethyst.

**1C1269**—3 pieces, full finished pot glass, ground polished bottoms, asstd. amber, green, blue and amethyst. Set comprises:
1 only 6¼ in. handled tray.
1 " 3¾ x 3¼ in. open sugar.
1 " handled creamer.
Asstd. 1 doz. in carton. Doz **$9.25**
**25 lbs.**

*Butler Brothers catalogue (Mid-Winter, 1927).*

The No. 10 round candy box which was used for so much cut ware was also made in a divided version in late 1925, capitalizing upon the same advantages alleged for the sectional relish dish. This new article, called the No. 107 Three-Compartment Candy Box, was advertised in several trade publications.

In the late summer of 1925, New Martinsville's No. 723 Bridge Sugar and Cream Set was advertised in *Pottery, Glass and Brass Salesman* (August 13, 1925) and, later, in *Crockery and Glass Journal* (November 19, 1925). The colonial-style creamer and open sugar bowl were designed to fit snugly on a tray with a basket-like handle. These were made in the typical New Martinsville colors [see Fig. 325]. They appeared in Butler Brothers catalogues a little over a year later.

## SPECIALTY ARTICLES

In addition to the various glasswares lines above, the New Martinsville Glass Manufacturing Company also made a number of specialty articles in the early and mid-1920s when Ira Clarke was general manager. Among these were novelty plates, ashtrays and smokers' sets; vanity or dresser sets; lamps; beverage sets; and other unique articles. The information available on some of these items is quite remarkable—patent records, original trade journal ads, etc. For others, it is frustratingly inadequate. For example, the New Martinsville firm sent a "small glass revolver" to the National Association of Manufacturers of Pressed and Blown Glassware on November 23, 1921, but no details are available; it could have been a candy container.

New Martinsville's novelty plates included the No. 10 Souvenir Plate with fleur-de-lis border [see Fig. 252], which was obviously intended as a blank to be etched or otherwise decorated. Three so-called A-B-C plates were also produced: the rather plain No. 530 has a star in its center [see Fig. 254], but No. 531 has the figure of long-haired boy [see Fig. 253] and No. 532 features a dog [see Fig. 255]. The numbers for these latter three plates are consistent with many of the items made from old Higbee moulds, but these plates are not on the mould list, so they could have been developed at New Martinsville.

During the entire time of Clarke's tenure at New Martinsville, the firm produced ashtrays and other items as smoker's accessories. These ranged from the standard Nos. 1 through 4 from the earlier stationers' line (see p. 46) to a number of patented ashtrays and elaborate smoker's sets on trays. A few New Martinsville ashtrays can be found in the Butler Brothers catalogue for January, 1924, and an extensive array of ashtrays and other smokers' items appeared in a Mid-Winter, 1927, catalogue.

Between 1922 and 1925, Ira Clarke was granted design patents for six different ashtrays. Two of these, both circular in shape, saw double duty as covers for a jar designed to hold loose cigarettes or to serve as a humidor for pipe tobacco. Other ashtrays had cleverly-designed holders for boxes or books of safety matches, and one featured a pipe rest (some of these may have been made especially for the Diamond Match Company). These ashtrays were made in most of New Martinsville's characteristic colors—amber, blue, green and amethyst—as well as crystal and black. The humidors with covers may also be found with light cutting decorations.

In 1925, the New Martinsville firm began to market smoker's sets which consisted of several individual articles and an accompanying tray. The first such offering, the No. 10/728 set, had a tobacco jar plus ashtray and a match box holder. The oblong tray was also used later for some of the firm's vanity sets.

The No. 149 set featured a holder designed especially for the soft package in which cigarettes were then sold by major American tobacco companies. This holder was available in crystal, amber, green, blue and amethyst, and it may be decorated with either cutting or hand-painting. The 1926 company catalogue shows one of these holders in black glass with a vivid hand-painted decoration (see p. 124).

The New Martinsville firm showed its No. 149 set with Chesterfield brand cigarettes and even attached the appellation "Chesterfield" to it in a full-page ad in *Pottery, Glass and Brass Salesman.* Two small ashtrays flanked the holder on a tray; these small ashtrays, which often bear the NM mark, were also marketed individually as pin trays, and the large tray also saw service in some of New

62,476. COMBINED HUMIDOR AND ASH TRAY. IRA M. CLARKE, New Martinsville, W. Va., assignor to New Martinsville Glass Manufacturing Co., New Martinsville, W. Va., a Corporation of West Virginia. Filed May 31, 1922. Serial No. 2,479. Term of patent 7 years.

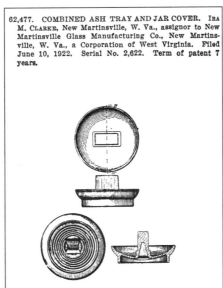

62,477. COMBINED ASH TRAY AND JAR COVER. IRA M. CLARKE, New Martinsville, W. Va., assignor to New Martinsville Glass Manufacturing Co., New Martinsville, W. Va., a Corporation of West Virginia. Filed June 10, 1922. Serial No. 2,622. Term of patent 7 years.

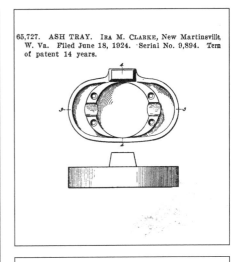

65,727. ASH TRAY. IRA M. CLARKE, New Martinsville, W. Va. Filed June 18, 1924. Serial No. 9,894. Term of patent 14 years.

63,152. ASH TRAY. IRA M. CLARKE, New Martinsville, W. Va., assignor to New Martinsville Glass Mfg. Co., New Martinsville, W. Va., a Corporation of Virginia. Filed Nov. 28, 1922. Serial No. 4,436. Term of patent 7 years.

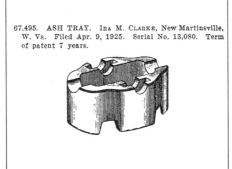

67,495. ASH TRAY. IRA M. CLARKE, New Martinsville, W. Va. Filed Apr. 9, 1925. Serial No. 13,080. Term of patent 7 years.

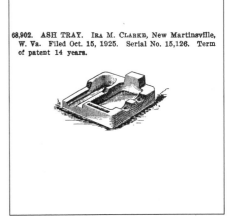

68,902. ASH TRAY. IRA M. CLARKE, New Martinsville, W. Va. Filed Oct. 15, 1925. Serial No. 15,126. Term of patent 14 years.

*Design drawings for various ashtrays and a humidor patented by Ira M. Clarke. All of these were made at New Martinsville in the mid-1920s.*

## No. 14
### New Safety Ash Tray

GONE FOREVER are burned tables and ruined tablecloths when this ash tray is used. Made specially for cigarette smokers and designed so that cigarette cannot drop off the tray. Fine pot glass, highly finished all over.

New, very popular and a profit making item.

#### THE NEW MARTINSVILLE GLASS MFG. CO.
NEW MARTINSVILLE, W. VA.

---

### NEW MARTINSVILLE
## No. 13 Card Table Ash Tray

While designed originally for the bridge table, this unique little ash tray is handy on any card table.

¶ It is quite new in design, made from fine, fire polished, clear, pot glass, and is finding favor wherever it is displayed.

Packs 12 dozen per package
Weight of package 150 lbs.

#### THE NEW MARTINSVILLE GLASS MFG. CO.
NEW MARTINSVILLE, W. VA.

---

## Another Home Run!

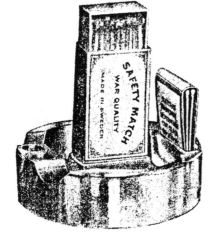

### No. 7 Smokers' Tray and Match Stand

This tray has all the new improvements—cigarette snuffers, cigar rests, slot for paper matches, and stand for safety matches. Is four inches in diameter, perfectly round, and most convenient for use on card tables. Is also desirable for use by mounters. Packs twelve dozen to package; weight 150 lbs. Samples on application.

## New Martinsville Glass Mfg. Co.
### New Martinsville, W. Va.
Malone & Nicholson, 125 Fifth Avenue, New York

---

### Combination
## Ash Tray and Match Holders

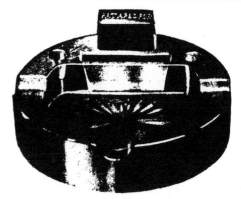

No. 6—6-inch Diameter

Perfectly round for Mounter's Use.
Holds either paper or safety boxes of matches.
Has three Cigar Rests—two Cigarette Snuffers.
Clear Crystal Pot Glass. Size and Price is right. Ask us for sample.
Packs 12 doz. to ½ bbl. Weight 175 lbs.

## New Martinsville Glass Mfg. Co.
### New Martinsville, W. Va.

---

*Four New Martinsville ashtrays from various trade publications, 1922-1925.*

# CRYSTAL ASH TRAYS

| DIAMOND PATTERN ROUND ASH TRAY | COMBINATION ROUND TRAY | "FOUR IN ONE" POT GLASS TRAY |
|---|---|---|

"FOUR IN ONE" POT GLASS TRAY
Ash tray, match box holder, cigar rests and snuffers.

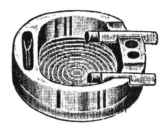

**1C96**—5 in. diam., clear crystal, diamond pattern, deep match box holder, cupped tray. 1 doz. in pkg.
Doz. 92c

**1C2436**—4 in. diam., good crystal, extra deep, match box holder and 3 cigar rests. 2 doz. in pkg.
Doz **$1.25**
(Total $2.50)

**1C92**—"Four in One," 4 in., finest pot glass, smooth finish bottom, will not scratch polished surfaces. 1 doz. in box.
Doz **$1.25**

*New Martinsville ashtrays from a Butler Brothers catalogue (January, 1924).*

Martinsville's vanity sets [see Figs. 333-335].

Later, a similar cigarette pack holder was modified by the addition of an arm to hold a box of safety matches; this was advertised as the No. 149/4 "Van's Own" Smokers' Companion in April, 1926. The larger, slightly upturned base served as an ashtray. These sets and individual holders were offered with several different decorations in the 1926 New Martinsville catalogue [see pp. 121 and 124]. Among the most interesting is the four-piece No. 10/3016 set, which consists of four shallow rectangular trays decorated with the clubs, diamonds, hearts and spades found on playing cards [see p. 124].

## The Latest Novelty in Glass Smokers' Articles

(Patent applied for.)

A jar, the cover of which is an ash tray and match stand. Decidedly unique; thoroughly practical; will sell like "hot cakes."

Comes in three sizes—for Cigarettes, Cigars, Tobacco. Clear crystal POT GLASS. Sizes and Prices are right.

**Send for Samples and Prices**

### New Martinsville Glass Mfg. Co.
New Martinsville, W. Va.

Pottery, Glass and Brass Salesman *(June 8, 1922).*

## No. 10/728 Smoker Set in Green Glass

OFFERING you our new Smokers' Set. A brand new novelty. How do you like it? Some merchants whose judgment we rely upon a lot tell us it's a "humdinger." It is made in the fascinating New Martinsville green glass. There is an oblong tray 9¼ by 8¼ inches mitred the long way on the bottom to simulate an optic effect. There is a blown covered tobacco jar, and an individual match box holder and ash tray. It is a popular combination and that's the reason why we think it's going to be a big seller. Incidentally, and very important, *the price is right.*

### New Martinsville Glass Mfg. Company

*From Pottery, Glass and Brass Salesman (August 30, 1925).*

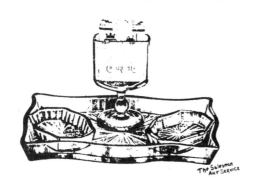

## No. 149 Cigarette Smokers' Set in Colored Glass

THE first buyer we showed this set to ordered 3,000. And he's a pretty wise bird. Said he thought it would be another ten-strike winner like the vanity set. We hope he's right. Certainly, the set looks good to us, and incidentally, to a couple of other able operators who have bought it.

The illustration gives a fair idea of what it looks like. So that you can visualize it, we might mention that the tray is 9½ by 6 inches, and the cigarette holder just big enough to hold a package of Chesterfield cigarettes. That's the reason we are calling it the "Chesterfield." Obtainable in either green or amber glass—rich shades in both colors. With all its novelty and attractiveness it sells at a popular price. Write us for prices and details as to packages, etc.

*From* **Pottery, Glass and Brass Salesman** *(September 17, 1925).*

## No. 149-4 Cigarette Holder
### *Decorated or Plain*

This patented smoker's companion, named "Van's Own" after its designer, combines into a single item cigarette holder, ash tray and two holders for paper or box matches.

"Van's Own" is a big seller, so order now and gain the advantages of "first run" sales. Write for prices on plain colors and decorated, in quantities.

## THE NEW MARTINSVILLE GLASS MFG. CO.
### NEW MARTINSVILLE, W. VA.

**Crockery and Glass Journal** *(September 9, 1926).*

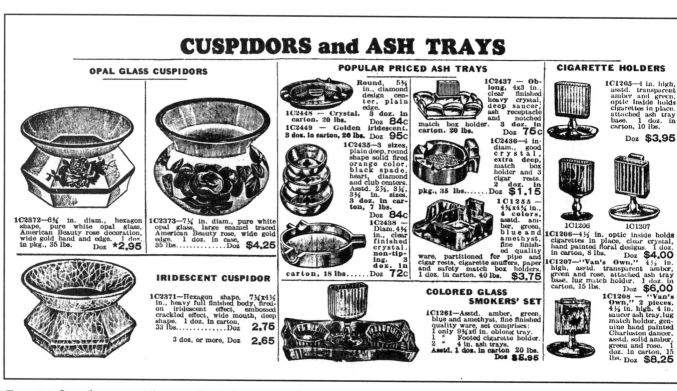

*Except for the cuspidors, all of these smokers' items in a Butler Brothers catalogue (Mid-Winter, 1927) were manufactured at New Martinsville. The small round ashtrays at center are painted orange and have playing card decorations.*

Vanity sets emerged as an important part of New Martinsville's production during the latter part of Clarke's time there. Some of the articles, such as puff boxes for face powder, had been used in conjunction with smokers' sets or were first intended for foodstuffs. Clarke filed an application to register the design for a "glass jar or similar container" on January 7, 1926, and this item could certainly function as a puff box (design registration #74,417 was not granted until February 4, 1928, after Clarke had left the firm). Several trays from smokers' sets did double duty as trays for vanity sets. Other items, such as perfume bottles, were developed specifically for New Martinsville's vanity sets. Production of vanity sets continued well beyond the Clarke years as new ones were introduced, and readers interested in this area should be sure to consult the next chapter of this book as well as the Whitmeyer's *Bedroom and Bathroom Glassware of the Depression Years*.

The first set displayed by the New Martinsville firm in early 1926 was probably its No. 1926, a plain affair consisting of a round puff box with domed lid, two bulbous perfume bottles with flat-topped applicator stoppers and a rectangular tray (the 1926 catalogue reveals that these were sold with or without the tray). When the sets were advertised again in *Crockery and Glass Journal* (October 7, 1926), the company claimed that "thousands of dozens of these ... were sold the first month they were introduced."

New Martinsville's No. 1926/2 "Mysterious" Vanity Set was featured in a full-page advertisement in *Pottery, Glass and Brass Salesman* during March, 1926. The large knob-like cover on the round puff box was actually a separate container for rouge ("Pat. Apld. For" appears inside this area). The ad copy described it as follows: "You see that knob on the cover of the puff box? Well, try and lift said cover. Ah-ha! You lift NOT the cover of the puff box BUT the cover to a miniature rouge box which is superimposed on the larger cover." In a later ad in *Crockery and Glass Journal* (October 28, 1926), the firm called this feature "a special covered rouge or cologne powder refill holder mounted on top of the puff box cover." The design for this article was registered by Clarke on August 31, 1926 (#70,952). These sets, along with New Martinsville's rather plain Queen Anne, were shown in Butler Brothers catalogues in July, 1928.

The idea of multiple containers in a vanity set apparently proved popular, for Clarke decided to add yet another to the set. He obtained both a registered design (#70,784; granted August, 10, 1926) and a patent (#1,598,365; granted August 31, 1926) for the firm's No. 1926/3 vanity set which combined puff box, rouge container and perfume bottle. Full-page ads picturing this article appeared in *Pottery, Glass and Brass Salesman* about four months apart (June 3 and September 9, 1926). The Fostoria Glass Company of nearby Moundsville had produced puff box/perfume bottle combinations, but Clarke's "threesome" may be unique.

New Martinville's other vanity sets included the No. 2001, which was decorated. This set was illustrated in the 1926 catalogue [see p. 125]. The perfume bottles for the No. 2001 set are similar to those made by other firms, although New Martinsville's have eight-sided stoppers and a narrow ring just below the body of the bottle above the base. Some perfume bottles have the NM mark on the underside of the foot.

New Martinsville's No. 10-2 Queen Anne Dresser Sets included two perfume bottles and a plain puff box with eight-sided finial. According to the 1926 catalogue, the Queen Anne sets were available in amber, green, blue and amethyst. A similar set consists of the same perfume bottles accompanied by a slightly smaller puff box; this set usually has an oval tray.

In April and June, 1926, Ira Clarke sought patents for a flower bowl with holder and a method of making the flower holder (called a "flower frog" by collectors today) integral to the bowl rather

## No. 1926/2 "Mysterious" Vanity Set

*From* **Pottery, Glass and Brass Salesman** *(March 25, 1926)*.

## A Colorful Vanity Set
### to Retail for $1.00

THE decoration of the No. 2001 Vanity Set is an eye catching combination of brilliant colors, red, yellow, blue and black. Three useful pieces that you can retail at profitable low prices in big quantities.

**Packs 12 dozen per bbl.
Shipping wt. 160 lbs.**

## THE NEW MARTINSVILLE GLASS MFG. CO.

### NEW MARTINSVILLE, W. VA.

## Fast Selling Vanity Set

THOUSANDS of dozens of these No. 1926 Vanity Sets were sold the first month they were introduced. Don't fail to include this item in your future orders.

Made of clear pot glass, fine polished, in crystal for decorators and for the retail trade in the popular colors, green, blue, amber and amethyst.

**Packs 6 dozen sets to the barrel
Shipping weight 160 lbs.**

## THE NEW MARTINSVILLE GLASS MFG. CO.

### NEW MARTINSVILLE, W. VA.

No. 1926-2

## Latest Improved Vanity Set

THIS 1926-2 Vanity Set includes two colognes, puff box, tray and has a special covered rouge or cologne powder refill holder molded on top of the puff box cover. No others like it and it's patented. Made in crystal, blue, green, amber and amethyst.

**Packs 6 dozen per bbl.
Shipping wt. 175 lbs.**

## THE NEW MARTINSVILLE GLASS MFG. CO.

### NEW MARTINSVILLE, W. VA.

70,784. COMBINATION HOLDER FOR TOILET PREPARATIONS. IRA M. CLARKE, New Martinsville, W. Va. Filed May 11, 1926. Serial No. 17,658. Term of patent 3½ years.

The ornamental design for a combination holder for toilet preparations, substantially as shown.

*New Martinsville vanity sets from various issues of* Crockery and Glass Journal *in October, 1925; Clarke's design drawing for the tri-partite set is at the lower right.*

## No. 1926/3 Vanity Set

SOME critics say that in producing the above-pictured Vanity Set we have "painted the lily." And, with tremendous success. Here is the reason for their tribute:

Early in the year we produced a rouge puff box that was an instantaneous hit. As will be recalled it was a combination of a gracefully shaped puff box with a little covered rouge puff compartment surmounted on the box. Now we have gone this one better by placing on top of the rouge puff a dainty perfume bottle—with ground-in stopper and cut knob—a veritable three-in-one compact for milady's boudoir. It is 5¾ inches high. We regard this as the biggest thing in its sphere on the market at the present moment. In the new "Peach Melba" glass it is very beautiful, especially in the frosted finish. It is to be had, however, in our full range of colors. Needless to say, we have patented it. Prices on request—you'll want a quick shipment when you receive them.

TRADE MARK

QUALITY
AND
SERVICE

# New Martinsville Glass Mfg. Company
## New Martinsville, W. Va.
### Ira M. Clarke, General Manager

Frederick Skelton, 200 Fifth Ave., New York City
L. H. Simpson & Co., 17 No. Wabash Ave., Chicago, Ill.
Harry Gabriel, 718 Mission St., San Francisco, Cal.
I. M. Ober, 211 Jacobson Bldg., Denver, Colo.
G. J. Rosenfield Co., 116 Bedford St., Boston, Mass.

James P. Gordon, Seneca Hotel, Rochester, N. Y.
Geo. R. West Sales Co., 954 Liberty Ave., Pittsburgh, Pa.
Chas. Mullis, 2912 Victoria Ave., Hyde Park, Cincinnati, Ohio.
R. E. L'Ecuyer, 1845 S.W. Seventh St., Miami, Fla.
Morris Lando, 139 Colonial Arcade, Cleveland, Ohio.

Henry C. Hubley, Transportation Bldg., Los Angeles, Cal.

*From* **Pottery, Glass and Brass Salesman** *(September 9, 1926).*

No 727.—Two-piece Glass Lamps—Made in Eight Sizes—Patented.

# Aladdin's Well-Known Lamp Has Nothing on This One

*From* Pottery, Glass and Brass Salesman *(July 3, 1924).*

1,596,716.   FLOWER BOWL AND FLORAL SUPPORT.
IRA M. CLARKE, New Martinsville, W. Va.   Filed Apr,
22, 1926.   Serial No. 103,752.   2 Claims.   (Cl.
47—41.)

*This drawing accompanied Clarke's application for a patent on the flower bowl with integral flower frog.*

than as a separable part. The method was ingeneous; after the bowl was moulded with the flower frog on the outside of the base, the sides of the bowl were completely re-shaped while the glass was still hot, resulting in the flower frog being on the inside of the base. The process was rather like turning a hat of flexible material inside out! Clarke's patents (#1,596, 716 and #1,603,025) were granted, and such bowls were indeed made at New Martinsville [see Fig. 403].

The patented threaded connector (U. S. Patent #1,057,899) used for staple goods also served as the basis for a line of kerosene lamps. Many

Americans had gas or electric lighting by this time, of course, so the New Martinsville firm suggested that their lamps were, "when the gas freezes or the electricity short circuits," the perfect source of emergency light. A full-page ad appeared in the July 3, 1924, issue of *Pottery, Glass and Brass Salesman*. Like the staple goods made with this connector, these lamps carried the factory designation No. 727. According to *Pottery, Glass and Brass Salesman* (July 31, 1924), New Martinsville's patented lamps were soon on display at a major establishment in Chicago:

*Lewis H. Simpson & Co., Shops Building, 17 North Wabash Avenue, have recently put on the market a new line of two-piece glass lamps made by the New Martinsville Glass Manufacturing Company, of New Martinsville, W. Va. These lamps have the merit of being simple in construction, which means that they are not of the dirt-catching variety. A nickel-plated metal screw-thread connection—a patented device absolutely controlled by the New Martinsville concern—adds to the appearance and at the same time makes for easy packing, as the lamps can be knocked down, which means a material reduction in the freight charge.*

On December 31, 1924, Ira Clarke made application for a patent on a "stand for floor lamps, smokers' stands and the like." The text of this invention's description is not particularly enlightening, but its accompanying drawing suggests a tall lamp composed of five bowling pin-shaped glass sections connected by metal hardware. Arch Hill's column in the December, 1924, issue of the *American Flint* contains this note: "We are making a floor lamp here now out of glass and it sure is a fine one. The base of it is pressed and the rest is blown and made from different colors of glass. Not different colors in each lamp, but lamps of crystal, blue, green, and about the color of mahogany." One wonders if any of these survive to the present day! Clarke's patent (#1,613,382) was granted on January 4, 1927, several months after he had left the firm.

Containers for various beverages were nearly staple items for any glass firm in the 1920s, so it is not surprising that the New Martinsville Glass Manufacturing Company was active in this area. The No. 10-2 water bottle, designed for hotel use, was surely a staple item as was the No. 727 hotel water tray and No. 10 Hall Boy jug [see Fig. 300 for a similar jug].

In addition to producing half-gallon or 3-quart pitchers which could be sold with matching tumblers for water, lemonade or iced tea sets, the firm also made so-called "guest sets," smaller pitchers with a single tumbler. When inverted, the tumbler fit smoothly into the top of the pitcher for overnight storage. These were intended for bedside tables in guest rooms. Production of these continued after Clarke left, so readers should be sure to see the next two chapters of this book and the Whitmeyer's book, *Bedroom and Bathroom Glassware of the Depression Years*.

New Martinsville advertised plain guest sets in *Pottery, Glass and Brass Salesman* as early as January, 1924, and such sets with cut decorations were probably on the market soon thereafter. Sets with a ribbed optic (No. 140-1) are in the firm's 1926 catalogue. A similar set (called No. 728) had a tray to hold a covered pitcher and a matching tumbler; these were shown in Butler Brothers catalogues.

The first liquor set made at New Martinsville was probably the firm's No. 10/3 set, which was featured in a full-page advertisement in *Pottery, Glass and Brass Salesman* (July 30, 1925). The set, which was then available only in green, consisted of a decanter with stopper and six whiskey tumblers. Other colors were probably available shortly thereafter, for the company advertised its No. 728

1,613,382. STAND FOR FLOOR LAMPS, SMOKERS' STANDS, AND THE LIKE. IRA M. CLARKE, New Martinsville, W. Va. Filed Dec. 31, 1924. Serial No. 759,042. 2 Claims. (Cl. 248—41.)

*This drawing was filed with Clarke's application for a patent on the floor lamp made at New Martinsville in 1924-25.*

*Butler Brothers catalogue (Mid-Winter, 1927)*

Liquor Set about six months later (*Crockery and Glass Journal*, December 31, 1925), offering it in amber, green, blue and amethyst. Amber and green were available through the Butler Brothers catalogue in Mid-Winter, 1927, for $1.39 per set.

## No. 10/3 Liquor Set, Green, Optic

**Pottery, Glass and Brass Salesman** *(July 30, 1925).*

The No. 728 set may also have been called "Marty" in the company's advertising.

Among the most interesting New Martinsville products intended for beverages are the "Volstead Pup" and the "Nice Kitty" novelty decanters [see Figs. 308 and L]. The canine debuted with a full-page ad in *Pottery, Glass and Brass Salesman* (May 27, 1926), which apparently named it the "Sympathetic Pooch" before mentioning the "spontaneous humor that this sad-eyed pup arouses" and describing "dashes of color boldly applied which accentuate the gawky, forlorn figure itself." An ad in *Crockery and Glass Journal* alluded to "a sobbing, gurgling noise" produced by the decanter when pouring. These decanters are usually found in decorated crystal [see Fig. 308] or green today, although one ad mentioned "a full range of colors." By mid-1928, New Martinsville's Volstead Pup was in Butler Brothers catalogues. A similar decanter in two sizes was made by the Cambridge Glass Company, probably a few years before New Martinsville introduced its "Volstead Pup" (see the NCC's book, *Colors in Cambridge Glass*, pp. 12-13 and 22-23).

At the time New Martinsville introduced this decanter, the United States was in the midst of that great historical contradiction in terms: the "Roaring 20s" and "Prohibition." The nationwide

*Butler Brothers catalogue (Mid-Winter, 1927).*

## Pep Up Your Sales for 1926

### Our 728 Liquor Set as Illustrated Will Do the Trick

Absolutely new, strikingly attractive, beautifully finished in every detail.

You can picture the immediate appeal of this finely proportioned flagon, the graceful fluted tumblers and tray all to match in a choice of exquisite shades of Amber, Green, Blue, and Amethyst. There is nothing to equal it on the market for the price.

**Be the first to stock it in your locality.**

*Orders will receive prompt attention for delivery after January 1.*
*Packed 2 doz. sets to a barrel.*

**This and many other surprises await you at**

**Our Display from January 11th to 30th, Pittsburgh Exhibit, Rooms 712 and 714.**

## New Martinsville Glass Mfg. Co.

### New Martinsville, W. Va.

IRA M. CLARKE—General Manager

*From Crockery and Glass Journal (December 31, 1925).*

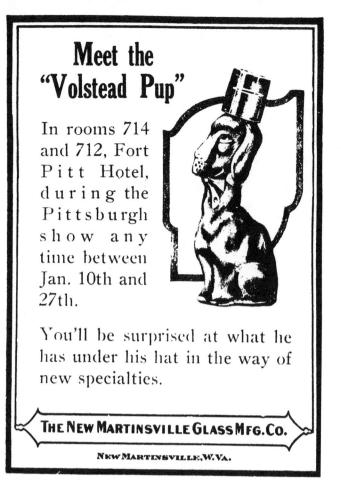

*Ads for New Martinsville's Volstead Pup as shown in* Pottery, Glass and Brass Salesman *(left) and* Crockery and Glass Journal.

ban of all alcoholic beverages under the Eighteenth Amendment had been in effect since January 29, 1920. Enforcement of the amendment was through the Volstead Act, which occured on October 28, 1919. New Martinsville's outright reference to the legislative efforts of Congressman Andrew J. Volstead was clearly a vote in favor of the Roaring 20s but against Prohibition! Like virtually all the American glass factories, New Martinsville freely advertised its liquor and wine sets.

The Nice Kitty set was introduced in October, 1926, with a French flair: "Le Chat Noir—et Blanc" (trans: The white cat—and the black). Actually, the Nice Kitty was available in decorated crystal and no fewer than five colors—black, amber, blue, green and a hue called "rose." The rose shade, probably a pale pink rather than ruby red, was also available with a frosted satin finish, the color probably called Peach Melba when used for vanity sets. Both the Nice Kitty and the Volstead Pup were expected to retail for about one dollar each, but wholesale buyers could purchase

J9719—8 piece set, 14x9½ in., silver plated stand, peach crystal comic dog with silver plated hat cover, 6 optic glasses! 1 set in box.
Was $6.95    Now
SET (8 pcs) $5.95

*From Butler Brothers catalogue (July, 1928).*

them "packed 3 dozen to a barrel—assorted dogs and cats."

## THE 1926 CATALOGUE

Among the most important sources in ascertaining New Martinsville's products during the Clarke years is a color catalogue showing the company's wares available in 1926. Although the catalogue is not particularly lengthy, just 12 pages, it shows a number of New Martinsville items and provides excellent documentation of the colors and items then being produced.

Through the courtesy of the Corning Museum of Glass, this catalogue is reproduced in color in this book (see pp. 115-126; the original catalogue sustained some water damage in the Corning flood of 1972, but it is still quite readable and useful to students of glass). A factory price list keyed to this catalogue has also been helpful. Incidentally, the Corning Museum's copy of this catalogue was originally sent from the New Martinsville Glass Manufacturing Company to the Pittsburgh Cut Glass Co. of Beaver, Pa., in response to the latter's request in October, 1926. The Pennsylvania firm may have been contemplating the purchase of blanks from New Martinsville.

References to the 1926 catalogue are made throughout this chapter, but there are some remaining articles which deserve special mention here. Reports from New Martinsville in the *American Flint* during this time mentioned that the firm had just one iron mould shop, a group of skilled glassworkers who would make such blown articles as large vases and jugs (pitchers) with handles. Among the men at New Martinsville who could do such work were George Frye, John Forbes, and Louis Zohnd, who had the position of handler when jugs were made. They were likely responsible for much of the production of liquor and wine decanters as well as the No. 190-4 and No. 198-7 jugs [see p. 115], the No. 725 fan vases [see p. 115] and perhaps the No. 150/3010 sweet pea vase [see p. 124].

The 1926 catalogue shows several items from the well-established No. 10 line, including the large round candy box [see p. 116] and four sizes of plates [see p. 123]; these plates were also advertised in the April 15, 1926 issue of *Crockery and Glass Journal*. The catalogue also pictures a lemon plate, designated No. 160/3019 [see p. 124].

## CLARKE TAKES HIS LEAVE

Although the New Martinsville plant was making a great variety of goods in the mid-1920s, competition in the industry was incredibly keen. The Fenton Art Glass Company of Williamstown, West Virginia, was certainly a major player in the tableware segment of the trade as was the Diamond Glass-Ware Co. of Indiana, Pa. Other important firms included the Imperial Glass Co. (Bellaire, Ohio), the Cambridge Glass Co, (Cambridge, Ohio), A. H. Heisey and Co. (Newark, Ohio) and the Fostoria Glass Co. (Moundsville, West Virginia).

Other factors which may have led to Clarke's departure were the climate of restlessness among the workers and the outright animosity between the workers and the factory's management. Both the company's correspondence with the National Association of Manufacturers of Pressed and Blown Glassware and the worker's columns in the *American Flint* reflect the tension under which the New Martinsville plant operated in the early and mid-1920s. For instance, after the Higbee moulds came to the New Martinsville plant, numerous disputes arose between the glassworkers and management over the wages to be paid to the gathers and pressers and over the "move" (number of pieces to be made in a turn or shift). These disagreements were ultimately adjusted, but sometimes only with the assistance of the national AFGWU officers or the staff of the manufacturers' group, the National Association of Manufacturers of Pressed and Blown Glassware.

On October 17, 1923, Clarke wrote to Charles Voitle, executive secretary of the National Association for advice about some men he regarded as troublesome employees. Clarke did not name them, but his letter clearly reflects his frustration:

*The writer wants to ask your advice in the matter of one or two men that we have working for us that are absolutely undesirable and do not have the interests of this company at heart. They try to block our progress in every way possible but do it in a way we can't take any exception to so as to fire them and what we would like you to do is to tell us if we are obliged to keep men such as this. Can't we make some excuse of reducing our force or something of that kind whereby we can discharge these men? We object to keeping them until they die unless they do something that is wrong.*

In November, 1923, Clarke and his management team were so concerned about general slackness—especially frequent absenteeism and lateness in reporting for work—that they sought counsel from William P. Clarke, national president of the AFGWU. Although the union officer felt strongly that the matter should be adjusted and settled locally, he wrote to both Ira Clarke and Charles E. Ward, secretary of Local Union No. 16 in New Martinsville. The following paragraph is from William P. Clarke's letter to Ward, dated November 14, 1923:

*There must be a certain amount of discipline in every plant, otherwise it cannot be operated successfully. Again, the management must have respect for the workmen and the workmen must have respect for the management or the plant cannot be operated successfully. If the plant is not operated successfully, then both the management and the workmen suffer. Therefore, it behooves all to display a spirit of co-operation based on equality and fair play.*

On several occasions, New Martinsville's managers sent discharge notices to some members of Local Union No. 16 for being incompetent workers. The cause of these fired workers was nearly always taken up by the AFGWU chapter, and many official "protests" were filed. Some of these matters dragged on for months at a time as management documented a particular worker's poor performance, while the union countered with complaints about working conditions and allegations of inconsistent enforcement of work rules.

Every controversy has at least two sides, of course, and New Martinsville's workers did not hesitate to express themselves. As early as the July, 1921, issue of the *American Flint*, William Cross wrote that eveyone was "busted and disgusted." A few months later, Cross was more specific: "Since the new factory started, December 20, 1920, the workers have been working under difficulties, poor snaps, poor punties and a general lacking in the way of facilities, and when we ask for anything to work with, it takes us a lot longer to get it than it took George Washington to cross the Delaware" (*American Flint*, September, 1921).

Glassworker Arch Hill, who had come to New Martinsville from the Higbee plant where he worked under Ira Clarke, was among the most optimistic of the employees. His column in the *American Flint* lauded the "very steady run for seventeen months" (January, 1924). Even when conditions were down, Hill was upbeat: "As expected, we have been on half-time for the last four weeks and can't see any change in sight yet. We are all hoping though that we will be on full again soon" (July, 1924).

Hill's generally positive outlook was in sharp

## NEW MARTINSVILLE, W. VA.

### By W. O. W.

Since my last report things have got worse here. We went along full time for twelve weeks when the tank sprung several leaks and was out on May 6 and are going to rebuild it all over. I think they were getting short of orders, so it didn't affect them very much. We are working three days and three nights each week. I mean we go out to work those days or nights, but we never get a full night's work. Never heard of such a way of working, as the men must be here all the time, whereas if we worked week about, the men could do something the week they were off. I think if ever a factory should have the name of "Black Cat" this factory sure should have it. Our old friend, John Gillett, quit his job here and is going back to Belgium. Bob Martin has taken a job spare here.

Most of the men here are busy with their gardens, and since we are on half time they will find plenty of time to work them.

Brothers Russ Emch and Charlie Powell are building new homes. Houses are very scarce here and rents rather high, although there are quite a few new ones being built.

Our local put on the great labor picture called "Contrast" and made a big success out of it, as they had a crowded house to see it.

"Oh, yes! Guy Wilt bought a Ford touring car and believe me, he goes some. The first time he came to work in it he knocked over a stone wall, but came right through it. He didn't have quite as much luck, though, when he tried to climb the telegraph pole. Our firm has opened a display room down town and have a fine display of their cut glass samples and also other samples. We are all hoping for a fine run of work when our tank is finished, but guess that will be two more months.

*This column in the June, 1922, issue of the* American Flint *captures the mood of New Martinsville's glassworkers and provides an insight into conditions in the town.*

contrast to that of longtime New Martinsville glassworker Russell C. Emch, whose column first appeared in the *American Flint* in March, 1926:

*I know that reports from here from time to time have left the trade at large under the impression that everything down this way has been lovely, while the fact of the matter is somewhat to the contrary, and does not exactly harmonize with the reports of members who have worked here and left. Now, I don't say that any particular party is to blame for the situation, but I do know that there is a certain amount of dishonesty displayed, and we know that where there is dishonesty, peace flees. The truth is that peace fled from here quite a while ago. ... The company has good orders, and it is true we are working steady but there just seems to be a general misunderstanding.*

Emch's view was probably an accurate one, for glassworker Frank Schultz had appeared before Justice of the Peace M. R. Daugherty in New Martinsville on October 15, 1924, to file a list of charges against factory manager Theodore ("Dory") Schwing. Among other things, Schultz accused Schwing of intimidation and threatening behavior against him and others. Schultz, Paul Martin and other workers criticized Schwing for improper application of work rules and for inconsistency and abrasiveness in his treatment of the workmen. A general meeting of Local Union No. 16 was held, and these charges were later presented to general manager Ira Clarke, who took some actions designed to ameliorate the workers' concerns.

Nonetheless, the situation continued to fester until early April, 1926, when executive officers from both the American Flint Glass Workers Union and the National Association of Manufacturers of Pressed and Blown Glassware came to New Martinsville for several days of meetings. National AFGWU officers and Local Union No. 16 met throughout the afternoon and evening on April 2, 1926. In a lengthy letter to Ira Clarke, charges were again levied against manager Theodore Schwing as well as another manager, Ross Schwing, who was Theodore's brother. The letter was signed by these members of the local union's factory committee: William Cross; C. Powel; F. Frizzell; E. D. Horstman; Guy Wilt; Charles Frey; George Workman; and Raymond Hoskins. The crux of their letter is this paragraph:

*The workmen are determined that the condition that has existed for so many years at your factory must be corrected, and that they will no longer tolerate the abusive attitude displayed by your managers. A definite settlement must be made of the situation and we are hopeful that you as general manager will set about to remedy the matter.*

On April 3, 1926, a committee of New Martinsville's workers met with Clarke and officials from the AFGWU and the National Association of Manufacturers of Pressed and Blown Glassware. The parties decided that all future disputes regarding wages/moves and any matters relating to grounds for discharge would be presented directly to general manager Ira Clarke. The workers pledged to "do all in their power to creat harmony in the factory," and all parties agreed that "no profane language shall be used by either side in any manner."

About this time, Charles Voitle, executive secretary of the National Association of Manufacturers of Pressed and Blown Glassware, apparently suggested confidentially to Clarke that the company would do well to obtain a new factory manager, either by promotion of a respected man from within the ranks of the skilled glassworkers at New Martinsville or by securing the services of an outsider. Clarke immediately sought someone to hire, but he was unable to do so until late August, 1926, when Voitle recommended Wilbur Rider, who was then working in Lancaster, Ohio. Rider accepted the position and came to New Martinsville in early September, 1926. The company also altered Theodore Schwing's job, relieving him of his managerial responsibilities but putting him in charge of glassmaking, the furnaces and the lehrs.

Despite these efforts to create better relations between the workers and management, all was not well at the New Martinsville plant. On August 26, 1926, Clarke wrote to AFGWU vice-president Joseph Gillooly, seeking advice as to the proper procedure for a reduction of the company's work force. Clarke said that the plant had been operating with eight shops (in contrast to 14 in better times) and felt obligated to reduce the number even further to six.

Ira M. Clarke remained as treasurer and general manager until late September, 1926. Company correspondence on October 1, 1926, was signed by Robert McEldowney with his title given as "General Manager," although Clarke's name still appeared on the letterhead. A new chapter in the life of the New Martinsville Glass Manufacturing Company was about to begin.

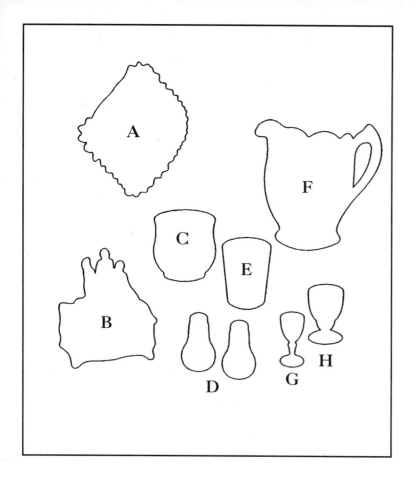

## FRONT COVER:

**A.** Salmon Muranese square crimped berry bowl.

**B.** Martha Washington trinket box in jade/black combination.

**C.** No. 88 Carnation spooner with amber stain.

**D.** Turquoise No. 57 (Vining Rose) salt and pepper shakers.

**E-F.** No. 717 (Horseshoe Daisy) tumbler and pitcher with gold and ruby-stain decoration.

**G-H.** No. 37 (Moondrops) cordial in ruby and footed juice tumbler in amber.

## BACK COVER:

**I.** Turquoise No. 800 (By the Sea) miniature lamp.

**J.** No. 204 (Scalloped Plume) coaster with gold decoration.

**K.** Opal Muranese sauce dish.

**L.** Green "Nice Kitty" Good-Night Set (decanter and tumbler).

**M.** Salmon No. 160 (Vining Rose) decorated molasses can.

**N.** Pink Muranese sauce dish.

**O.** No. 4543-1SJ Janice Swan (crystal neck/ruby body).

**P.** Blue No. 15 decanter with crystal fan-shaped stopper.

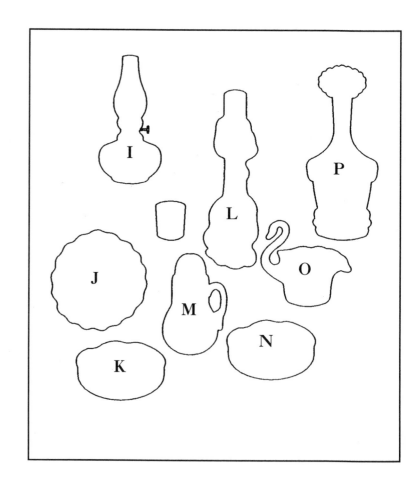

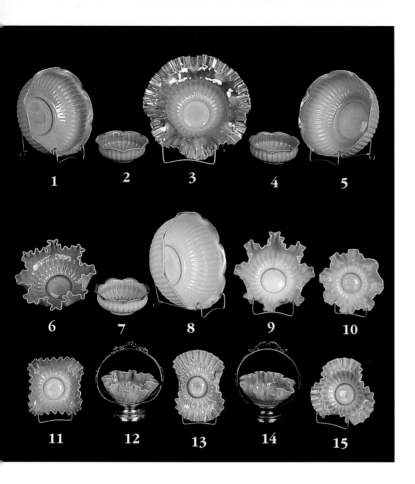

**1-3.** Salmon Muranese bowl, sauce dish and large, crimped bowl with vibrant gold iridescence. **4-5.** Pink Muranese sauce dish and bowl with some gold on rims.

**6.** Salmon Muranese crimped bowl. **7-9.** Opal Muranese sauce dish, bowl and crimped bowl. **10.** Pink Muranese crimped sauce dish.

**11.** Salmon Muranese square crimped sauce dish. **12 and 14.** Pink Muranese crimped sauce dishes in silver-plated holders. **13.** Unusual Salmon Muranese crimped sauce dish. **15.** Unusual opal Muranese tri-corner crimped sauce dish with greenish interior.

**16 and 19.** Salmon Muranese crimped bowls. **17.** This Salmon Muranese piece has an acidized, satin finish. **18.** Muranese crimped bowl.

**20-21.** Salmon Muranese shades. **22 and 25.** Pink Muranese shades. **23-24 and 26.** Muranese crimped bowl and shades.

**27-28 and 30.** Various pink Muranese crimped sauce dishes in silver-plated holders. **29.** Muranese sauce dish with silver-plated holder and spoon.

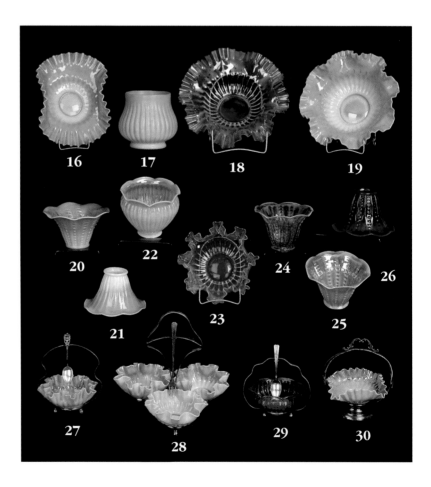

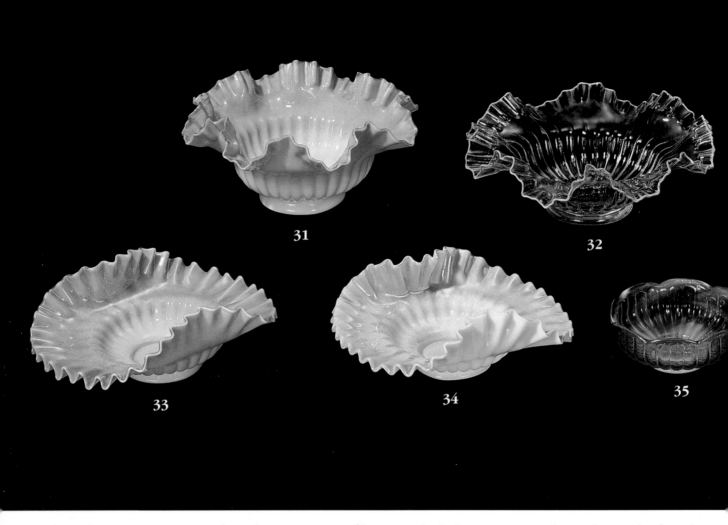

31

32

33

34

35

These five Muranese pieces show the great range of hues in which this interesting glass color can be found. For many years, all of these colors were simply lumped together under the general term "New Martinsville Peachblow." Henceforth, the original name for this line, Muranese, should be restored and used. Additionally, the original terms for three particular colors within the Muranese line—pink, salmon and opal—can be linked to specific colors as shown here. Items 32 and 35 might be from the Muranese line as continued by Mooney and Kavanaugh after Joseph Webb left New Martinsville.

**31.** This is a crimped bowl in pink Muranese, which may have been the initial Muranese color developed by glassmaker Joseph Webb at New Martinsville about 1902 (the Millers called this color "Sunburst"). These pieces range from a soft pink, as shown here, to a deep pink exterior with gold highlights on the edges and/or interior.

**32.** Although it is almost crystal clear, this Muranese bowl displays some greenish iridescence, especially near its edges; other pieces have deeper, all-over iridescence. The original name for this color, if any, is not known, but the Millers called it "Sunrise."

**33.** This crimped bowl with upturned sides is the Salmon Muranese mentioned by the New Martinsville Glass Manufacturing Company in its 1904 catalogue; some of these pieces feature bright gold edges and interior highlights (the Millers called this "Sunglow").

**34.** Opal Muranese was also mentioned by the New Martinsville Glass Manufacturing Company in its 1904 catalogue; this piece is quite light, but others have warm yellow interiors, often with gold highlights and gold rims. The Millers called this "Sunlite."

**35.** This Muranese sauce dish is shaded from yellowish to orange-red. The Millers called this "Sunray."

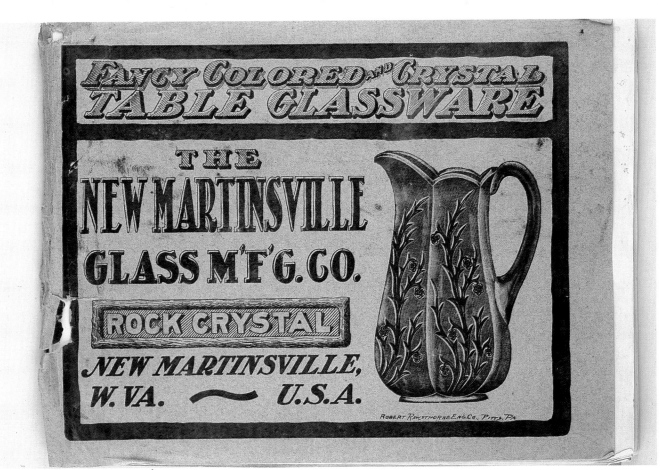

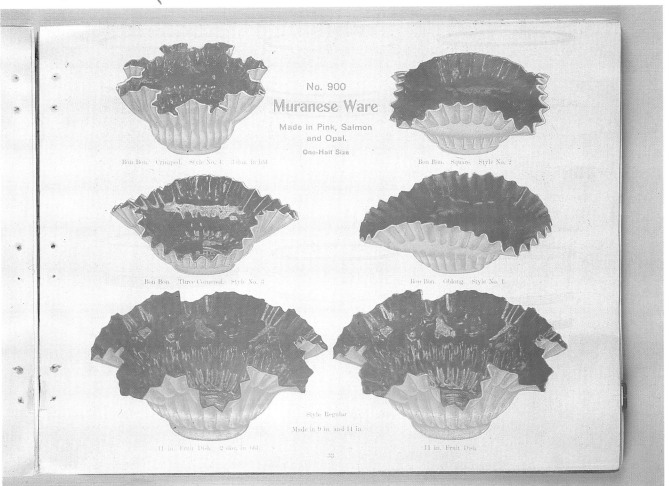

Courtesy of the Corning Museum of Glass.

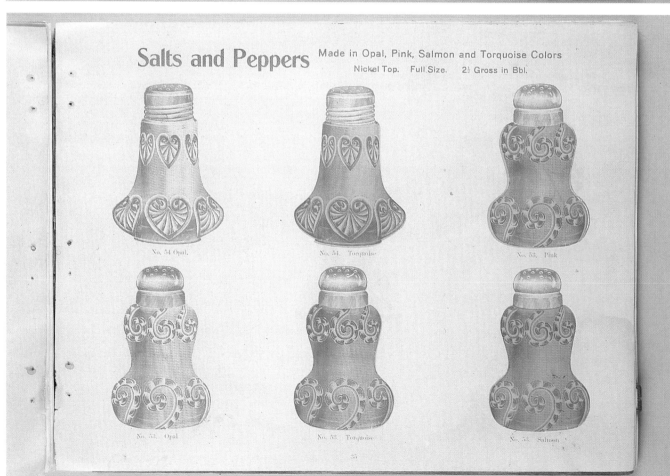

Courtesy of the Corning Museum of Glass.

Courtesy of the Corning Museum of Glass.

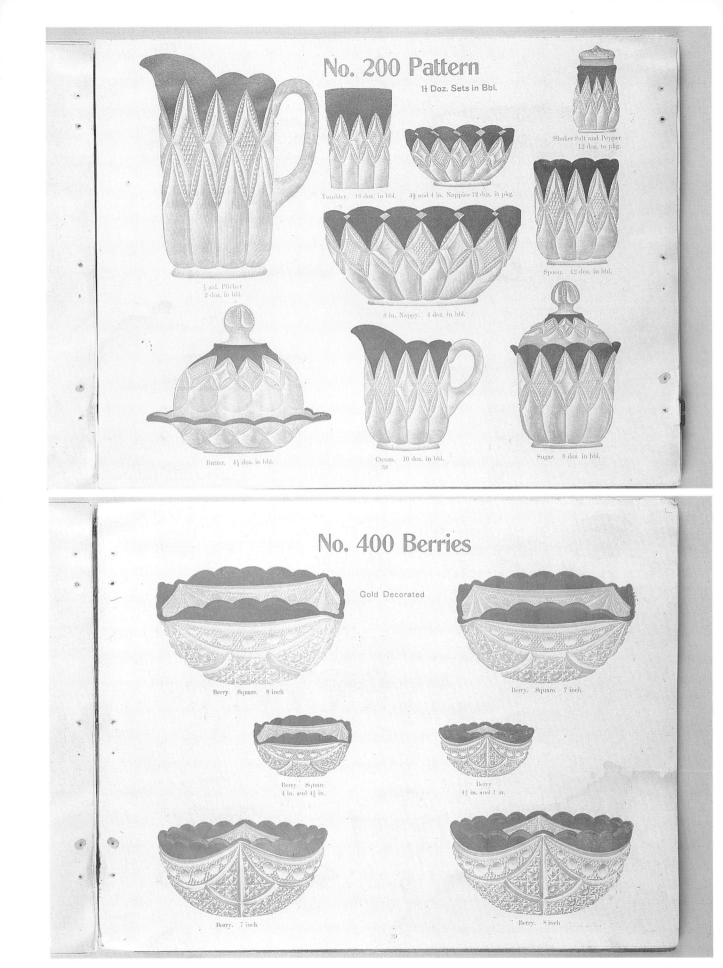

# No. 200 Pattern

1½ Doz. Sets in Bbl.

Shaker Salt and Pepper
12 doz. to pkg.

Tumbler. 18 doz. in bbl.

4½ and 4 in. Nappies 12 doz. in pkg.

Spoon. 12 doz. in bbl.

½ gal. Pitcher
2 doz. in bbl.

8 in. Nappy. 4 doz. in bbl.

Butter. 4½ doz. in bbl.

Cream. 10 doz. in bbl.
38

Sugar. 8 doz. in bbl.

# No. 400 Berries

Gold Decorated

Berry. Square. 8 inch

Berry. Square. 7 inch

Berry. Square.
4 in. and 4½ in.

Berry
4½ in. and 4 in.

Berry. 7 inch

Berry. 8 inch

39

Courtesy of the Corning Museum of Glass.

96

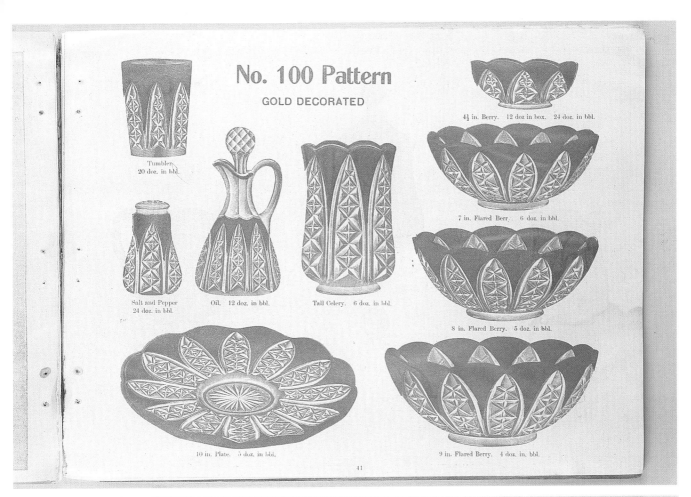

# No. 100 Pattern
## GOLD DECORATED

Tumbler.
20 doz. in bbl.

Salt and Pepper
24 doz. in bbl.

Oil.   12 doz. in bbl.

Tall Celery.   6 doz. in bbl.

4½ in. Berry.   12 doz in box.   24 doz. in bbl.

7 in. Flared Berry.   6 doz. in bbl.

8 in. Flared Berry.   5 doz. in bbl.

10 in. Plate.   5 doz. in bbl.

9 in. Flared Berry.   4 doz. in. bbl.

41

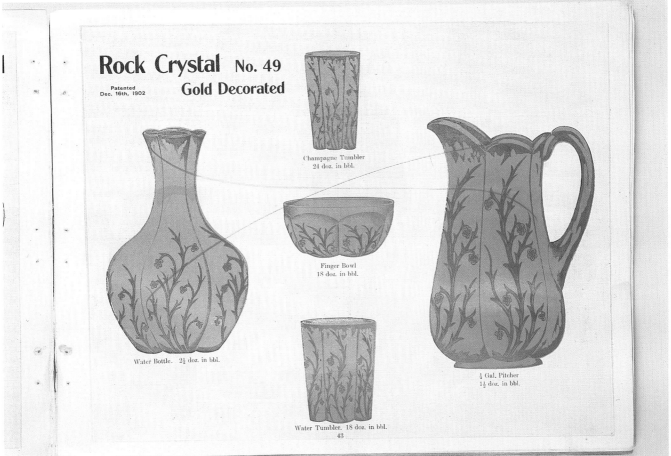

# Rock Crystal  No. 49
**Patented**
**Dec. 16th, 1902**
## Gold Decorated

Champagne Tumbler
24 doz. in bbl.

Finger Bowl
18 doz. in bbl.

Water Bottle.   2½ doz. in bbl.

Water Tumbler.  18 doz. in bbl.
43

½ Gal. Pitcher
1½ doz. in bbl.

Courtesy of the Corning Museum of Glass.

No. 600 Pattern--Gold Decorated
No. 43

No. 600 Celery

Plain Bowl Sugar Shaker, Tin Top

Tall Tankard Cream

Sugar

Cream

Spoon

Butter

49

No. 600 Ware
Decoration No. 20

4½ in. Berry, Cupped

4½ in. Berry

8 in. Berry, Cupped

Tall Celery

8 in. Berry

Butter and Cover

Spoon

Cream

Sugar and Cover

52

Courtesy of the Corning Museum of Glass.

# No. 600 Ware

## Decoration No. 20

No. 150 Sugar Shaker

No. 600 Salt and Pepper

No. 600, 5 in. Berry Crimped

No. 150 Mol. Can

No. 600, 9 in. Berry Crimped

No. 600 Tumbler

No. 600 ½ Gal. Tankard

53

# No. 160 Lamps

## Plain or Decorated

Footed Hand. No. 1 Collar
6 doz. in bbl.

Flat Hand. No. 1 Collar
9 doz. in bbl.

C Sewing. D Sewing. No. 2 Collar
C—3 doz. in bbl. D—2¼ doz. in bbl.

O Stand. No. 1 Collar
5 doz. in bbl.

A Stand. No. 1 Collar
4 doz. in bbl.

60

Courtesy of the Corning Museum of Glass.

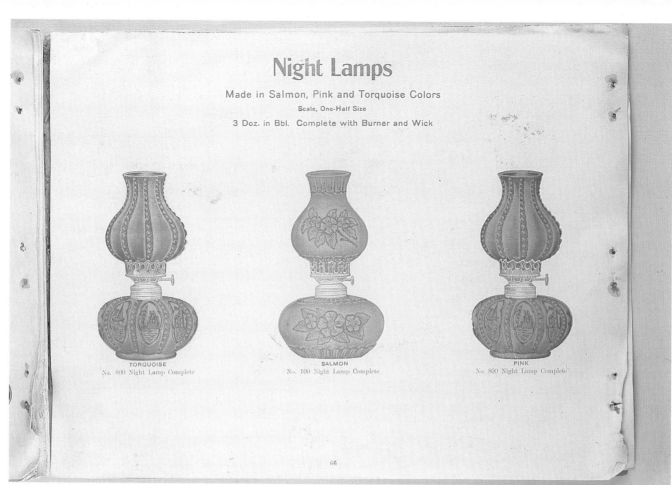

# Night Lamps

## Made in Salmon, Pink and Torquoise Colors

### Scale, One-Half Size

### 3 Doz. in Bbl.  Complete with Burner and Wick

TORQUOISE
No. 800 Night Lamp Complete

SALMON
No. 100 Night Lamp Complete

PINK
No. 800 Night Lamp Complete

66

No. 8 Electric
Coralene, Ruby, Tinted and Etched
Class F

Post Burner
No. 1000 Gas Shade
Pink Opaque
Made also in Salmon Opaque
Class H

No. 8 Electric
Ruby, Tinted and Etched
Class D

No. 1100 Gas Shade
1¼ Finish
Salmon, Opaque and Etched
Class G

No. 1150 Gas Shade
1¼ Fitting
Pink, Opaque and Etched
Class H

70

Courtesy of the Corning Museum of Glass.

These miniature "night lamps" date from about 1904, when opal, pink, salmon and turquoise were in production at New Martinsville. **36.** Swirl Rib. **37, 39 and 41.** No. 800 (By-the-Sea). **38 and 42.** Flowering Vine. **40.** Iris.

**43-44, 46 and 48.** Rock Crystal (Floral Panel) table set with overall gold decoration (originally called decoration No. 49). **45.** Salmon Rock Crystal (Floral Panel) swung vase. **47.** Rock Crystal (Floral Panel) individual sugar bowl.

These shakers show some colors and decorations associated with New Martinsville. **49-50 and 61-62.** No. 52 opal shakers. **51-52.** No. 702 (Placid Thumbprint) shakers. **53-54.** Rose Relievo shakers in turquoise and opal (attributed by Lechner). **55-57.** Leaf Drooping opal shakers. (attributed by Lechner). **58.** Turquoise No. 55 (Many Petals). **59.** Turquoise Top Hat (Lincoln Hat). **60.** No. 56 (Curly Locks).

63 64 65 66 67 68 69 70 71

72 73 74 75 76 77 78 79

80 81 82 83 84 85

86 87 88 89 90 91

**63-66 and 68-71.** Opal Curved Body shakers (note the various "S" and "P" decorations). **67.** Curved Body shaker in opaque pale turquoise.

**72-79.** No. 58 (Creased Waist) shakers in various shades of yellow, salmon, pink, opal and turquoise.

**80-85.** No. 54 (Palmette Band) shakers in opal (note various decorations) and pink.

**86-91.** No. 62 (Vine with Flower) shakers in various shades of turquoise, opal (note decorations) and salmon.

**92-94.** No. 61 (Rose Viking) shakers in opal (note decoration), pale yellow and pink. **95-97.** Pillar and Flower shakers in opal (note decorations) and turquoise.

**98-102.** No. 57 (Vining Rose) shakers in various shades of turquoise, salmon and opal (**100** is decorated with gold paint).

**103-107.** No. 53 (Scroll Two Band) shakers in opaque green, opal (note decorations), pink and turquoise.

**108-111.** No. 63 (Tall Aster) shakers in pink, opal (note decoration), turquoise and salmon.

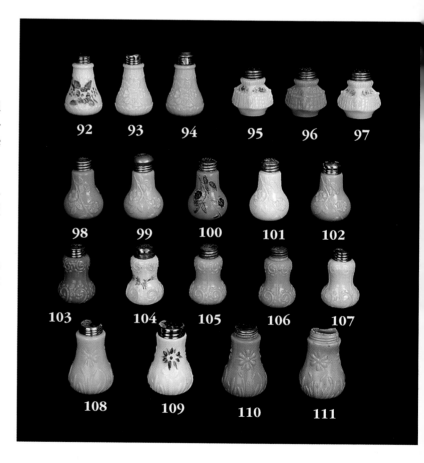

92 93 94 95 96 97

98 99 100 101 102

103 104 105 106 107

108 109 110 111

Ruby-stained glassware was an important feature of production at New Martinsville between 1907 and 1915, and many different patterns are shown here and on the next six pages.

**112.** No. 714 (Chateau) pitcher. **113-114.** No. 719 Old Glory tumbler and pitcher with green decoration. **115.** No. 719 Old Glory pitcher. **116-117.** No. 721 Studio tumbler and pitcher.

**118-124.** No. 88 Carnation spooner, covered sugar bowl, creamer, sauce dish, tumbler, pitcher, and butterdish.

**125-127.** No. 717 (Horseshoe Daisy) berry bowl, sauce and butterdish. **128.** No. 721 (Studio) covered sugar bowl (the lid may be ruby-stained in two different ways, as shown).

**129-131.** No. 711 (Leaf and Star) tumblers and pitcher. **132.** No. 704 (Placid Thumbprint) pitcher. **133-135.** No. 711 (Leaf and Star) wine, pitcher and tumbler with gold decoration.

**136-140.** No. 97 Old Colony table set (butterdish, spooner, covered sugar bowl and creamer), plus another butterdish with a slightly different ruby-stain decoration.

**141-145.** No. 711 (Leaf and Star) butterdish, salt/pepper shakers, toothpick, covered sugar bowl and creamer. **146.** No. 718 (Frontier) toothpick. **147.** No. 720 Florene pomade jar. **148.** Plain salt shaker.

**149-150.** No. 705 Klear-Kut tumbler and pitcher. **151-152.** No. 705 Klear-Kut tumbler and pitcher with gold decoration (note the design on the upper portion of the pitcher). **153-154.** No. 718 (Frontier) tumbler and pitcher.

**155-156.** No. 704 (Placid Thumbprint) berry bowl and sauce. **157-158.** No. 720 Florene berry bowl and sauce with gold decoration. **159-160.** No. 97 Old Colony berry bowl and sauce.

**161.** No. 707 (Horseshoe Medallion) olive dish with gold decoration. **162-165.** No. 719 Old Glory table set with gold decoration. **166.** No. 100 (Celtic) goblet with gold decoration.

**167-168.** No. 704 (Placid Thumbprint) celery holder and biscuit jar. **169-170.** No. 707 (Horseshoe Medallion) creamer and covered sugar bowl. **171-172.** No. 717 (Horseshoe Daisy) tumbler and pitcher.

**173-179.** No. 722 (Lorraine) covered sugar bowl, creamer, butterdish, sauce dish, spooner, tumbler and pitcher.

**180-184.** No. 715 Lenoir butterdish, spooner, creamer, sauce dish and berry bowl.

**185** **186** **187** **188** **189** **190**

**191** **192** **193** **194** **195**

**196** **197** **198** **199** **200**

**185-188.** No. 720 Florene pitcher, tumbler, spooner and creamer. **189-190.** No. 97 Old Colony tumbler and pitcher.

**191-194.** No. 715 Lenoir table set—butterdish, spooner, covered sugar bowl and creamer. **195.** No. 711 (Leaf and Star) butterdish.

**196-199.** No. 704 (Placid Thumbprint) table set—butterdish, spooner, creamer and covered sugar bowl. **200.** No. 721 (Studio) covered sugar bowl.

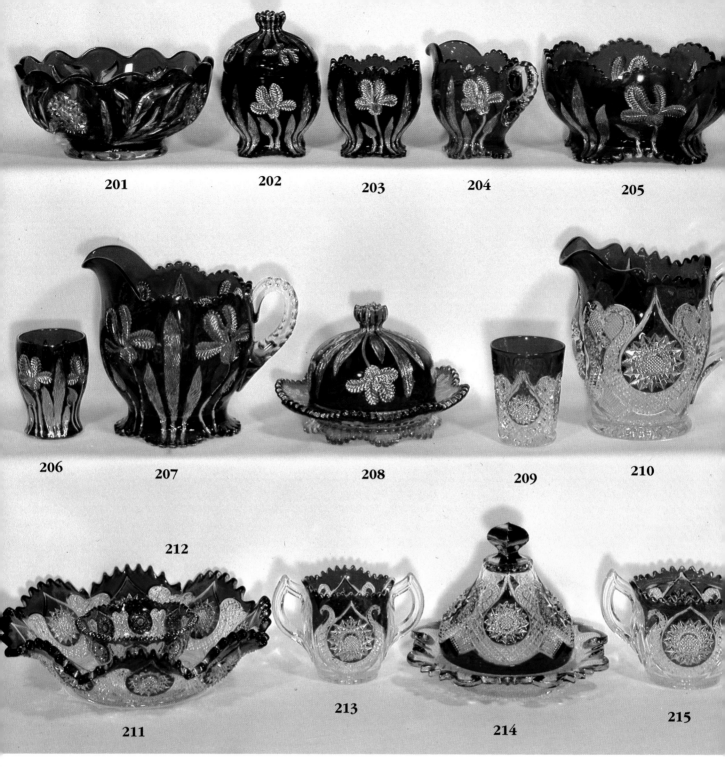

**201.** No. 88 Carnation berry bowl. **202-205.** No. 716 Rebecca (Japanese Iris) covered sugar bowl, spooner, creamer and berry bowl.

**206-208.** No. 716 Rebecca (Japanese Iris) tumbler, pitcher and covered butterdish. **209-210.** No. 707 (Horseshoe Medallion) tumbler and pitcher.

**211-215.** No. 707 (Horseshoe Medallion) berry bowl, sauce dish, spooner, butterdish and sugar bowl (no lid).

216 | 217 | 218 | 219 | 220 | 221

222 | 223 | 224 | 225

226 | 227 | 228 | 229

**216-221.** No. 724 (Heart in Sand) tumbler, pitcher and table set—spooner, covered sugar bowl, creamer and butter dish.

**222-224.** No. 724 (Heart in Sand) berry bowl, sauce dish and jelly compote. **225.** This metal server is fitted with two No. 724 (Heart in Sand) sauce dishes.

**226-228.** No. 705 Klear-Kut pitcher, covered sugar bowl and butterdish. **229.** No. 722 (Lorraine) pitcher.

# No. 724 Pattern
## DECORATED No. 36

Butter and Cover      Tumbler      Sugar and Cover

Spoon      4½ inch Berry      Cream

7 inch Berry

8 inch Berry      ½ Gallon Jug

This page, from an original New Martinsville Glass Manufacturing Company catalogue c. 1917, shows pattern No. 724 (Heart in Sand) with the decoration designated No. 36. This motif was described as "fired enamel floral decorations" in the January 14, 1915, issue of *Pottery, Glass and Brass Salesman*.

230    231    232    233    234    235    236

237    238    239    240    241    242    243    244

245    246    247    248    249    250    251

All of these articles are crystal glass.

**230-235.** Floral Oval goblet, wine, wine with flared rim, covered butterdish, punch cup and compote. **236.** Perkins cruet.

**237-241.** Rexford syrup jug, tall shaker, handled nappie, wine and covered compote. **242-244.** Paris salt/pepper shakers and sugar shaker.

**245-251.** Rexford toothpick holder, sauce dish, cruet, and four-piece child's set—covered sugar bowl, spooner, creamer and butterdish.

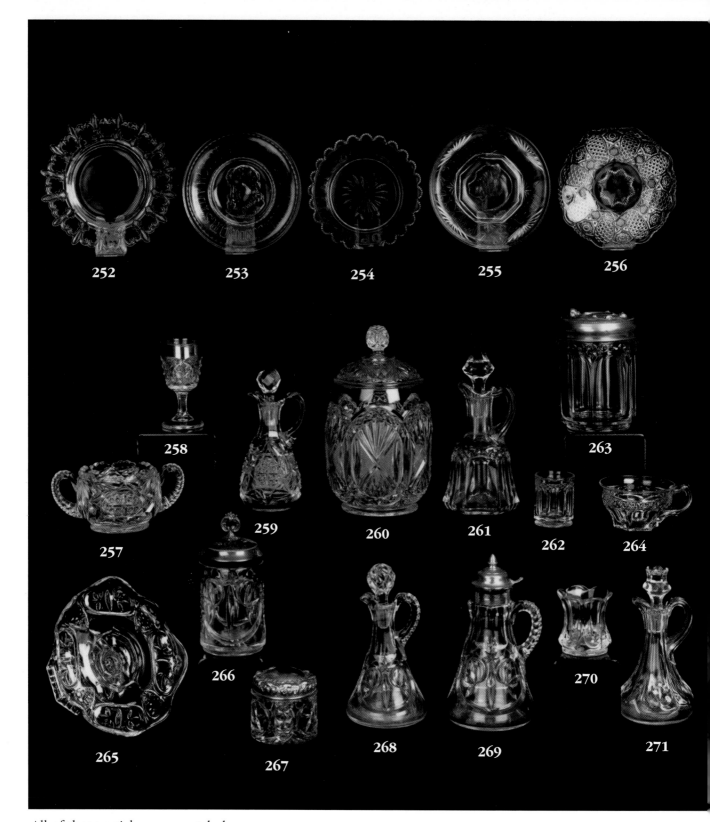

252 253 254 255 256

257 258 259 260 261 262 263 264

265 266 267 268 269 270 271

All of these articles are crystal glass.

**252.** No. 10 Souvenir plate. **253.** No. 531 Boy A-B-C plate. **254.** No. 530 Star A-B-C plate. **255.** No. 532 Dog A-B-C plate. **256.** No. 705 Klear-Kut 6" plate.

**257-259.** No. 500 Wetzel (Star of David) hotel sugar, wine and cruet. **260.** No. 30 (Fan in Oval) covered cracker jar. **261-264.** No. 718 Frontier cruet, toothpick holder, tobacco jar (note metal lid) and punch cup.

**265-269.** No. 711 (Leaf and Star) flared bowl, tobacco jar (note metal lid), hair receiver (note metal lid), cruet and syrup jug. **270-271.** No. 704 (Placid Thumbprint) toothpick holder and cruet (note shape of stopper).

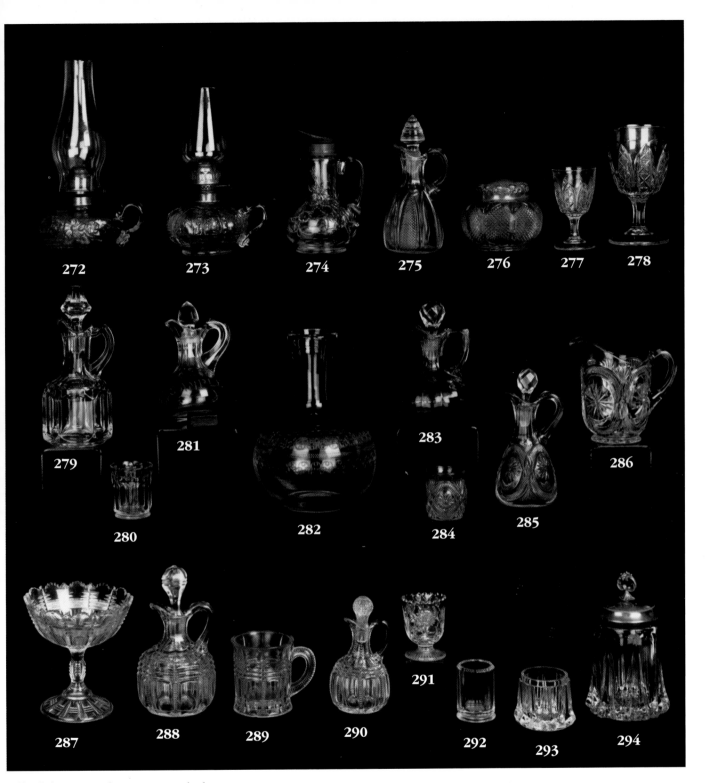

272 273 274 275 276 277 278

279 281 283 286

280 282 284 285

287 288 289 290 291 292 293 294

All of these articles are crystal glass.

**272.** Rose Viking hand lamp. **273.** No. 800 (By the Sea) hand lamp. **274.** No. 160 (Vining Rose) molasses can. **275.** No. 702 (Long Leaf Teasel) cruet. **276.** No. 312 (Panelled File) hair receiver (note metal lid). **277-278.** No. 100 (Celtic) wine and goblet.

**279-280.** No. 720 Florene cruet and toothpick holder. **281-282.** No. 708 Lusitania cruet (marked "SAMPLE") and water bottle (etching No. 2306). **283.** No. 728 Colonial cruet (marked NM on handle). **284-286.** No. 713 (Pleated Medallion) toothpick holder, cruet and creamer.

**287-290.** No. 116 (Zipper Cross) jelly compote, cruet and mug. **291.** No. 88 Carnation toothpick holder. **292.** No. 723 (Express) toothpick holder. **293-294.** No. 314 (Long Buttress) pomade jar (lacks metal lid) and tobacco jar (with metal lid).

113

All of these articles are crystal glass.

**295.** No. 10 4-inch handled candlestick. **296.** Plain bobeche (marked "SAMPLE"). **297.** Square ashtray (marked "FACTORY SAMPLE"). **298.** No. 10 pen tray. **299.** Christina basket. **300.** Large colonial-style creamer (marked "SAMPLE").

**301.** No. 758/742/735 10-pc. wine set (possibly made by Viking). **302-304.** No. 12 candlesticks in various sizes (the tallest has cut decoration). **305-306.** No. 714 (Chateau) child's berry dishes and bowl. **307.** No. 1000 cone holder. **308.** Volstead pup.

**309-311.** Janice basket (marked "SAMPLE") and Janice swans (the smaller is No. 4541-1HSJ and the larger is No. 4551-1SJ).

## Ice Tea - Water and Wine Sets - Guest Jugs and Bud Vases

No. 10-1-282
Wine Set—Green
Packs 2 Doz. to Bbl.

No. 10-1-282
Wine Set—Amethyst
Packs 2 Doz. to Bbl.

No. 140-1
Guest Jug and Tumbler—Optic—Amber
Packs 3 Doz. Sets to Bbl.

Blue    No. 723-8   Bud Vases    Amber
Packs 24 Doz. to Bbl.

No. 140-1
Guest Jug and Tumbler—Optic—Green
Packs 3 Doz. Sets to Bbl.

No. 190-4
Ice Tea Jug—Optic—Amber
Packs 2¼ Doz. to Bbl.

No. 113
12 oz. Tumbler—Optic—Amber
Packs 14 Doz. to Bbl.

No. 198-7
Water Jug—Optic—Amber
Packs 2 Doz. to Bbl.

No. 82
9 oz. Tumbler—Optic—Amber
Packs 20 Doz. to Bbl.

Courtesy of the Corning Museum of Glass.

115

# Candy Jars and Boxes

No. 149-2
One lb. Candy Jar and Cover—Amber
Packs 4⅔ Doz. to Bbl.

No. 10
1½ lb. Candy Box and Cover—Blue
Packs 4 Doz. to Bbl.

No. 149-3
½ lb. Candy Jar and Cover—Amber
Packs 5½ Doz. to Bbl.

No. 149-3
½ lb. Candy Jar and Cover—Amethyst
Packs 5½ Doz. to Bbl.

No. 10
1½ lb. Candy Box and Cover—Amber
Packs 4 Doz. to Bbl.

No. 149-3
½ lb. Candy Jar and Cover—Green
Packs 5½ Doz. to Bbl.

Courtesy of the Corning Museum of Glass.

# Console Sets

No. 10-10
Console Set—Amber
Packs 1½ Doz. Sets to Bbl.

No. 10-21
Console Set—Blue
Packs 1½ Doz. Sets to Bbl.

## Salad Sets

No. 160-8
Plate—Green

No. 728—7½
Plate—Amber

No. 160-12
Bowl and Plate—Green
Packs 1½ Doz. Sets to Bbl.

No. 728-12
Bowl and Plate—Amber
Packs 1½ Doz. Sets to Bbl.

## Relish Dishes

No. 10.   5 Part Relish Dish and Liner—Amber
Packs 2 Doz. to Trc.

No. 10.   5 Part Relish Dish and Liner—Amethyst
Packs 2 Doz. to Trc.

Courtesy of the Corning Museum of Glass.

# Queen Anne Dresser Sets

Packs 6 Doz. Sets to Bbl.

No. 10-2.  Amber

No. 10-2.  Green

No. 10-2.  Blue

No. 10-2.  Amethyst

Courtesy of the Corning Museum of Glass.

No. 2001
Vanity Set—Cold Color Decoration
Packs 12 Doz. to Bbl.

No. 1926
Vanity Set and Tray
Packs 6 Doz. without Tray, 4 Doz. with Tray

All items may be had in Crystal, Blue, Green, Amber and Amethyst.

Courtesy of the Corning Museum of Glass.

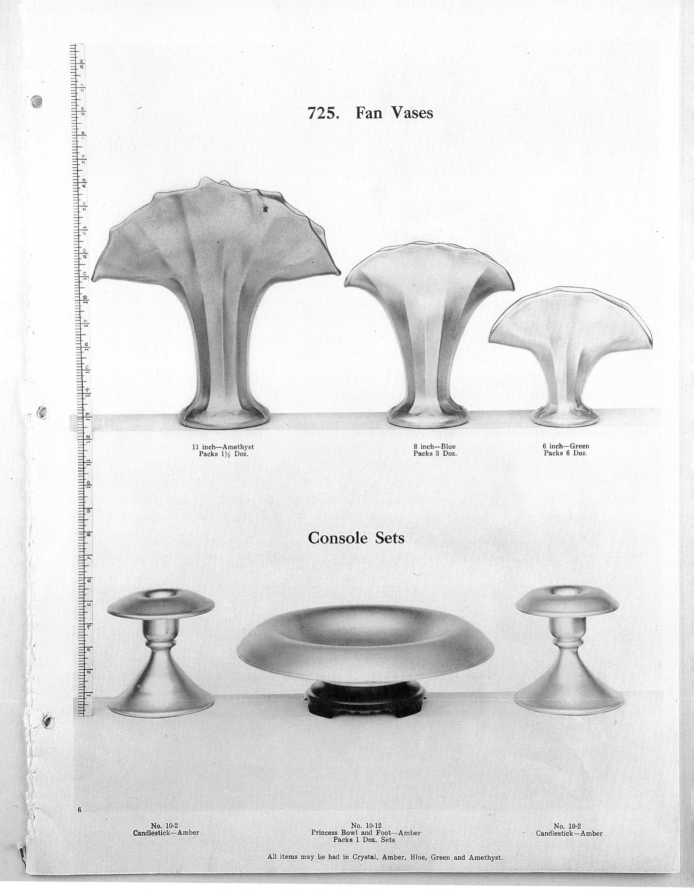

## 725. Fan Vases

11 inch—Amethyst
Packs 1½ Doz.

8 inch—Blue
Packs 3 Doz.

6 inch—Green
Packs 6 Doz.

## Console Sets

No. 10-2
Candlestick—Amber

No. 10-12
Princess Bowl and Foot—Amber
Packs 1 Doz. Sets

No. 10-2
Candlestick—Amber

All items may be had in Crystal, Amber, Blue, Green and Amethyst.

Courtesy of the Corning Museum of Glass.

No. 2003
Smoker Set.  Cold Color Decoration
Packs 12 Doz. Sets to Bbl.

No. 20
Ash Tray—Amber
Packs 12 Doz. to Bbl.

No. 149-2
Cigarette Holder—Green
Packs 18 Doz. to Bbl.

No. 10-2
Cigarette Set—Green
Packs 6 Doz. Sets to Bbl.

All items may be had in Crystal, Blue, Green, Amber and Amethyst.

Courtesy of the Corning Museum of Glass.

## Smoker Articles---Candlesticks

No. 728
Ash Tray—Amethyst
Packs 50 Doz. to Bbl.

No. 10-3
3 inch Candlestick—Amber
Packs 15 Doz. to Bbl.

No. 728
Match Stand—Green
Packs 50 Doz. to Bbl.

No. 10
4 inch Hld. Candlestick—Green
Packs 15 Doz. to Bbl.

No. 725
Tabacco Jar with Ash Tray Cov.—Amethyst
Packs 4½ Doz. to Bbl.

No. 725
Cigarette Jar with Ash Tray Cov.—Blue
Packs 12 Doz. to Bbl.

All items may be had in Crystal, Amber, Blue, Green and Amethyst.

Courtesy of the Corning Museum of Glass.

No. 10
6 inch Plate—Amber
Packs 24 Doz. to Bbl.

No. 10.  8½ inch Plate—Blue.  Packs 12 Doz. to Bbl.

No. 10
7½ inch Plate—Green
Packs 12 Doz. to Bbl.

No. 10.  10 inch Plate—Amethyst.  Packs 4 Doz. to Bbl.

No. 1926
Candy Box—Blue
Packs 6 Doz. to Bbl.

No. 728
Guest Set—Green
Packs 3 Doz. Sets to Bbl.

All items may be had in Crystal, Blue, Green, Amber and Amethyst.

Courtesy of the Corning Museum of Glass.

No. 149/4/3020.  Cigarette Holder.

No. 149/2/3019.  Cigarette Holder.

No. 10/3016.  Ash Tray Sets.
4 Trays in Box.

No. 2003.  Cigarette Set 3 Pieces.

No. 160/3019.  Lemon Plate and Fork.

No. 10/2/3000.  Smoker Set.

No. 150/3010.  Sweet Pea Vase.

Courtesy of the Corning Museum of Glass.

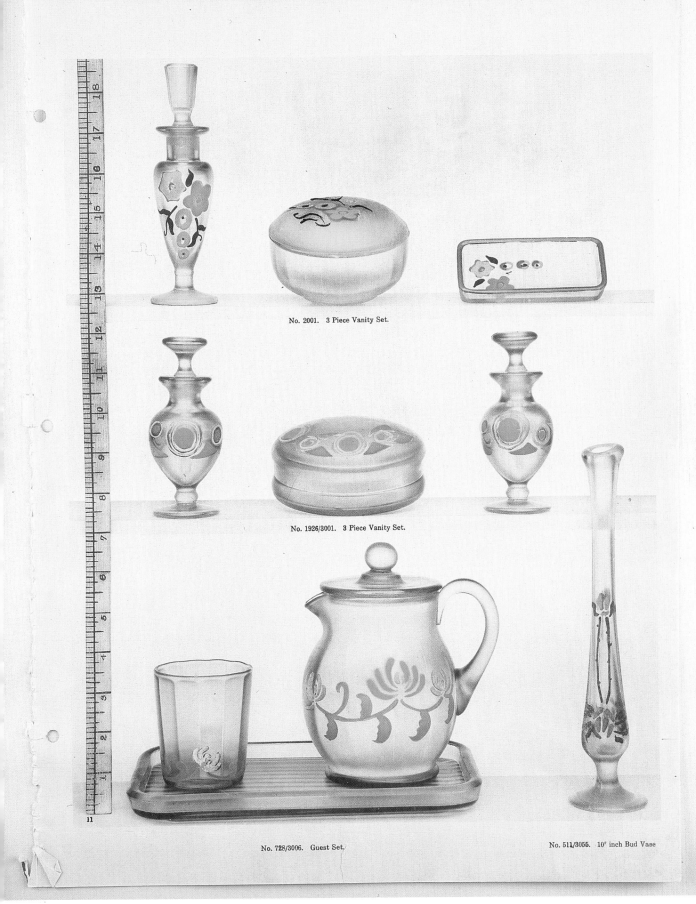

No. 2001. 3 Piece Vanity Set.

No. 1926/3001. 3 Piece Vanity Set.

No. 728/3006. Guest Set.

No. 511/3055. 10" inch Bud Vase

Courtesy of the Corning Museum of Glass.

No. 10/12″/3004. Princes Bowl.

No. 10/4/3004. 3″ Candlestick.

No. 10/2/3004. 5″ Candlestick.

No. 9/3000. Mint Jar.

No. 149/3/3002. ½ lb. Candy Jar.

No. 1926/3003. Candy Box.

No. 728/3011. ½ lb. Candy Jar.

Courtesy of the Corning Museum of Glass.

312  313  314  315

317  319  323

316  318  320  321  322  324

325  326  327  328

**312.** No. 728 Guest Set (covered pitcher, tumbler and rectangular tray) in pink. **313.** No. 10-2 Queen Anne Dresser Set in green (these appear in the 1926 catalogue without the tray). **314-315.** Square tray and No. 149-3 ½ lb. candy jar in amethyst.

**316.** Pale blue ashtray with etched decoration. **317 and 319.** Green Elephant incense burners (note decoration on Fig. 317; the top is missing on Fig. 319). **318.** Frosted pink decorated Elephant cigarette holder (compare the elephant's trunk with the incense burners). **320.** Pink Wise Owl pitcher with light cutting decoration. **321.** Cobalt blue No. 18 Saucer Candlestick. **322.** No. 1059 candlestick in opaque blue. **323.** Dancing Lady flower frog in frosted pink. **324.** Police Dog bookend (or lamp base) in frosted pink.

**325.** Cobalt blue No. 723 Bridge Sugar and Cream Set. **326-327.** Martha Washington trinket boxes in frosted pink and green (see also the front cover of this book). **328.** Blue No. 20 Ash Tray, says "PAT 68902" and "HOLLAND SOCIETY CIGARS".

**329.** Blue No. 33 Modernistic vanity set. **330.** Crystal No. 15 vanity set. **331.** Crystal vanity set with painted pink trim (probably made at New Martinsville). **332.** Vanity set in pink with hand-painted decoration.

**333.** Vanity set in green with hand-painted decoration. **334.** Frosted blue vanity set. **335.** Vanity set in frosted pink with gold band decoration.

**336.** Vanity set in pink. **337 and 339.** Puff boxes in frosted green and green. **338.** Sectional jar with lid (patented in 1923). **340.** Amber No. 10-2 Queen Anne Dresser Set (the perfume bottles and the puff box are marked NM).

**341-343.** No. 18/2 vanity sets in light blue, crystal/black and amber.

128

344 345 346 347 348 347 349 350 351

352 353 354 355 356 357 358

359 360 361 362 363 364 365

**344 and 351.** No. 33 Modernistic 8½" vases in frosted pink and frosted blue. **345-346.** Frosted blue No. 33 Modernistic candleholder and puff box. **347-348.** Frosted pink No. 33 Modernistic candleholders and console bowl (note the black painted decoration). **349-350.** Frosted green No. 33 Modernistic sugar and creamer (see Fig. 392 for the tray).

**352.** Canary No. 42 Radiance punch cup. **353.** Crystal No. 149-3 ½ lb. candy jar with orange paint and gold band decoration. **354-355.** No. 10/4 candleholders in green and blue. **356.** Blue No. 10-12 Princess console bowl with black base. **357-358.** Dark green batter jug and syrup jug with lid (these were part of the No. 2 Waffle Set).

**359-360.** Light blue No. 44 sugar and creamer. **361.** Ashtray made for Diamond Match Co. **362.** Amethyst No. 149 Allah or Chesterfield smoker's set. **363-365.** No. 37 (Moondrops) 2 oz. handled tumbler, 9 oz. tumbler and handled relish (note the different shades of green).

**366.** Jade green No. 36 vase with plate etching designed by Harry Barth. **367-368.** No. 3 (Addie) sandwich tray in black and bowl jade green with "Call of the Wild" silve deposit by the Lotus Glass Co. **369.** Jad green No. 35 (Fancy Squares) sandwich tra **370.** Black No. 33 Modernistic 8½" vase.

**371-372.** No. 34 (Addie) tumblers in blac (note silver deposit) and jade green. **373** Black No. 34 (Addie) plate. **374-375.** No. 3 (Addie) black saucer and jade green sherbe **376.** Jade green No. 33 Modernistic suga with "Call of the Wild" silver deposit by th Lotus Glass Co. **377.** Jade green No. 10/4 car dleholder. **378.** No. 728 Guest Set (covere pitcher, tumbler and tray) in jade green/blac combination.

**379-382.** No. 34 (Addie) cups and saucers **383-387.** Jade green No. 35 (Fancy Squares cup/saucer, comport, sugar and creamer.

**388-389.** Jade green plain decanter (note black stopper) and wine. **390.** Jade green No. 34 (Addie) sandwich tray with "Call of the Wild" silver deposit by the Lotus Glass Co. **391.** "Flapper Girl" or "Jackie" covered puff box in jade green/black combination.

**392.** Jade green No. 33 Modernistic sugar and creamer on handled tray in black. **393.** Jade green No. 1926 sugar, creamer and salt/pepper shakers on handled tray in black.

The other articles were made by the Fenton Art Glass Co. of Williamstown, West Virginia.

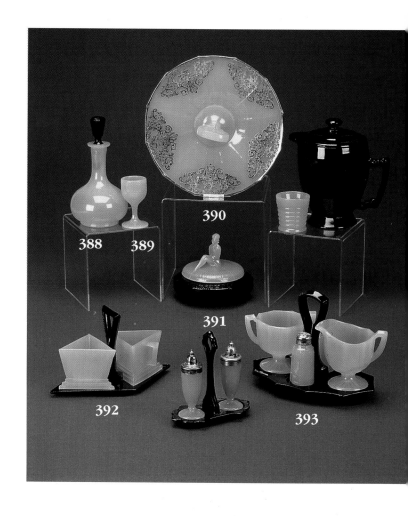

These items display various cutting motifs from the New Martinsville plant.

**394.** Blue No. 10-12 Princess console bowl with black base, c. 1926; both are marked NM. **395-396.** No. 10 sandwich trays in green and crystal, c. 1924. **397.** No. 600 spooner, c. 1904, with light cutting and gold decoration.

**398.** Octagon plate in pink, c. 1926. **399-400.** Amber No. 37 (Moondrops) sugar and creamer, c. 1933. **401-402.** Light green No. 33 Modernistic candleholders, c. 1929. **403.** Pink bowl with integral flower frog, c. 1926.

An excellent assortment of New Martinsville items in amber glass.

**404.** No. 101 vase. **405.** No. 149-3 ½ lb. candy jar. **406.** No. 42 Radiance plate with No. 26 Meadow Wreath (Flower Basket) plate etching. **407-408.** No. 37 (Moondrops) large handled mug and pitcher (the mug may be fitted with a silver top for use as a cocktail shaker; see Fig. 439).

**409.** No. 18 Crystal Eagle 15" oval bowl. **410.** No. 37/2 (Moondrops) 4" candlestick. **411.** No. 767 candelabra. **412-413.** No. 37 (Moondrops) candleholder and console bowl.

**414.** No. 18/2 vanity set (note similarity to Fig. 409 bowl above). **415-417.** No. 37 (Moondrops) three-footed divided bowl, 2 oz. handled tumbler (note the floral motif imparted by the mould) and cup. **418-419.** Ashtray (marked NM) and cigarette pack holder from No. 149 Allah smoker's set [see also Fig. 362].

**420-426.** Cobalt blue No. 37 (Moondrops) 12 oz. tumbler, stemmed sherbet, 4 oz. tumbler, decanter (note Beehive stopper), 3 oz. footed juice glass, 4" stemmed comport, and mayonnaise bowl.

**427.** Free-blown ruby glass vase with crystal stem and foot. **428 and 432.** Ruby No. 37 (Moondrops) handled relish and cordials. **429-430.** Ruby No. 4453 6" candlesticks. **431.** Crystal punch cup with applied ruby handle. **433.** Ruby No. 42 Roly Poly decanter with crystal stopper.

**434.** The mould for this "Krystal Klear" piece was used to make several articles in the 470-series (see p. 208) **435.** Crystal No. 14 cocktail. **436.** Cobalt blue No. 37/4 handled relish dish. **437.** Crystal No. 677 and No. 678 perfume bottles (made by Viking, these are sometimes found with ruby stoppers). **438.** Crystal candlestick (made by Viking about 1962).

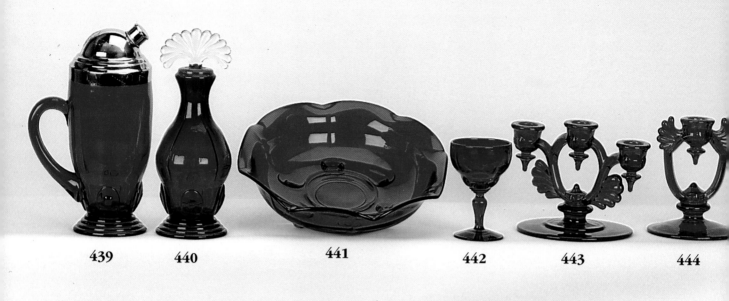

These items in ruby glass are from New Martinsville's No. 37 (Moondrops) line and were made between 1932 and 1936-37, except for Figs. 443-444, which continued in production well into the 1940s.

**439.** Handled mug with silver top for use as a cocktail shaker. **440.** Decanter (note fan-shaped stopper; see Fig. 423). **441.** 9½" ruffled bowl. **442.** Stemmed sherbet. **443.** No. 37/3 candelabra. **444.** No. 37/2 4" candlestick.

**445.** Three-footed, round bowl. **446.** Three-footed divided bowl. **447.** Footed sherbet. **448.** Oval bowl, 9¾" long.

**449-450.** Sugar and creamer. **451.** 4 oz. tumbler. **452.** Wine tumbler with tripod, "rocket" foot. **453.** 9 oz. tumbler. **454.** Butterdish with metal lid. **455.** Candy or bon bon dish with metal lid.

These articles in ruby glass are from New Martinsville's No. 42 Radiance line, which was in production between 1937 and 1943.

**456-459.** Punch bowl, underplate, ladle and punch cup. **460.** Large crimped bowl mounted on elaborate metal stand with decorative ruby prisms.

**461.** 2-light candelabra **462.** Salt/pepper shakers. **463-465.** Sugar, creamer and tray. **466-467.** Cup and saucer.

**468.** Plate, 7" d. **469.** Relish dish, 3 sections. **470.** Relish dish, 2 sections.

135

These articles are from New Martinsville's No. 45 (or 4500) Janice line. Original item numbers are given from company catalogues.

**471.** No. 4512 11" fruit bowl. **472.** No. 4554 5" candlestick. **473.** No. 4529 12" 2-handled plate. **474.** No. 4541-1SJ swan candy box (lacks crystal lid).

**475.** No. 4530 plate. **476-477.** No. 4580 cup and saucer. **478-479.** No. 4521-1SJ swan and No. 412-1SJ swan. **480.** No. 4552 handled basket. **481.** No. 4581 luncheon goblet.

**482.** No. 4532 creamer. **483.** No. 4582 low sherbet. **484.** No. 4520 2-handled plate. **485.** No. 4522 mayonnaise bowl (lacks underplate and ladle). **486.** No. 4534 2-compartment relish.

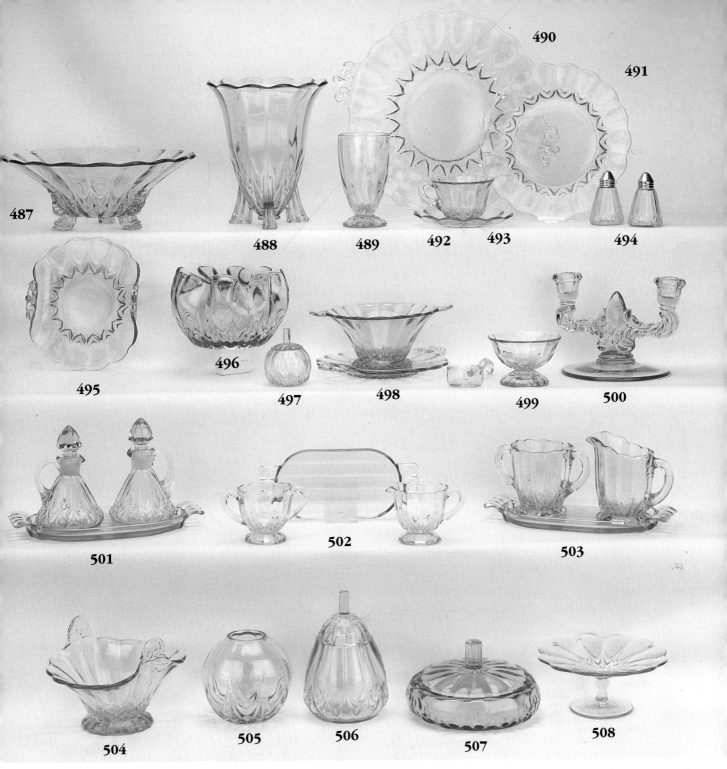

Except for Fig. 500, these items in pale blue are from New Martinsville's No. 45 (or 4500) Janice line. Original item numbers are given from company catalogues.

**487.** No. 4511 flared footed bowl. **488.** No. 4527 8" flared vase. **489.** No. 4581 luncheon goblet. **490-491.** No. 4516 and No. 4579 plates. **492-493.** No. 4580 cup and saucer. **494.** No. 4587 salt and pepper.

**495.** No. 4518 bon bon. **496.** No. 4574 flower bowl, crimped. **497.** Small covered jar from No. 4548 condiment set. **498.** No. 5422 3-pc. mayonnaise set. **499.** No. 4582 low sherbet. **500.** No. 4457 2-light candle.

**501.** No. 4583 Oil and Vinegar with tray. **502.** No. 4586 3-pc. individual sugar and cream with tray. **503.** No. 4532 sugar and cream with tray.

**504.** No. 4524 2-handled bon bon. **505.** No. 4575 ivy vase. **506.** No. 4577 jam jar and cover. **507.** No. 4541 6" candy box and cover. **508.** Cheese comport from No. 4528 set.

**509.** This unique 9-piece torte set in crystal glass was handpainted especially for the 1939 glass show in Pittsburgh. The low relief pattern on the underside of each plate is similar to New Martinsville's No. 38 line. Each of the central scenes is different, and the borders on the smaller plates are lines of various widths in either black or dark brown. These plates were placed on a white paper background in order to photograph them; there is no white paint on the plates themselves.

**510.** Cast iron base and glass Cat lamp; the Millers borrowed this piece from Theodore Hoskins (now deceased), a longtime New Martinsville glassworker. **511.** Blue No. 55 Fern Comport.

# CHAPTER FOUR
# THE McELDOWNEY YEARS

WHEN IRA CLARKE left the New Martinsville Glass Manufacturing Company in September, 1926, the position of general manager came quite naturally to Robert E. McEldowney. He had been with the firm since at least the early 1920s, for he was listed as "assistant sales manager" in company advertising in late 1920. Alongside Clarke, he represented the company at glass shows in Pittsburgh. When disputes arose with the glassworkers in 1924-26, McEldowney was present with Clarke at meetings with the shop committee of AFGWU Local Union No. 16. McEldowney was a lifelong New Martinsville resident and had been in the insurance business in 1910.

McEldowney was general manager of the New Martinsville Glass Manufacturing Company from late September, 1926 until Ira Clarke returned in August, 1932. About September, 1933, McEldowney, who then held the post of company secretary, left the firm to go to a competitor's glass plant at nearby Paden City. David Fisher, who had built the Paden City plant in 1916 after a success-

ful time in New Martinsville, had passed away in May, 1933, and McEldowney's experience in the glass industry helped fill that company's need.

Another young man who was to be vital to the New Martinsville concern was Harry Barth, whose first job was as a laborer in the packing room about 1918. His precise role in the 1920s is difficult to determine, but he became the company's purchasing agent and then assistant general manager later on. He was an important figure when the factory was sold in 1938 (see Chapter Six).

McEldowney's tenure as general manager (September, 1926-July, 1932) must have been a trying period in the firm's history. At its outset, the recent rifts between workers and management were fresh in everyone's memory, even though agreements had been reached which were designed to ameliorate the situation. In the midst of this period, the nation was plunged into an economic depression which had a profound effect upon the glass industry, closing many firms forever. At the end of McEldowney's time, the New Martinsville Glass Manufacturing Company's future was cloudy, indeed.

Nonetheless, the McEldowney years were marked by the production of glass in some remarkable shapes and interesting color combinations as well as the introduction of some new novelties. Patent and design records substantiate some of these, but the relative amount of advertising done by the company (and the resultant coverage by the trade press) dropped off considerably from the large quantity generated earlier in the 1920s. Correspondence between the New Martinsville firm and the National Association of Manufacturers of Pressed and Blown Glassware also proved valuable in identifying articles made during this period.

## STAPLE GOODS/PRIVATE MOULDS

As one might suspect, many of the articles previously made as staple goods continued to be made at New Martinsville. Among these were glassware for mounting and stationers' glassware. Production of beer mugs also continued, of course, and several different ones are shown in the firm's catalogues.

**Portrait of Robert McEldowney.**

# "Old Home Weeks"
## from Jan. 3rd to 29th 1921
# MONONGAHELA HOUSE
## *"Cradle of the Pittsburgh Glass Exhibit"*

*You Are Cordially Invited*

## The New Martinsville Glass Mfg. Co.
### New Martinsville, W. Va.

IRA M. CLARKE
General Manager

ROBT. McELDOWNEY
Assistant Sales Manager

From *Pottery, Glass and Brass Salesman* (December 16, 1920).

The liquid capacity of New Martinsville's No. 25 beer mug could be adjusted by changing the bottom plate in the mould during manufacture, creating a so-called "sham" bottom.

New Martinsville's No. 14 beer mug is similar to the standard bar glassware made by many other American glass factories.

Because of their importance to the firm, smokers' goods must be considered staple items during this period in the New Martinsville plant's history, too. Some of the ashtrays featured during the Clarke years were continued as market demand

warranted. The Diamond Match Company continued to be an active private mould customer [see Fig. 361], and this firm had some ashtrays especially made for particular hotels. One can expect to find New Martinsville ashtrays with any of these names, which were listed in an old record of moulds: Hotel Willard (Worcester, Pa.); Carleton Plaza (Detroit); McLure House (Wheeling); The Ten Eyck (Albany); and Le Bal Taberin (Hartford, Conn.). Another special ashtray made for the Diamond Match Company bears the legend "Sach's cigars—made in our own factory."

Several new smoker's accessories were developed, including a heavy "combination ash tray, matches support and pipe rest," the design for which was registered by Robert McEldowney on March 22, 1927. This article weighs about 19 ounces and was known as the Pipe Smokers Ash Tray. A similar article, the No. 20 ash tray, appeared in the 1926 catalogue (see p. 121), and it was also made with special lettering for private mould customers [see Fig. 328]. Pencil sketches (dated March 14, 1928) for the firm's No. 21, a simple round ashtray with slot for book matches, are in the files of the National Association of Manufacturers of Pressed and Blown Glassware.

In 1931, the New Martinsville firm was making a large ivy ball. Correspondence with the National Association of Manufacturers of Pressed and Blown Glassware indicates that the No. 15 Ivy Ball

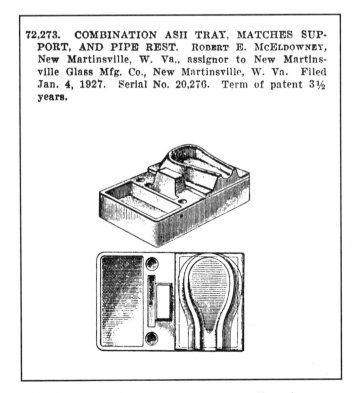

72,273. COMBINATION ASH TRAY, MATCHES SUPPORT, AND PIPE REST. ROBERT E. McELDOWNEY, New Martinsville, W. Va., assignor to New Martinsville Glass Mfg. Co., New Martinsville, W. Va. Filed Jan. 4, 1927. Serial No. 20,276. Term of patent 3½ years.

Design patent for a New Martinsville ash tray.

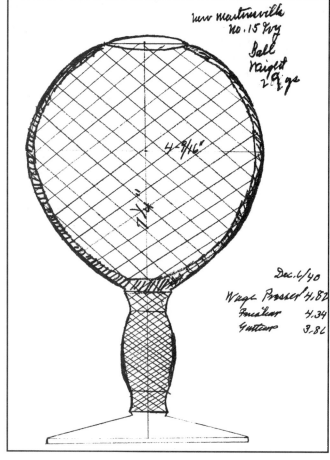

**Sketch of the No. 15 Ivy Ball.**

weighed 27 ounces and that a footed bowl was made from the same mould. The motif present on this piece is similar to that on the vanity sets which carry the same No. 15 designation.

Many glass companies depended upon "private mould" work for a steady source of income, especially during difficult economic times. Unlike the risks associated with putting a new pattern line in the marketplace, private mould work is simply the manufacture of a quantity of goods to meet a customer's order. Some moulds were made at independent mouldmaking establishments, while others were contracted to be made at the glass plant which was to make the article. In most cases, the customer owned the mould and had the right to remove it, usually shipping it to another glass factory which was willing to make the item for a lower price. When the private mould owner was unable to pay a bill, the glass factory often acquired the mould with the hope of adding the article to its own line or perhaps modifying the mould to make something that would sell.

A ledger containing mould records as early as 1917 is among the few original documents which survive from the New Martinsville Glass Manufacturing Company. The following firms had pri-

vate moulds in New Martinsville in the mid- to late 1920s: Ball Bearing Inkwell Co. (Paulding, Ohio); Cushman & Dennison (New York City); Carter Glass Butter Jar Co.; General Eclipse Co. (Danielson, Conn.); Jennings Silver Co. (Torrington, New Jersey); O. K. Manufacturing Co.; Rogers Silver Plate Co.; Reading Knob Works; Safety Night Lite Co.; and Western Electric Co. (New York). One of the more unusual items made was a glass mouse trap; the customer was Shoenheit & Pease.

The New Martinsville Glass Manufacturing Company also made glass for other glass companies. Some of this was in the form of "blanks" for firms that cut or otherwise decorated glass, such as Wheeling's Bonita Art Glass Co. or the Lotus Glass Company of Barnesville, Ohio. Sometimes, a glass manufacturing company lacked the capacity (in skilled workers or in lehr space) to fill orders during an especially busy time. In such a case, moulds might be sent to another company, which would be paid to make and ship the glass required. Although the companies were otherwise competitors, this sort of arrangement was more common than most glass collectors realize today. In the 1920s, the New Martinsville firm occasionally made glass for the nearby Paden City Glass Manufacturing Company and for the St. Mary's Glass Company, which was located in another West Virginia town further south along the Ohio River.

### INNOVATIVE COLORS AND PATTERNS

When McEldowney took over, the New Martinsville firm's reputation for colored ware was reasonably well-known. Without doubt, the most important colors were amber, blue, green and amethyst although canary, pink (called Peach Melba) and black were also made, probably in comparatively small quantities. Decorations in the form of hand-painting were well-established, and the firm had an active cutting shop. Acid was used to satin finish some glass, with pink, blue and green the colors typically treated this way.

Within the next several years, the importance of black glass would be enhanced, and two significant new colors—transparent ruby and opaque jade green—were added about 1930 or shortly thereafter. Although these colors may have enhanced the firm's repertoire of glassware products, they did not move the company into prosperity. Without them, however, the New Martinsville Glass Manufacturing Company might have come to an abrupt end.

**74,940. SANDWICH TRAY OR SIMILAR ARTICLE.** ROBERT E. McELDOWNEY, New Martinsville, W. Va., assignor to New Martinsville Glass Mfg. Co., New Martinsville, W. Va., a Corporation of West Virginia. Filed Feb. 8, 1928. Serial No. 25,265. Term of patent 3½ years.

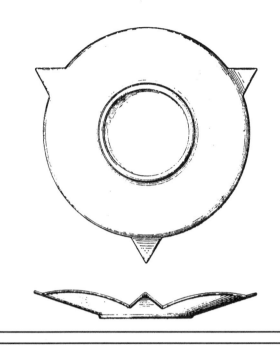

**75,272. SANDWICH PLATE OR SIMILAR ARTICLE.** ROBERT E. McELDOWNEY, New Martinsville, W. Va., assignor to New Martinsville Glass Mfg. Co., New Martinsville, W. Va., a Corporation of West Virginia. Filed Feb. 8, 1928. Serial No. 25,263. Term of patent 3½ years.

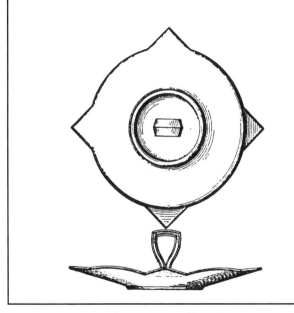

**Design patent drawings.**

Glass colors must be expressed in the form of objects, of course, and the New Martinsville firm had been able to introduce new lines and individual novelties on a regular basis for over a quarter-

century before Robert McEldowney became general manager. This ability continued, although the innovations were fewer in number and came less regularly.

On February 8, 1928, Robert McEldowney filed applications to register the designs for two sandwich trays. The first (#74,940) was essentially a plate which combined the geometric shapes of triangle and circle. The second (#75,272) was a handled tray which combined square and circle.

At least some of the octagonal shapes from the Clarke years were continued, and new articles were likely added to this line, which may have shared the No. 1926 designation with other articles then in production. Sketches for a creamer and sugar set (October 3, 1927) and a cheese comport (December 2, 1927) are in the files of the

**This assortment of cut ware in rose-pink glass appears to be the work of the Lotus Glass Co. of Barnesville, Ohio, which bought blanks from many different companies and decorated them before assembling various combinations. The octagonal sandwich tray, salad plate, and cheese and cracker set are likely New Martinsville products, as is the round covered candy dish (Butler Brothers catalogue, Mid-Winter, 1927). For a similar "No. 701 Octagon Assortment" by Lotus, see Weatherman's *Colored Glassware of the Depression Era 2*, p. 235.**

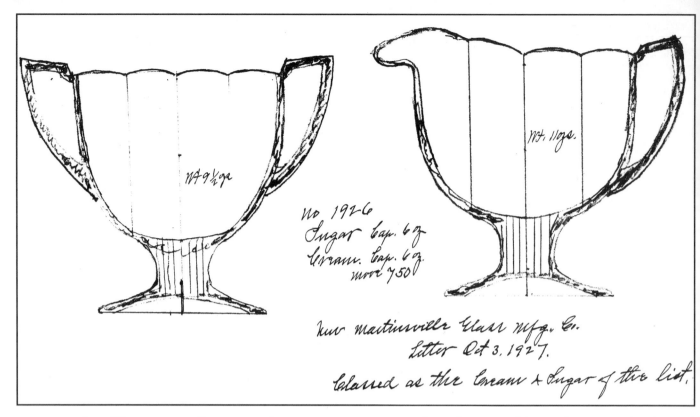

No 1926
Sugar Cap. 6 oz
Cream. Cap. 6 oz
more 750

New Martinsville Glass Mfg. Co.
Letter Oct 3, 1927.
Classed as the Cream & Sugar of this list.

**New Martinsville's No. 1926 sugar and creamer are octagonal in shape and have distinctively-shaped handles which rise above the rims (for a set in jade green, see Fig. 393).**

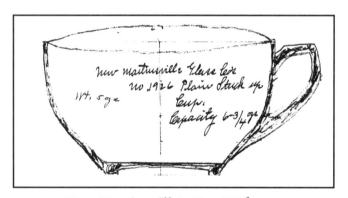

New Martinsville Glass Co.
No 1926 Plain Stuck up
Cup.
Capacity 6-3/4 oz
Wt. 5 oz

**New Martinsville's No. 1926 cup.**

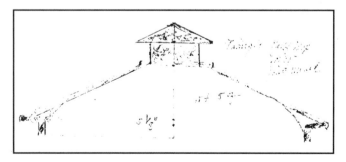

**This undated sketch of the cover for New Martinsville's "triangle puff box" was probably the work of Charles E. Voitle, executive secretary of the National Association of Manufacturers of Pressed and Blown Glassware (note the 5⅛" measurement; another box, 7" on a side, is also known).**

National Association of Manufacturers of Pressed and Blown Glassware. An assortment of "Rose Color Art Glass" in the Butler Brothers Mid-Winter, 1929, catalogue includes some New Martinsville octagonal pieces.

The No. 1926 designation was also applied to a rather plain cup. According to sketches and correspondence from January, 1929, in the files of the National Association of Manufacturers of Pressed and Blown Glassware, this cup weighs about 5 ounces and was made as a "stuck up" item (this means that the base will be ground and polished).

McEldowney also registered designs for some unusual articles which employ triangles for their basic shapes. The designs for a sandwich tray and a large console bowl were approved on October 23, 1928, and three other articles—powder puff box (5⅛" on side), candlestick holder and compote—were registered by June, 1929. The triangular shapes and the three "steps" on the base and/or finial of each item are distinctive. This was New Martinsville's No. 33 line, and the firm called it "Modernistic." Original company records relating to castings and other mould work refer to "Modernistic," but other documents, such as catalogues or advertising, have yet to be found which use this term. The mould records, maintained by mouldmaker Ed Scully, indicate that many

144

moulds for the No. 33 Modernistic line were cast in September, 1928, at Lanam's Foundry. New moulds for the No. 33 Modernistic candy box and cover were completed in December, 1929.

There is little information about these pieces in previous books on glass, although some items have been pictured (see Stout's *Depression Glass in Color, Number One*, plate twenty and *Depression*

**76,699. CONSOLE BOWL OR SIMILAR ARTICLE.** ROBERT E. McELDOWNEY, New Martinsville, W. Va., assignor to New Martinsville Glass Mfg. Co., New Martinsville, W. Va., a Corporation of West Virginia. Filed July 25, 1928. Serial No. 27,580. Term of patent 3½ years.

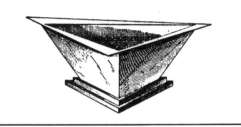

This patent drawing for the No. 33 Modernistic console bowl shows the base with just two steps (see Fig. 348 for the bowl as actually manufactured; the three equal steps are clearly visible).

**77,110. POWDER-PUFF BOX OR SIMILAR ARTICLE.** ROBERT E. McELDOWNEY, New Martinsville, W. Va., assignor to New Martinsville Glass Mfg. Co., New Martinsville, W. Va., a Corporation of West Virginia. Filed Sept. 7, 1928. Serial No. 28,067. Term of patent 3½ years.

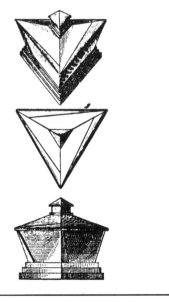

Patent drawing for the No. 33 Modernistic puff box. Although no dimensions are given, this appears to be the box which measures 5⅛" on its side (see Figs. 329 and 346).

**77,971. CANDLESTICK HOLDER OR SIMILAR ARTICLE.** ROBERT E. McELDOWNEY, New Martinsville, W. Va., assignor to New Martinsville Glass Mfg. Co., New Martinsville, W. Va., a Corporation of West Virginia. Filed Jan. 2, 1929. Serial No. 29,481. Term of patent 3½ years.

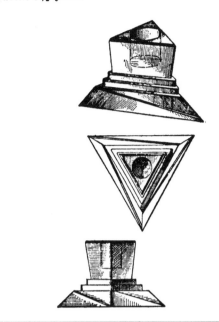

In this patent drawing for the No. 33 Modernistic candleholder, the taller bottom step appears to be "sliced" in a way unlike those pieces actually made. The candleholder actually has two short steps above one taller step (see Figs. 345, 347 and 401-402).

**78,835. COMPOTE OR SIMILAR ARTICLE.** ROBERT E. McELDOWNEY, New Martinsville, W. Va., assignor to New Martinsville Glass Mfg. Co., New Martinsville, W. Va., a Corporation of West Virginia. Filed Dec. 24, 1928. Serial No. 29,394. Term of patent 3½ years.

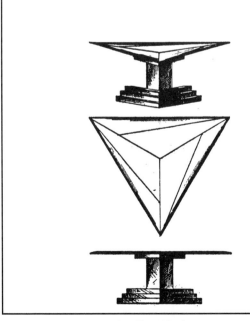

No. 33 Modernistic compote.

**No. 33 Modernistic sandwich tray.**

*Glass in Color, Number Three,* plate 9 and p. 20; Weatherman's *Colored Glassware of the Depression Era 2,* p. 397; Toohey's *Collector's Guide to Black Glass,* Fig. 207 and Heacock's article in *Glass Collector's Digest,* vol. 1, no. 1, p. 65).

These pieces have been variously called "Triad" or "Pyramid," but the latter name is now strongly associated with a different glassware pattern produced by the Indiana Glass Company of Dunkirk, Indiana. Perhaps the best course now is for collectors to adopt the original name, No. 33 Modernistic. In addition to the articles illustrated in the design drawings for the No. 33 Modernistic line, these articles are known: 8½" tall vase; small creamer/open sugar set on a tray; candy box (7" on side); perfume bottle with stopper; tray for vanity set; tumbler; and pitcher (the original records list a "Modernistic night jug").

Perhaps the most striking aspect of No. 33 Modernistic is the range of colors and decorations in which it occurs. Articles in blue, pale green and pink can be found, and most will have an acidized satin finish [see Figs. 344-351]. A pair of candleholders shown in this book [see Figs. 401-402] has cutting on the lowest step. Pieces in New Martinsville's very dark, dense black glass are sometimes decorated with gold along the raised portions near each corner. Items in No. 33 Modernistic occur in New Martinsville's jade green, too, and the creamer/sugar set employs a black tray [see Fig. 392]. A No. 33 Modernistic sugar bowl with the "Call of the Wild" silver-deposit motif (by the Lotus Glass Co.) is also known [see Fig. 376].

The large satin-finished pink bowl and accompanying candleholders in No. 33 Modernistic are

sometimes decorated with black paint [see Figs. 347-348]. A bowl decorated with hand-painted dancing figures is pictured in Gaston's *Collector's Guide to Art Deco,* although no information about its manufacturer is given, and a similarly decorated vase has been reported.

Not long after No. 33 Modernistic was in production, the firm anticipated putting out a diamond-shaped line, probably in many of the same colors, although satin-finished blue or green are most often seen. McEldowney made application to register this design in April, 1929, and the design patent was issued on August 20, 1929 (previous writers have erroneously reported that this design dates c. 1924). The narrow base slopes sharply to meet the body of the article; there are no steps similar to No. 33 Modernistic. Although McEldowney's design was for a "powder puff box or similar article," there do not seem to be any other pieces which accompany or match this lone item, which might well be dubbed "New Martinsville's Diamond" when more is learned about it (see the Whitmyers' *Bedroom and Bathroom Glassware of the Depression Years,* p. 118).

In early 1930, the New Martinsville enterprise embarked upon a relatively ambitious new line, No. 34. This was intended as a complete "luncheon set," encompassing handled sandwich tray, plates, juice glasses and tumblers (6 oz. and 9 oz.), cups and saucers, creamer and sugar, and a small comport which today's collectors would call a sherbet dish. A 5" d. mayonnaise bowl and a 3½" candlestick may have been added to the No. 34 line sometime before April, 1932, as the firm corre-

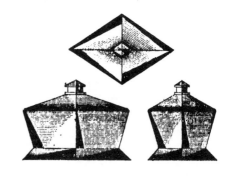

**Design patent drawings.**

sponded with the National Association of Manufacturers of Pressed and Blown Glassware.

The twelve subtle points around the rim or edge of each piece are the No. 34 line's most distinctive feature. When the item is pressed, the plunger produces an interior rib optic effect. The late William Heacock (*Collecting Glass*, vol. 1, p. 68 and vol. 2, p. 68) named this pattern "Addie" in Mrs. Miller's honor.

The twelve-pointed rim also occurs on the shade for New Martinsville's No. 100 lamp which was shown in the January, 1932, issue of *Crockery and Glass Journal* (see p. 150). The base is a modified version of one of New Martinsville's other items, probably the No. 10 handled candlestick. The Houze Convex Glass Company of Point Marion, Pa., made a similar lamp, but the rim of its shade has what the Whitmyers describe as a "square sawtooth rim."

Several pieces of No. 34 (Addie) were shown in trade journals during March-April, 1930, and the luncheon set was said to be available in black as well as "pink, green or combination of crystal and black." The jade green and black combination shown in this book [see Figs. 380-381] was probably made about the same time or shortly thereafter. In her *Price Trends 2*, Weatherman shows a c. 1930 notice for a No. 34 set in crystal glass with an etching she named "Lorelie Lace."

Some pieces of New Martinsville's No. 34 (Addie) in jade green or black are known with a silver deposit treatment. This was applied by the Lotus Glass Company of Barnesville, Ohio, and it comes in several different design motifs [see Figs. 368, 371, 376 and 390]. One of the most interesting was dubbed "Call of the Wild" in the Lotus firm's advertising (this treatment is also known on

New Martinsville's No. 149 cigarette holder; see Weatherman's *Colored Glassware of the Depression Era 2*, p. 242). Some No. 34 (Addie) cups were decorated with a plate etching (see Toohey's *Collector's Guide to Black Glass*, p. 33), but this was done at the New Martinsville plant.

Another line being made in the early 1930s was New Martinsville's No. 35. The sketch of an "after dinner coffee cup" in the files of the National Association of Manufacturers of Pressed and Blown Glassware provides one of the few clues thus far available about this line. An agreement (dated June 5, 1931) between New Martinsville's shop committee and the plant management lists these items in No. 35: sugar, cream, cup, and "A[fter] D[inner]" cup. A subsequent letter (dated November 19, 1931) mentions a No. 35 vase.

The sketch of the cup matches those typically found with saucers called "Fancy Squares" today (see Heacock's *Glass Collector*, vol. 6, pp. 30-31). There seems little doubt that plates and other items would accompany these pieces, of course, and the jade green No. 35 (Fancy Squares) articles are a close match in color (especially under ultraviolet light) to jade green items in New Martinsville's No. 34 (Addie) line as well as No. 33 Modernistic. In addition to cups and saucers, these other items were made in the No. 35 (Fancy Squares) line: luncheon plate, handled sandwich tray, sugar bowl, creamer, and small comport [see Figs. 369 and 383-387].

In late April, 1932, the Lincoln Theatre in New Martinsville announced its plans for a glassware give-away. The glass, of course, almost certainly came from the New Martinsville Glass Manufacturing Company. Beginning Saturday May 7,

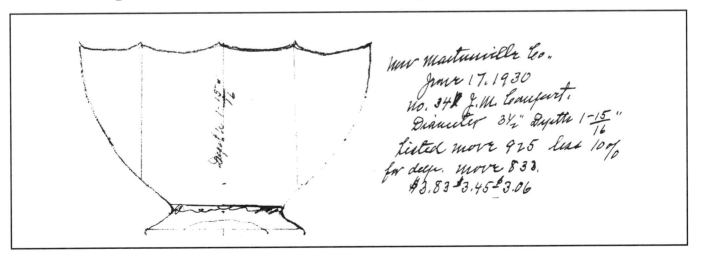

**Sketch for New Martinsville's No. 34 comport from the files of the National Association.**

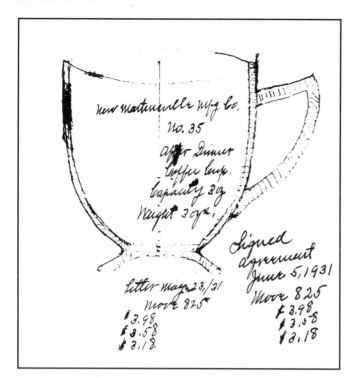

Sketch of the No. 35 "after dinner coffee cup" from the files of the National Association. Workers were required to make 825 of these (the "move") in a 4½ hour turn; the presser was paid $3.98, the finisher $3.58, and the gatherer $3.18.

1932, ladies would be given one item from a 39-piece luncheon set in ruby glass. If a lady attended for 39 consecutive Saturdays, her set would be complete! To stimulate interest, displays of the luncheon set were placed in the theatre lobby as well as Oneacre's Drug Store, which also had its own promotions, such as drawings for two $5.00 gold pieces each Saturday night as well as a free automobile (winner's choice of a 1933 Plymouth, Ford or Chevrolet) to be given away on Christmas Eve, 1932.

The feature film on May 7 was "Young America" (starring Spencer Tracy, Doris Kenyon, Tommy Conlon, Ralph Bellamy and Beryl Mercer), and the evening concluded with a two-reel comedy, "Mickey Mouse and Medbury in Voodoo land." The *Wetzel Democrat* (May 5, 1932) mentioned the Lincoln Theatre's "truly wonderful profit-sharing plan" on its front page. On May 12, 1932, the *Democrat* reported that "a very large number of ladies" had attended the show and begun their luncheon sets. A week later, the newspaper noted once more that attendance at the Lincoln Theatre "has increased appreciably" (*Wetzel Democrat*, May 19, 1932). The theatre's advertising mentioned "Glassware Night" for the next month or so. One wonders what the glassware

was? It might have been either the No. 34 (Addie) or the No. 35 (Fancy Squares) line in ruby glass. Another possibility, of course, is that the company was readying its No. 37 (Moondrops) line for the marketplace and decided to make it available locally (this pattern flourished from late 1932 to about 1936 and is discussed in the next chapter).

Despite the difficult economic times, New

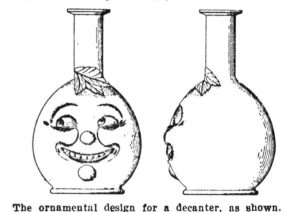

74,183. DECANTER. ROBERT E. McELDOWNEY, New Martinsville, W. Va., assignor to New Martinsville Glass Mfg. Co., New Martinsville, W. Va., a Corporation of West Virginia. Filed Oct. 22, 1927. Serial No. 23,849. Term of patent 3½ years.

The ornamental design for a decanter, as shown.

**Design patent for "Silly Toby."**

76,409. PITCHER OR SIMILAR ARTICLE. ROBERT E. McELDOWNEY, New Martinsville, W. Va., assignor to New Martinsville Glass Mfg. Co., New Martinsville, W. Va., a Corporation of West Virginia. Filed Jan. 31, 1928. Serial No. 25,099. Term of patent 3½ years.

**Design patent for the "Wise Owl."**

Martinsville's designers apparently retained the sense of humor present in the earlier Volstead Pup when they created the decanter now known as "Silly Toby" as well as the "Wise Owl" night set. McEldowney secured a design patent for the Silly Toby on January 3, 1928. The Wise Owl was registered in September, 1928, although the application was filed on January 31, 1928. The range of colors is not yet known for Silly Toby, but the Wise Owl occurs in crystal, amber, blue, green, amethyst, pink [see Fig. 320] and New Martinsville's opaque jade green. Usually, the Wise Owl has "Pat. Applied For" on its base. The Whitmyers (p. 223) show a Wise Owl in frosted pink glass with floral decoration as well as an example in jade green.

Despite the documentation available, some aspects of New Martinsville's production remain difficult to determine. The Elephant incense burner [see Figs. 317 and 319] and cigarette holder [see Fig. 318], for example, was probably first made about 1930, based upon the colors and treatments in which they occur, as well as the testimony of former New Martinsville workers who have vivid memories of this article (Garman and Spencer's *Glass Animals of the Depression Era* suggests a 1940 date).

The graceful Dancing Lady flower frog [see Fig. 323] and the Police Dog [see Fig. 324] also originated c. 1930, although the latter continued in production for many years, including versions with different bases made by the Viking Glass Company in the 1970s-80s. These are most often found in frosted pink glass.

### VANITY SETS

During the late 1920s and throughout the 1930s, vanity sets were an integral part of New Martinsville's production. These typically consisted of a powder (or so-called "puff") box flanked by two perfume bottles on a tray (or a mirror which the New Martinsville plant purchased from a supplier). The New Martinsville Glass Manufacturing Company developed several different designs during McEldowney's tenure, and these were offered in variety of colors and color combinations. Some were also decorated with hand-painted enamel.

About a month after McEldowney became New Martinsville's general manager, he filed an application to register the design for an elaborate perfume bottle stopper (#71,807; granted January 4, 1927). The drawing shows that this was intended

71,807. BOTTLE STOPPER. ROBERT E. MCELDOWNEY, New Martinsville, W. Va., assignor to New Martinsville Glass Mfg. Co., New Martinsville, W. Va., a Corporation of West Virginia. Filed Nov. 2, 1926. Serial No. 19,571. Term of patent 3½ years.

**Design patent for stopper.**

to be a stopper which also served as an applicator. The top of the stopper is quite fancy, and this could have been a very difficult object to produce.

No. 33 Modernistic, which was discussed earlier in this chapter, also manifested itself in a vanity set. These consisted of two perfume bottles and a puff box on a triangular tray with sharply-pointed corners [see Fig. 329]. The perfume bottles carry out the design perfectly, including a three-step base and triangular stoppers (these are ground flat on top and do not come to a point as does the cover on the puff box).

The No. 33 Modernistic vanity sets occur in blue, pink and green—all of which may be either transparent or frosted glass, although the frosted versions are more frequently found. The No. 33 Modernistic set also comes in splendid jade green/black combinations, usually featuring a black tray plus jade green perfume bottles with black stoppers and a puff box in jade green with black lid (see the Whitmyers *Bedroom and Bathroom Glassware of the Depression Years*, p. 118). Due to the thickness of the glass, the opaque jade green appears to be somewhat darker than the shade typically found in pieces from the No. 34 (Addie) or No. 35 (Fancy Squares) lines mentioned earlier.

Several other New Martinsville vanity sets were probably being made about the same time, and two of them occur in the same colors as No. 33 Modernistic, including the black/jade green combination. The first was described by the Whitmyers as eight-sided or octagonal, but they noted that the geometry is not that of a perfect octagon. There are eight panels on the perfume bottles, and narrow and wide panels alternate [see Fig. 332]. The stoppers have eight sides, too, and they seem to be similar to those used in the Queen Anne sets featured in the firm's 1926 catalogue. The puff box and the tray reflect one another in shape.

A second set features perfume bottles with interior swirl and flat stoppers with scalloped edges as well as a puff box of distinctive shape whose finial matches the stoppers [see Fig. 334]. The tray used for this set is similar to, but smaller than, the one employed in the No. 149 Allah smoker's set.

Still another set combines perfume bottles from the earlier Queen Anne set with a smaller, more graceful puff box with an eight-sided finial. These sets may be found on any of several trays: round [see Fig. 336], oval, triangular with rounded corners, or a shape similar to the No. 149 Allah smoker's set [see Figs. 333 and 335]. The typical New Martinsville colors occur—pink, blue and green (transparent or frosted)—as well as darker blue, cobalt blue, and a darker green [see Fig. 339], which may also be frosted [see Fig. 337].

The range of colors and the admixture of trays suggest that this set was popular and in production for some time.

New Martinsville's No. 15 vanity set was introduced in January, 1932. The oval tray has two small handles, and the diamond-like pattern on part of its underside matches that featured on the perfume bottles and puff box. Weatherman gave fanciful names to these sets ("Judith," "Leota," etc), but the original factory designations, albeit in the form of numbers, may be preferable for those who wish to keep the historical record clear. The No. 15 set is shown in a c. 1938 catalogue but is noted as "discontinued" in the accompanying price list.

The No. 15 vanity set comes in numerous color combinations. Typically, crystal perfume or cologne bottles accompany a crystal powder box [see Fig. 330], sometimes on a crystal tray or a mirror. The powder box lid and stoppers for the bottles may be ruby, black or jade green, and the finials are known in several different styles [compare Figs. 330 and 331]. These sets are also known with crystal stoppers and lids which have been

**This ad, from *Crockery and Glass Journal* (January, 1932) shows New Martinsville's No. 100 Lamp as well as the No. 15 Vanity Set (Weatherman called this set "Judy").**

painted pale pink [see Fig. 331] or pale green.

The base for a "Colonial Girl Powder Box" is among the sketches in the files of the National Association of Manufacturers of Pressed and Blown Glassware. Unfortunately, the dimensions are not given, but a letter (dated June 1, 1928) which accompanied the sketch from general manager McEldowney says that "we understand the United States Glass Co. makes this item in a *larger* size" [emphasis added].

The lid is not part of the sketch, but this base is indeed similar to that of the "Curtsy" figural powder jars discussed by the Whitmyers (see *Bedroom and Bathroom Glassware of the Depression Years*, pp. 26-27). Moreover, the colors listed for Curtsy—frosted pink, frosted green, frosted blue and "jadeite" [light opaque green]—correspond to those in production at New Martinsville. In January, 1929, glassworker Edward D. Horstman informed his readers in the *American Flint* that "Most of our work has been on Christmas lines, such as vanity sets, comb trays, powder boxes, etc. These have been made in colors mostly and then cut, decorated or frosted, all of which makes a very fine line of gifts."

The powder box called "Flapper Girl" by Heacock (*Glass Collector's Digest*, vol. 1, no. 1, p. 66) and "Jackie" by the Whitmyers may be another New Martinsville product [see Fig. 391]. The colors available—frosted green, frosted pink and jade green/black combination—are certainly characteristic of New Martinsville. The Whitmyers note some similarities between Flapper Girl/Jackie and another powder jar called Gretchen, and their discussion opens yet another opportunity for continued research into New Martinsville's products.

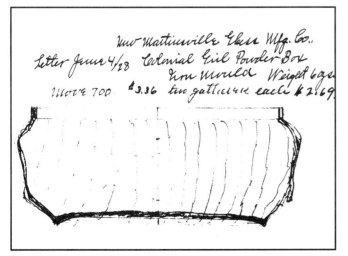

**Sketch for the base of the "Colonial Girl Powder Box" from the files of the National Association.**

## PEAKS AND VALLEYS

In view of the severe labor-management rifts which plagued the New Martinsville plant from 1924 to 1926, it may be useful to survey the comments made by New Martinsville's workers during the McEldowney years. Columns from New Martinsville appeared regularly in the *American Flint* from 1927 through 1930, usually over the by-line of union activist Edward Horstman.

In 1927, the plant operated at about half-time from January through September, and the glassworkers and management were compelled to perform the available work according to the long-standing "division of time" rule in the industry's collective bargaining agreement. This meant that work was divided among all the shops rather than subjecting an individual shop to layoff. Everyone's pay envelope was slimmer than usual, but no one was out of a job completely. Orders were plentiful for colored ware made from pot glass, but the workers were hoping for big orders of tank glass so the plant could run day and night.

From October to December 1927, the plant operated full-time or close to it, and both the mouldmakers and the cutters had plenty of work, too. In early, 1928, Horstman reported that "work has been fairly good here for the past four months, nine to eleven turns a week [45-55 hours] being the order" (*American Flint*, January, 1928). These conditions prevailed for several months, but things "slowed up some here" in May and remained so for the summer. After Labor Day, a large tank was started to meet increased demand for colored glass, and the plant ran smoothly until May, 1929, when half-time became the norm. In the *American Flint* (May, 1929), Horstman reported that most of the company's ware was "made for frosting"; the articles then in production included No. 33 Modernistic as well as several different vanity sets.

In January, 1930, Edward Horstman's column in the *American Flint* included a list of workers then employed at New Martinsville. With the assistance of Charles "Bud" Mason and Harold Ruble (both of whom have worked at the glass factory in New Martinsville from the 1930s to the present and knew many of these men), nicknames and other parenthetical information has been added here:

*Mould shop: Ed Scully; Ed Seelback (mould room foreman); Elmer Miller (later became plant superintendent); George Crimmel and apprentice Carl Suter.*

*Cutting Shop: M. Gunto; Kenneth "Ky" Wolfe; F. Burkett; P. Marshall; C. Sullivan; Charlie Johnson (stopper grinder) and Anthony Howell, apprentice.*

*Press shops: William "Daddy" Forbes (presser); David White (finisher; active in the union); Howard "Hoot" Crist; Clark Schwing; Elam Hoskins; Theodore "Dory" Hoskins; Alex Kilgore (made home brew); J. Smith; R. Ritz; Guy Ingram; A. McFadden; F. Sawyer; Elzie Miller (longtime presser); Thomas Haught (gatherer); George Workman (finisher); Frank Mosser (finisher); J. Goodwin; E. Fuller; F. Morgan; William "Jack" Deighton; Frank Bond (finisher); Lee Wade (gatherer and finisher); Arch Hill (presser); Max Schwing (finisher); Oliver "Odd" Mason (Charles Mason's father); Dave Potts (finisher); Louis "Louie" Zohnd (finisher); William "Bill" Cross (presser; lost an eye in factory accident but returned to work); Edward Horstman (active in the union); Charlie Powell (gatherer); Raymond Hoskins (presser); J. Hoskins; Guy Wilt; and O. Sawyer.*

*Iron Mould Blow Shop: George Frye; Jack Forbes; C. Bowden; and Louis Zohnd (handler when jugs were made).*

*Working spare were T. Carlyle and J. Oelschlegar. Other members are George Bresock; Dave Lively; Frank Chuffy; and Russell Emch.*

In early 1930, Horstman said that "things do not look any too bright at present," as the glassworkers were employed just "three days a week" while a furnace was down for repairs (*American Flint*, February, 1930). Two months later, "things have picked up and we are getting full time" (*American Flint*, April, 1930). The next report was nearly a year later, when David White said the firm was "working about half time with no night turn" (*American Flint*, February, 1931). Four months later, the work force had been cut from twelve shops to eight, and several broken pots in the main furnace had to be replaced.

In May, 1932, George Workman probably reflected the feeling of many New Martinsville glassworkers when he said that "we here have sure felt the depression." Nonetheless, he concluded somewhat optimistically, noting that "in the last few weeks things have been going a little better" (*American Flint*, May, 1932).

By late spring, 1932, the New Martinsville Glass Manufacturing Company was in the midst of very hard times, indeed. For nearly six months, the firm had paid its workers with a combination of cash and "scrip" in the form of certificates signed by the company's treasurer and president. In

**This bit of advertising bravado appeared in the March, 1931, issue of *Pottery, Glass and Brass Salesman*.**

effect, workers were forced to wait at least 60 days for a portion of the wages due them. Scrip continued to be issued from week to week, and some workers soon accumulated small stacks of these certificates. As their personal financial pictures became bleak, they redeemed certificates in the stores of those town merchants who would accept them—at less than face value, of course.

The nation was in the grip of the Great Depression and table glassware was not really a necessity. Like many plants, the New Martinsville firm found it difficult to market its wares. The expenses of running the business mounted as income from sales dwindled. Creditors and suppliers pressured the firm for payment of bills long since past due. Bankruptcy and closure seemed inevitable. The end of glassmaking in New Martinsville was at hand. Or was it?

# CHAPTER FIVE
# RECEIVERSHIP AND RENAISSANCE

JUST WHEN THE fortunes of the New Martinsville Glass Manufacturing Company seemed at their lowest, a well-known figure from the company's past, Ira M. Clarke, agreed to the stockholders' request that he come back to New Martinsville. Perhaps the board of directors and the stockholders regretted that Clarke had departed in 1926. Perhaps the balance of power had shifted and re-shifted among the stockholders. Perhaps now Clarke's experience and expertise could save—or at least salvage—the glassmaking enterprise. In any case, on August 1, 1932, Clarke returned to New Martinsville as general manager of the glass plant.

Clarke's whereabouts between October, 1926, and July, 1932, are not easy to ascertain. He was in Columbus, Ohio in August, 1931, and he might have been affiliated with the large Federal Glass Company there. He was also reported to have been a salesman for the Imperial Glass Company of Bellaire, Ohio, an Ohio River glassmaking center not far from New Martinsville (*China, Glass and Lamps*, August, 1931). The Imperial firm was reorganized in 1931, and Clarke's role in it has yet to be determined. In any event, Clarke moved quickly to stabilize the New Martinsville company's financial affairs. According to the *National Glass Budget* (as quoted in the *Wetzel Democrat*, January 26, 1933), the firm's creditors agreed on August 3, 1932, to a moratorium on their efforts to make collections of bills due them. This agree-

ment provided some financial breathing room so that Clarke and the company could focus upon producing a line of glassware that might generate big sales.

About six weeks after Clarke returned, the *Wetzel Democrat* (September 8, 1932), carried this headline: "Prospects Bright for Factory Re-Opening." The article revealed, however, that the plant had "closed down several months ago." The newspaper observed "that the depression will be almost licked in New Martinsville when the glass factory is started again is the opinion of many merchants and business men." Nevertheless, the reporter was optimistic: "Whatever the cost in money or effort at present, New Martinsville can not afford to let the local factory remain idle. The people will not let it remain idle either."

A glass industry trade publication, *China, Glass and Lamps*, was more guarded in its September, 1932, issue: "Stockholders and principal creditors of the New Martinsville Glass Mfg. Co., New Martinsville, W. Va., are working on plans for reorganization of the company which has long been known as a manufacturer of pressed tableware and specialties. Ira M. Clarke, who left the company in 1926, has returned as general manager." Shortly thereafter, the same trade journal reported that Clarke had been to New York, "getting a line on the general situation with reference to the wants of customers and familiarizing himself with current trade conditions ...." The article concluded by

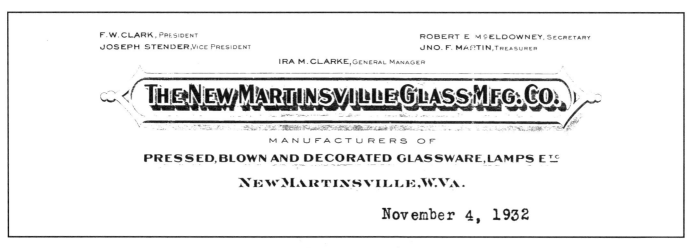

F. W. CLARK, PRESIDENT
JOSEPH STENDER, VICE PRESIDENT
ROBERT E. McELDOWNEY, SECRETARY
JNO. F. MARTIN, TREASURER
IRA M. CLARKE, GENERAL MANAGER

# The New Martinsville Glass Mfg. Co.

MANUFACTURERS OF

PRESSED, BLOWN AND DECORATED GLASSWARE, LAMPS Etc

NEW MARTINSVILLE, W.VA.

November 4, 1932

*Letterhead from November, 1932.*

noting that "Ira now is on duty at factory headquarters where he is busily engaged mapping out plans and arranging lines for the ensuing season."

Robert McEldowney remained at New Martinsville as company secretary until he joined the Paden City Glass Manufacturing Company in 1933, and Harry Barth probably became assistant general manager about that time. Barth got on well with Clarke, and it may have been Clarke who encouraged Barth upwards from his first job in the packing room. After Barth became assistant general manager under Clarke, he was also active as a designer of both glassware articles and patterns to be used for decorative plate etchings. Ira Clarke's son-in-law, Fred Schlens, was also associated with the company in a managerial post. The New Martinsville plant was scheduled to re-open on September 19, 1932.

The *Wetzel Democrat* had an optimistic account of the plant's future in its October 6, 1932, issue. The newspaper said that the factory would operate to "the fullest extent possible" by year's end and further noted that "enough orders are on hand to keep the plant running ... for several months." Apparently, a group of local businessmen (described by the newspaper as a "citizen's committee") was seeking to establish a fund "to tide the company over the inevitable tight places." This effort must have been unsuccessful, for Ira Clarke was appointed by the Wetzel County Circuit Court in New Martinsville to act as "receiver" for the New Martinsville Glass Company on January 3, 1933.

In effect, Clarke was in full charge of the company's financial affairs as well as its day to day operations and plans for the future. For about the next four years, Clarke made regular financial reports to the court, complete with detailed accounts of income and expenses. On the few occasions when a small quarterly profit was shown, partial payments were made to those creditors who were part of the moratorium agreement effected August 3, 1932, by Clarke.

The *National Glass Budget* carried an article about the New Martinsville plant in January, 1933, and the *Wetzel Democrat* reprinted it on the front page of its January 26, 1933, edition. The *Budget's* article recounted the legal maneuvers which installed Clarke as receiver, and it noted that the firm's exhibit at the Pittsburgh glass show had elicited considerable praise from the buyers there. The *Democrat* concluded that all of this was "a fine

boost for the local glass plant and its management." These encouraging words were all to the good, of course, but what the New Martinsville plant really wanted was a solid seller in glassware.

## MOONDROPS AND MAGIC

When production resumed in late September, 1932, the New Martinsville factory continued to make articles from its No. 34 (Addie) line, which had been introduced about 1930. Correspondence with the National Association of Manufacturers of Pressed and Blown Glassware (dated December 2, 1932) lists these articles in the No. 34 line: 6 oz., footed tumbler; 9 oz., footed tumbler; 7" footed bowl; and a 3½" candlestick. The No. 35 (Fancy Squares) line was surely in production also. Sales of No. 34 and No. 35 were probably steady, but hardly spectacular.

If ever a glass tableware plant needed a new line of goods which could catch and hold the public's fancy, the New Martinsville Glass Manufacturing Company had such a situation in late 1932. The need was soon met. On November 29, 1932, Ira Clarke's application for a design registration was approved (#88,398). The drawing submitted depicts a tumbler in New Martinsville's No. 37 line, which debuted in late 1932, although it was in production somewhat earlier. Collectors today call this "Moondrops," and the magic of its public allure may have been the most significant and profitable venture in the history of the company.

In December, 1932, the New Martinsville firm unveiled its two new lines, No. 16 and No. 37. The former was described as "a miter-effect band with a punty-like treatment on the flat ware." According to *Pottery Glass and Brass Salesman*, No. 16 was available in crystal as well as "the New Martinsville range of colors," which probably included

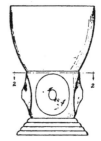

88,398. TUMBLER OR SIMILAR ARTICLE. IRA M. CLARKE, New Martinsville, W. Va., assignor to New Martinsville Glass Mfg. Co., New Martinsville, W. Va., a Corporation of West Virginia. Filed Oct. 5, 1932 Serial No. 45,230. Term of patent 7 years.

*Design drawing for No. 37.*

# Two Corking New Lines for 1933!

We have a host of new things to offer the trade for 1933 and, believe us, they are veritable winners—snappy, up to date and popular in price

See our display in Rooms 706-708, Fort Pitt Hotel, Pittsburgh
During January Show

Ira M. Clarke, General Manager, in charge.

# New Martinsville Glass Manufacturing Company
NEW MARTINSVILLE, W. VA.

*This ad, from* **Pottery, Glass and Brass Salesman** *(December 18, 1932), launched New Martinsville's No. 16 and No. 37 lines; the former was apparently short-lived, but No. 37 was a great hit and continued in production for several years.*

**Crockery and Glass Journal** *(December, 1932)*.

***From* Crockery and Glass Journal.**

amber, blue, green, amethyst and ruby. No further mention of the No. 16 line is to be found, but it may be of interest to note that moulds from this line were being used by Dalzell-Viking of New Martinsville in 1993 to produce articles for their "Collectors Classics" line in several colors.

New Martinsville's No. 37 featured raised circles on the lower portions of the bowls or bases of the items then being made: low footed tumblers in six sizes, sherbet, goblet, wine, champagne and cordial. An ad in *Pottery Glass and Brass Salesman* promised that "a full line of tableware and dinnerware will be added January 1 [1933]." Original records from mid-September, 1932, indicate that moulds for many articles in the No. 37 line had been completed by that time.

A set consisting of a footed sherbet which fit neatly into a shallow well in a plate was shown in the February, 1933, issue of *Crockery and Glass Journal*. A 15" long tray was also among the items shown in 1933. This article, like the plates and some other shallow items in the No. 37 line, lacks the distinctive "Moondrops" on the sides and may be difficult to recognize. Original mould records suggest that this may have been intended as a meat platter. In any case, the swift introduction of additional items to the No. 37 line is proof positive that sales were strong.

Correspondence between the New Martinsville firm and the National Association of Manufacturers of Pressed and Blown Glassware also reflects the importance of the No. 37 line to the company. Agreements were reached on moves and wages for various tumblers in October-November, 1932. In February, 1933, agreements for seven sizes of saucers and plates were forwarded to the National Association by Ira Clarke. In November,

1933, an 8¼" tall vase was being made. Candleholders in the No. 37 line were still being produced in February, 1937, but the tableware pieces were probably phased out in 1936. Except for the candleholders and an occasional relish dish [see Fig. 436], there are no No. 37 (Moondrops) tableware articles in company catalogues issued after 1938.

Numerous advertisements for No. 37 (Moondrops) appeared in trade publications. An ad in *Crockery and Glass Journal* (December, 1932) showed a tumbler and mentioned these colors: crystal, Ritz Blue, amber, rose, ruby and jade. "Rose" refers to New Martinsville's typical light pink shade, of course, and "jade" is opaque jade green. "Ritz Blue" is likely the dark cobalt blue [see Figs. 420-426 and 436] eagerly sought by collectors today. The very pale blue that collectors call "ice blue" today was probably made a bit later when No. 37 was well into production. [see Figs. 359-360 and 487-514 for other New Martinsville patterns in this color].

No. 37 (Moondrops) was also made in amethyst, black and two shades of transparent green as well as a cloudy crystal called "smoke" by collectors.

*From* Pottery, Glass and Brass Salesman, *March 15, 1934 [see Fig. 436].*

Jade green, black and smoke are hard to find, but ruby and Ritz Blue (cobalt blue) seem to be the most popular colors today. Items in amber are sometimes found decorated with light cutting [see Figs. 399-400] or plate etching, and some may have a faint floral motif that is imparted by the mould [see Fig. 416]. Articles may also be fitted with metal parts [see Figs. 439 and 454-455].

The number of articles available in No. 37 (Moondrops) is impressive indeed. In addition to

*The No. 37/3 console set, as shown in the December 7, 1933, issue of* Pottery, Glass and Brass Salesman. *Note the reference to "Evergreen."*

*This full-page ad from* **Crockery and Glass Journal** *(December, 1933) shows the "rocket" decanter and matching liquor glasses in the No. 37 line. Note the fan-style stopper.*

158

# Royal Hostess Set in Crystal Glass
## OUTSTANDING FOR 1935

**37 LINE 3**
**RETAIL**
**$4.98**

TRAY 20x9    —    MIRROR 11x8
FOUR OUTSTANDING RELISH DISHES CUT
IN BOTTOM WITH FRUIT DECORATIONS
NO. 37 DECANTER    6—4 OUNCE GLASSES

PITMAN-DREITZER & CO., 1107 BROADWAY, NEW YORK
FREDERICK SKELTON, 200 FIFTH AVENUE, NEW YORK
GEORGE BORGFELDT CORP., 46 EAST 23RD ST., NEW YORK
MARTIN M. SIMPSON & CO., MERCHANDISE MART, CHICAGO

At the
PITTSBURGH SHOW
FORT PITT HOTEL
ROOM NOS. 706-708

# NEW MARTINSVILLE GLASS MFG. CO.
### Ira M. Clarke, General Manager
**NEW MARTINSVILLE**                    **WEST VA.**

*From* Crockery and Glass Journal *(January, 1935).*

viewing those articles pictured in this book [see Figs. 363-365, 399-400, 407-408, 410, 412-413, 415-417, 420-426, 428, 432, 436 and 439-455], collectors should also consult some of the important books devoted to depression-era glassware. Florence's *Collector's Encyclopedia of Depression Glass* (eleventh ed., 1993) lists over 70 different items! Collectors should try to find earlier editions of Florence's book, too, for the photographs are different in each version, and many different pieces of No. 37 (Moondrops) can be seen. Florence also discussed and pictured Moondrops in the first edition of his *Elegant Glassware of the Depression Era* (1983), but it has not been treated in subsequent editions of this particular book.

As its No. 37 (Moondrops) pattern grew in popularity, the New Martinsville firm quickly added pieces to the line. Stemware was soon to be had in various sizes, and decanters were available in 1933, too. A full-page ad in the December, 1933, issue of *Crockery and Glass Journal* showed the new No. 37/4 decanter with matching glasses. These are distinguished by the interesting tripod-style base, and today's collectors call this "rocket" because of its resemblance to the rocket ships of science fiction [see Fig. 452]. Decanters may have either round, beehive-shaped stoppers [see Fig. 423] or fan-style stoppers [see Fig. 440], both of which were also used in conjunction with various New Martinsville beverage sets as well as some vanity sets in the 1930s. The front cover of Weatherman's *Price Trends 2* has a No. 37 (Moondrops) butterdish with beehive-shaped finial in the lower left.

The three-piece console set, designated No. 37/3, was advertised in the December 7, 1933, issue of *Pottery, Glass and Brass Salesman*. This impressive combination, with its large, three-light candlesticks, was available in a variety of colors including "Evergreen," which is probably the darker of New Martinsville's transparent green hues [see Fig. 363]. A little over three months later, the No. 37/4 relish dish with compartments was featured in *Pottery, Glass and Brass Salesman*. It was offered in crystal and "all the regular colors" at a suggested retail price of one dollar, although ruby "is a little more expensive." The ad also said the tray was available with "deep plate etching," the earliest mention of this type of decorating from the New Martinsville firm. Assistant general manager Harry Barth was interested in such decorations, so this may be an early sign of his work.

In January, 1935, the No. 37/3 decanter with fan-style stopper was shown with six matching 4 oz., glasses accompanied by four rectangular relish dishes ("cut in bottom with fruit decoration"), all of which was held by a handled tray made of walnut-finish wood with a mirror under the decanter and glasses. This was called the "Royal Hostess Set." Another decanter, which looks like a large, handled mug fitted with metal top [see Figs. 407 and 439], was advertised as "The Butler's Delight" in *Pottery, Glass and Brass Salesman* (December 20, 1934). It was accompanied by stemware in No. 37 and the same rectangular relishes on the wooden tray with mirror.

From its inception in late 1932 until production was phased out in favor of other lines in the latter half of 1936, New Martinsville's No. 37 was a resounding winner in the national marketplace. The line was well-advertised, and it served to put the New Martinsville plant back on the map as a major player in the glass tableware industry. The success of No. 37 (Moondrops) was also felt locally. A front-page article in the *Wetzel Democrat* (April 20, 1933) carried this headline: "Business Picking Up In Glass Factories In This Vicinity."

## BEVERAGE SETS

The repeal of the Eighteenth Amendment in 1933 spurred sales of articles intended for use with

90,869
**DESIGN FOR A TUMBLER OR SIMILAR ARTICLE**
Ira M. Clarke, New Martinsville, W. Va., assignor to The New Martinsville Glass Mfg. Co., New Martinsville, W. Va., a corporation of West Virginia
Application July 29, 1933. Serial No. 48,874
Term of patent 7 years

The ornamental design for a tumbler or similar article, substantially as shown and described.

*Design drawing for No. 38.*

*From* Pottery, Glass and Brass Salesman *(July 12, 1934). Note the plain measuring jigger in the top row.*

alcoholic beverages, although many factories (including the New Martinsville plant) had, of course, made similar items and sets throughout Prohibition years. About a year after the No. 37 line debuted, Clarke registered the design for that

which was to become New Martinsville's No. 38, a Georgian-style motif.

The first article in the No. 38 line was a twelve ounce "Pilsener Glass," shown next to a bottle of beer in the May 11, 1933, issue of *Pottery, Glass and*

## A WINNER IN PILSENERS

Here is our No. 38 twelve-ounce Pilsener Glass (patent applied for)—the picture tells the story. Look at its graceful contour; its punties; which add to its attractiveness and make for firm gripping. It comes packed six to a carton, crystal or colors.

By the way, it can also be had in ten-ounce size with sham bottom. Write us for prices and shipping particulars.

Better get in your order NOW so we may ship you promptly.

New Martinsville Glass Mfg. Co.
NEW MARTINSVILLE, W. VA.

*This ad appeared in* **Pottery, Glass and Brass Salesman** *(May 11, 1933).*

*Brass Salesman.* A No. 38 pretzel container soon followed, and several sizes of decanters and a cocktail shaker with matching whiskey tumblers were shown in July, 1934, under the name "Repeal Set." A water set was advertised in the March, 1934, issue of *Crockery and Glass Journal,* and the ad claimed that No. 38 was "an authentic reproduction of a prize collector's set ... a century old." Items in No. 38 could be had in crystal as well as eight colors, but only four were specified—amber, ruby, green and cobalt blue. The measuring jigger for the Repeal Set was in the firm's beverage service line for many years as the No. 11 graduated jigger (this piece was apparently part of the No. 37 line also; see Florence's *Very Rare Glassware of the Depression Era,* second series, p. 130).

In late 1935, *Pottery, Glass and Brass Salesman* (November 21, 1935) showed the No. 38

*New Martinsville's assistant general manager, Harry Barth, is shown with Ann Toole in this c. 1934 photo taken at the glass show in Pittsburgh's Fort Pitt Hotel. Both No. 37 and No. 38 articles are visible in the left foreground.*

*Note the clear indication that New Martinsville's No. 38 line was based upon "antique" glassware in this ad from the March, 1934, issue of Crockery and Glass Journal.*

"Hostmaster Service," calling it "one of the big selling numbers of the New Martinsville Glass Manufacturing Company." This set consisted of "quart-size bar bottle, six old-fashioned cocktail glasses of 7-ounce capacity with muddlers to match tipped with color, ice tub with tongs, bitters bottle of correct size and a highly decorative tray 11½ by 18 inches." The No. 38 ice tub was the same article that had been intended for pretzels in 1933. According to original mould records, the No. 38 line moulds were machined and later used for the No. 14 line.

The No. 237/61 Liquor Set with cut decoration was shown in the October 12, 1933, issue of *Pottery, Glass and Brass Salesman.* (a plain, undecorated set was called "Michael" in Weatherman's *Colored Glassware of the Depression Era 2*, p. 294). The beehive-style stopper is similar to those found in No. 37 (Moondrops) decanters. The distinguishing feature of New Martinsville's No. 237/61 is the simple floral motif in the cutting; No.

*From* **Pottery, Glass and Brass Salesman** *(October 12, 1933).*

237 was probably the number for a plain set, and "61" designated the particular cutting. The beehive-style stopper was also utilized in New Martinsville's No. 42 "Novelty Roly Poly Whiskey

163

*From* **Crockery and Glass Journal (February, 1934).**

*From* **China, Glass and Lamps (July, 1934).**

*According to* **Crockery and Glass Journal (March, 1934), this unidentified New Martinsville decanter and glasses in amber glass were available from Frederick Skelton's New York showroom. Note the large bowknot in the plate etching decoration.**

Set," which was pictured in the February, 1934, issue of *Crockery and Glass Journal*. The Roly Poly was also available with a crystal fan-shaped stopper similar to that used in some vanity sets [see Fig. 433].

The fan-style stopper appears in an un-named, un-numbered New Martinsville liquor set (decanter and six small glasses) which was dubbed "Roberto" by Weatherman (*Colored Glassware of the Depression Era 2*, p. 296). This set was pictured in amber glass in the March, 1934, issue of *Crockery and Glass Journal*, and it featured a plate etching with a large bowknot motif.

Yet another beverage set was shown in the July, 1934, issue of *China, Glass and Lamps*, just prior to the New York City China and Glass Show, which was held from July 29 to August 4, 1934. Designated New Martinsville's No. 40/2/82, this set consisted of a tall decanter and six small glasses (1 oz. or 2½ oz.). The set was apparently available only in crystal glass with a cut motif of criss-cross design (this was cutting No. 82). Weatherman shows two other 1936 New Martinsville cocktail sets (*Colored Glassware of the Depression Era 2*, p. 297). The No. 125 shaker (called Sir Cocktail by Weatherman) is decorated with plate etching No. 25, an all-over floral motif of daisies. The decanter shown with Weatherman's "Cozy Cordial" set resembles the shape of the No. 42 Novelty Roly Poly from 1934.

## VANITY ARTICLES

The production of vanity sets continued to be an important facet of the New Martinsville plant's output during the 1930s. Glassworker Harold Ruble, who joined the New Martinsville firm as a carrying-in boy in 1934 and was later in the selecting, packing and shipping departments, recalls this time period, stating simply "we shipped those vanity sets by the boxcar load."

Among the vanity sets on the market in 1933 was a plain set which usually consists of crystal parts accompanied by colored stoppers and lid for the puff box (the set was called "Leota" by Weatherman). This set, whose original number or name has yet to be found, comes on a mirror.

The No. 18/2 vanity set was an extension of the so-called "Crystal Eagle" line introduced in December, 1935, which is discussed later in this chapter. The vanity set consisted of two identical cologne/perfume bottles accompanied by a puff box, which is about 5½" long. These were made in crystal, amber [see Fig. 343 and 414], pale green,

# Something New

**FOUR PIECE VANITY SET**
in crystal, and crystal with jade
or bright green covers and stoppers.
These retail at $1 each
– great promotional items!

*From an advertisement which appeared in 1933. In addition to the "jade or bright green" lids and stoppers, this set is also known with these parts in black or ruby glass.*

pink, ruby and a pale blue called "sky blue" [see Fig. 341]. The crystal set may have lids and stoppers made from either jade green or black glass [see Fig. 342]. There is also a larger, deeper covered puff box (about 6" long) which matches this set. Original catalogues c. 1938 show the No. 18/2 vanity set along with the No. 15 set [see Chapter Four and Fig. 330] and two others—No. 25 and No. 28. Instead of a tray, these were furnished with a 7" x 14" mirror.

New Martinsville's No. 603 puff box was probably the one called "Martha Washington" today [see the front cover and Figs. 326-327]. On November 8, 1932, the company wrote to the National Association of Manufacturers of Pressed and Blown Glassware about problems in making this article, stating simply "we ... have not been getting very good results." This distinctive item has been found in the jade/black combination (jade lid, black base), as well as other characteristic New Martinsville colors: crystal, blue, green and pink (any of which may be satin-finished).

A lengthy article in the January 24, 1935, issue of *Pottery, Glass and Brass Salesman* carried this enthusiastic account of the glassware then being made at New Martinsville, giving particular attention to the vanity sets and related articles:

*"Color! Color! And more color! That is the impression one gets from viewing the new line of the New Martinsville Glass Manufacturing Company, which was first displayed in Pittsburgh this January and is now on show at all the various agencies of the concern. The New Martinsville Company has featured color for many years, and here one finds lovely rubies, deep blues, regal purples, rich ambers and brilliant greens, together with a whole host of the more delicate colors that find favor to such an extent [probably the colors called ice blue and light green today]. Then, too, for those that want it, there is crystal. In many instances, crystal and color are combined, sometimes in the same set and sometimes even in the same items. There is nothing new about this, but some very striking and rich creations have been developed in the new array.*

*Practically everything that can be made in pressed glass is included in the New Martinsville showing, as is always the case. Perhaps the array of liquor ware is outstanding, and some very unusual sets are included in the concern's offering this season. Then, there is another feature in the line that New Martinsville has long emphasized—that is, the boudoir articles. Here, too, has the line been increased and improved from many different angles. As new items are constantly being added to the*

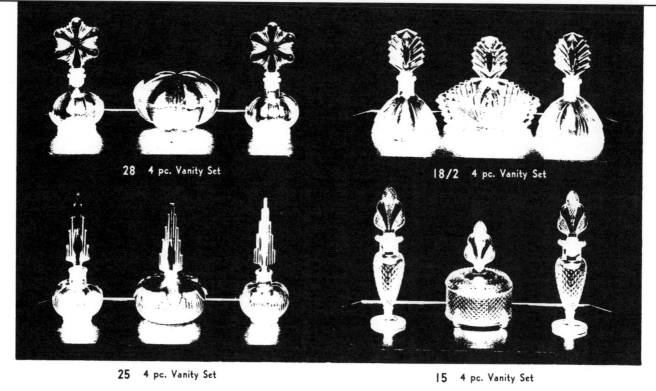

28   4 pc. Vanity Set    18/2   4 pc. Vanity Set

25   4 pc. Vanity Set    15   4 pc. Vanity Set

**NEW MARTINSVILLE GLASS COMPANY**    New Martinsville, W. Va.

*Vanity sets from c. 1938 catalogue.*

*array, it is not advisable at this time to comment on any as being outstanding compared with the rest, but descriptions of some of these individual items will appear in these columns from time to time.*

### A RADIANT SUCCESS

Although No. 37 (Moondrops) seems to have been an unqualified sales winner and probably kept the factory from closing, there were other items and lines launched during Ira Clarke's management in the 1930s. Foremost among the pattern lines was No. 42, which was also called Radiance. It was ready for the market in December, 1936, and the New Martinsville firm placed a full-page ad in *Crockery and Glass Journal* to laud the new line.

Unlike most ads in the glass trade periodicals, the New Martinsville firm's introduction of Radiance did not feature a photograph or drawing of the glassware. The ad said the firm "would rather have the trade see them [the new articles] first in Pittsburgh in January." The ad also noted that each article "is so designed as to allow ample space for decorations and cuttings," and it stated further that a plate etching called Meadow Wreath would be available (Meadow Wreath was plate etching No. 26). The line was well into production

**Crockery and Glass Journal** *(December, 1936); note the reference to the "Meadow Wreath" etching.*

214/7176—Assortment of 3 Styles. Hand made ruby glass in "R.diance" pattern. Consists of scalloped edge bowl, diameter 12 inches, round shallow fruit or flower centerpiece, diameter 13 in :hes; footed flared edge bowl, diameter 11 inches. ½ dozen assorted 3 kinds in carton. (Matches 214/7164 Luncheon Set, 214/7177 Salad Set and 214/7178 Console Set) WE DO NOT BREAK CARTONS. .................................................. Per dozen $24.00

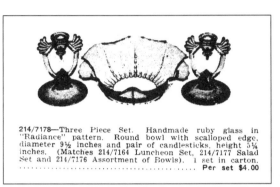

214/7164—15 Piece Luncheon Set. Ruby red glass in "Radiance" pattern, scalloped edge. Four 8½ inch salad plates, four cups, four saucers, sugar, creamer and cake or sandwich plate, diameter 14 inches. (Matches 214/7177 Salad Set, 214/7178 Console Set and 214/7176 Assortment of Bowls) 1 set in carton. ............................Per set $10.00

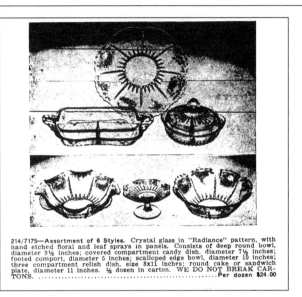

214/7178—Three Piece Set. Handmade ruby glass in "Radiance" pattern. Round bowl with scalloped edge, diameter 9½ inches and pair of candlesticks, height 5¼ inches. (Matches 214/7164 Luncheon Set, 214/7177 Salad Set and 214/7176 Assortment of Bowls). 1 set in carton. ............................................... Per set $4.00

214/7175—Assortment of 6 Styles. Crystal glass in "Radiance" pattern, with hand etched floral and leaf sprays in panels. Consists of deep round bowl, diameter 9½ inches; covered compartment candy dish, diameter 7½ inches; footed comport, diameter 5 inches; scalloped edge bowl, diameter 10 inches; three compartment relish dish, size 8x11 inches; round cake or sandwich plate, diameter 11 inches. ½ dozen in carton. WE DO NOT BREAK CARTONS. ........................................... Per dozen $24.00

*Blackwell Wielandy Company catalogue (1940-41).*

in February, 1938, as many agreements for moves and wages on specific articles are recorded in the files of the National Association of Manufacturers of Pressed and Blown Glassware.

Like No. 37 (Moondrops), New Martinsville's Radiance line was made for some years, and it is difficult to ascertain exactly when particular pieces were made in a given color. Crystal, amber, cobalt blue, light blue (ice blue) and ruby were surely made in the 1930s, probably along with a few articles in canary [see Fig. 352], rose (pink) and green. Production of No. 42 Radiance (sometimes also called the "4200 line") certainly continued at New Martinsville from late 1936 through about 1943 or 1944, although the plant was closed on several occasions for weeks at a time due to such matters as Ira Clarke's death and consequent legal problems inherent in the receivership and sale proceedings as well as several Ohio River floods.

A catalogue issued for 1940-41 by the St. Louis firm of Blackwell Wielandy Company includes a number of articles from the No. 42 Radiance line. An assortment of a half-dozen crystal pieces was shown with the No. 26 (Meadow Wreath) plate etching. A complete 15-piece luncheon set was

available for $10.00 in ruby glass, and other No. 42 Radiance items were also available in ruby. Perhaps most interesting is a console set consisting of a No. 42 Radiance bowl accompanied by two No. 37/2 4" candlesticks [see Fig. 444], which were originally part of the No. 37 (Moondrops) line.

The Viking Glass Company, which operated the New Martinsville plant from 1944 to 1986, revived the Radiance pattern, and pieces in ruby glass have been found with original Viking labels [see Figs. 484-485] as have pieces in a dark emerald green. Nonetheless, original black-and-white advertising sheets and catalogue pages (which date from 1937 to 1944) allow a discussion of this pattern here. Readers should also consult the various editions of Florence's *Collector's Encyclopedia of Depression Glass* as well as the first edition of his *Elegant Glassware of the Depression Era* (1983) and his *Very Rare Glassware of the Depression Years*, second series (1991).

No. 42 Radiance was quite a lengthy line, but it initially encompassed items considered tableware: several sizes of plates for both serving and individual use, cups/saucers, sugar and cream set on tray,

(continued on p. 177)

42/28 – 10" BOWL

4213/28 BOWL

4266/28 BOWL

4265/28 BOWL

4457/28

42/28 – 10" BOWL

4457/28

4227/28 RELISH

4428/28 RELISH

4226/28 RELISH

4211/28 BOWL

S-1-28 ASSORTMENT

ROSE & ROBIN ETCHING

*No. 42 Radiance items with plate etching No. 28 Rose & Robin, except for the No. 4457 two-light candlesticks, which were part of the later No. 44 line.*

S-1-28
ASSORTMENT

42/28 MAYONNAISE

42/28 CHEESE & CRACKER

42/28 CANDY BOX & COVER

42/28 SALVER

42/28 SUGAR & CREAM SET

4218/28 FOOTED BOWL

42/28-14" PLATE

42/28-11" PLATE

*No. 42 Radiance items with plate etching No. 28 Rose & Robin. Note the shape of the finial on the cover of the candy box and the characteristic solid handles on the creamer and sugar.*

# LINE No. 42

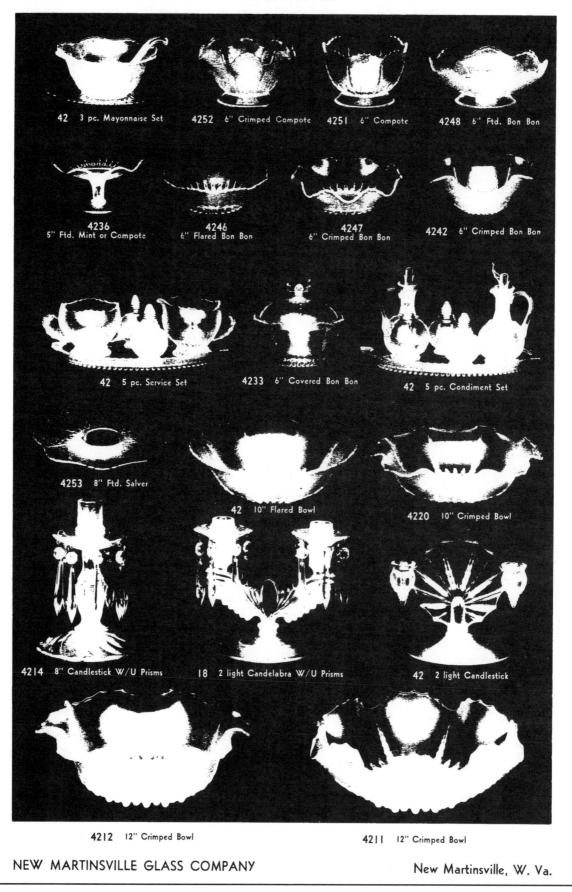

42    3 pc. Mayonnaise Set     4252   6" Crimped Compote     4251   6" Compote     4248   6" Ftd. Bon Bon

4236   5" Ftd. Mint or Compote     4246   6" Flared Bon Bon     4247   6" Crimped Bon Bon     4242   6" Crimped Bon Bon

42    5 pc. Service Set     4233   6" Covered Bon Bon     42    5 pc. Condiment Set

4253   8" Ftd. Salver     42   10" Flared Bowl     4220   10" Crimped Bowl

4214   8" Candlestick W/U Prisms     18   2 light Candelabra W/U Prisms     42   2 light Candlestick

4212   12" Crimped Bowl     4211   12" Crimped Bowl

**NEW MARTINSVILLE GLASS COMPANY**     New Martinsville, W. Va.

*This original catalogue sheet shows many pieces in the No. 42 line. Note the candlesticks in the second row from the bottom; the No. 18 in the center is a holdover from an earlier line c. 1936, but those on the right and left were part of the No. 42 line [see Fig. 460].*

170

# LINE No. 42

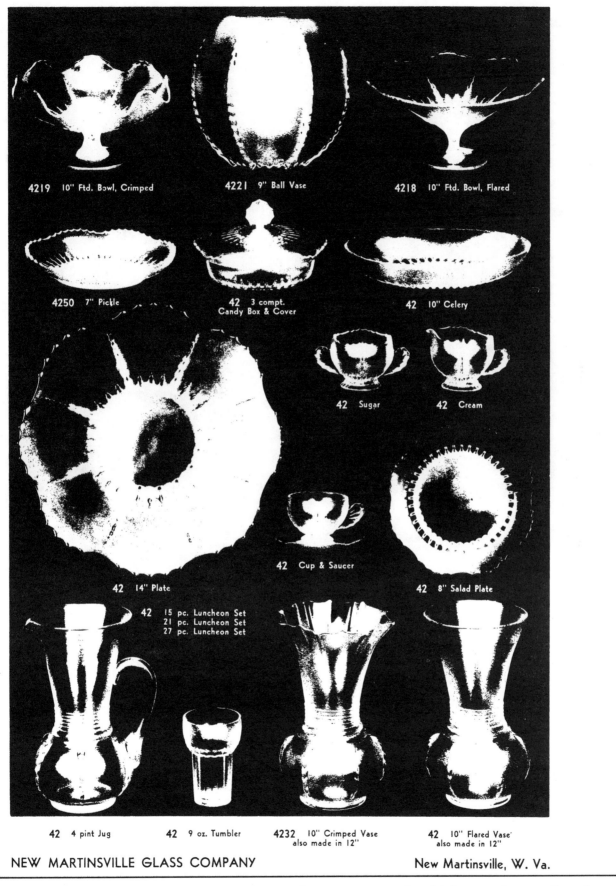

4219  10" Ftd. Bowl, Crimped

4221  9" Ball Vase

4218  10" Ftd. Bowl, Flared

4250  7" Pickle

42  3 compt.
Candy Box & Cover

42  10" Celery

42  Sugar

42  Cream

42  14" Plate

42  Cup & Saucer

42  8" Salad Plate

42  15 pc. Luncheon Set
21 pc. Luncheon Set
27 pc. Luncheon Set

42  4 pint Jug

42  9 oz. Tumbler

4232  10" Crimped Vase
also made in 12"

42  10" Flared Vase
also made in 12"

NEW MARTINSVILLE GLASS COMPANY

New Martinsville, W. Va.

*This original catalogue sheet shows the 9" ball vase (top row, center), which was also marketed as a punch bowl [see Fig. 456]. The pitcher and the 10" vases in the bottom row were all made from the same mould.*

171

42/401 C/Box and Cover 7½" 3 pt.

42/401 Cheese and Cracker 11½"

42/401 14" Plate

42/401 10" Vase

42/401 3 pc. Mayo. Set

42/401 Sugar, Cream and Tray

4462/401 12" 2 Hdl. Plate

MADE BY THE
NEW MARTINSVILLE GLASS CO.

VIKING

NEW MARTINSVILLE
WEST VIRGINIA

*New Martinsville's No. 401 cutting was a simple floral motif. It is shown here on items from the No. 42 Radiance line and a two-handled plate from the later No. 4400 line (lower left).*

# CUT No. 409 PATTERN

42  3 Compt.
Candy Box & Cover

42  Sugar, Cream & Tray

42
Mayonnaise Set

42
11" Cheese & Cracker

4554
5" Candlestick

4213
12" Flared Bowl

4453
6" Candlestick

42
14" Plate

42
10" Flared Vase

4462
12" 2 Hdl. Plate

4211
12" Crimped Bowl

4457
2 Light Candlestick

4265
11" Flared Bowl

**NEW MARTINSVILLE GLASS COMPANY**                    New Martinsville, W. Va.

*New Martinsville's No. 409 cutting combined a simple flower with wide lines of varying lengths. Most of the items shown are from the No. 42 Radiance line.*

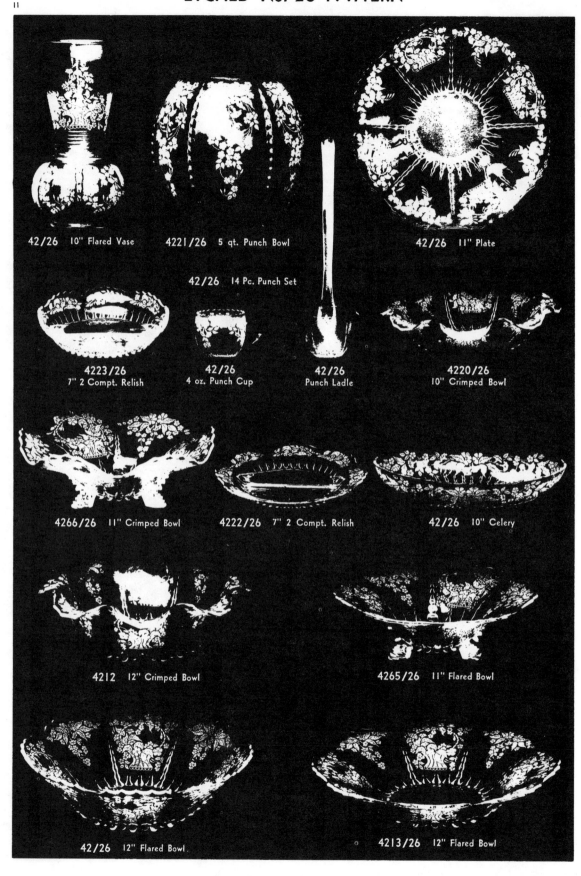

42/26　10" Flared Vase

4221/26　5 qt. Punch Bowl

42/26　11" Plate

42/26　14 Pc. Punch Set

4223/26
7" 2 Compt. Relish

42/26
4 oz. Punch Cup

42/26
Punch Ladle

4220/26
10" Crimped Bowl

4266/26　11" Crimped Bowl

4222/26　7" 2 Compt. Relish

42/26　10" Celery

4212　12" Crimped Bowl

4265/26　11" Flared Bowl

42/26　12" Flared Bowl

4213/26　12" Flared Bowl

**NEW MARTINSVILLE GLASS COMPANY**　　　New Martinsville, W. Va.

*No. 26 Meadow Wreath plate etching on items in New Martinsville's No. 42 Radiance line. Note the punch bowl (top row), which was available as a set with 12 cups and ladle.*

# ETCHED No. 26 PATTERN

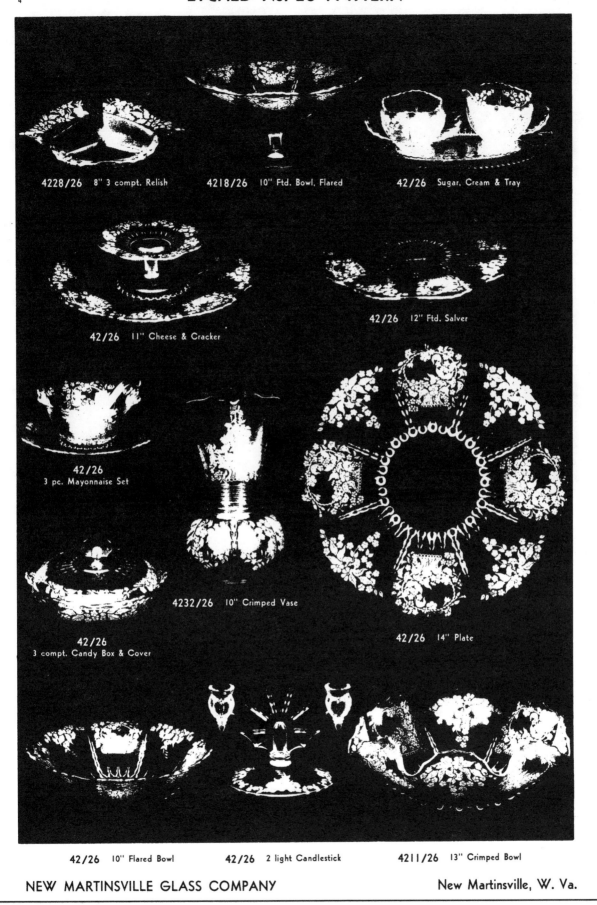

4228/26   8" 3 compt. Relish

4218/26   10" Ftd. Bowl, Flared

42/26   Sugar, Cream & Tray

42/26   11" Cheese & Cracker

42/26   12" Ftd. Salver

42/26 3 pc. Mayonnaise Set

4232/26   10" Crimped Vase

42/26 3 compt. Candy Box & Cover

42/26   14" Plate

42/26   10" Flared Bowl

42/26   2 light Candlestick

4211/26   13" Crimped Bowl

NEW MARTINSVILLE GLASS COMPANY          New Martinsville, W. Va.

*No. 26 Meadow Wreath plate etching on items in New Martinsville's No. 42 Radiance line. Note the shape of the finial on the candy box as well as the distinctive candlestick in the bottom row.*

175

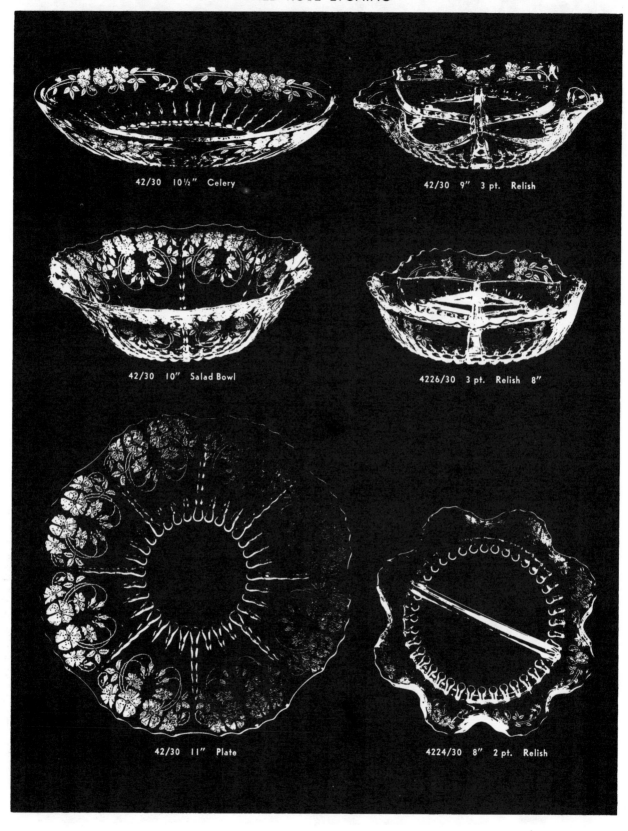

42/30   10½"   Celery

42/30   9"   3 pt.   Relish

42/30   10"   Salad Bowl

4226/30   3 pt.   Relish   8"

42/30   11"   Plate

4224/30   8"   2 pt.   Relish

MADE BY THE
NEW MARTINSVILLE GLASS CO.

VIKING

NEW MARTINSVILLE
WEST VIRGINIA

*No. 30 Wild Rose plate etching on items in New Martinsville's No. 42 Radiance line.*

salt/pepper shakers, and a variety of bowls and relish dishes (many of these can be seen in the S-1-28 Assortment with No. 28 Rose & Robin plate etching on two facing pages of this book (see pp. 168-169); see also Figs. 456-470). According to original catalogue pages, the fan-shaped finial was used only on the No. 42 Radiance butter dish. The finials on other covered pieces and the stoppers in the oil bottles were similar in shape to the large, flat central area of the No. 42 two-light candlestick [see Fig. 461].

Within a few years, the No. 42 Radiance line had grown considerably. Two undated catalogue sheets (see pp. 170-171) show a variety of compotes and bon bons as well as vases, a pitcher/tumbler set, and a 9" ball vase which did double duty as a punch bowl. The origins of the No. 42 Radiance punch bowl go back a few years. In correspondence with the National Association of Manufacturers of Pressed and Blown Glassware (August-October, 1936), New Martinsville's assistant general manager, Harry Barth, inquired about the move and wages for a ball-shaped No. 108 plain bowl in crystal or ruby which "is used by a silver manufacturer for a punch bowl." According to a log of private moulds, the No. 108 punch bowl mould was owned by the Keystone Silver Company. It may have been the inspiration for the similarly-shaped No. 42 Radiance punch bowl, or the mould itself may have been acquired later by the glass company and machined to add the pattern elements of the No. 42 line.

As its first advertising had proclaimed, the No. 42 Radiance line was intended to be decorated with cutting or plate etching. Some undated catalogue sheets show assortments of the No. 42 line with cuttings No. 401 and No. 409 (see, respectively, pp. 172-173). Other undated catalogue sheets show assortments of the No. 42 line with plate etchings such as No. 26 Meadow Wreath and No. 30 Wild Rose (see, respectively, pp. 174-175 and 176).

The No. 42 Radiance line certainly helped New Martinsville's glass enterprise maintain its position in the industry during the difficult 1930s. Other glass companies were not so fortunate and closed their doors for good during this dark period in the nation's economic history. To be sure, No. 42 Radiance and No. 37 (Moondrops) had been the kingpins, but there were other articles made at the New Martinsville factory during this time which contributed to the firm's stability.

## OTHER ITEMS AND LINES

Several interesting vases were marketed in 1934-36. The first of these was New Martinsville's No. 101, a massive flower vase with two birds at its base [see Fig. 404]. Weatherman (*Colored Glassware of the Depression Era 2*, p. 296) called this "Morning [sic] Dove." According to New Martinsville's ad in *Pottery, Glass and Brass Salesman*, the No. 101 vase was available in "all our beautiful colors and crystal." One retired New Martinsville glassworker thinks this vase may have been designed by Harry Barth. Interestingly, the Shawnee Pottery Company of Zanesville, Ohio, later produced a close facsimile of this vase as part of a low-priced line.

In the March, 1935, issue of *China, Glass and Lamps*, the New Martinsville plant displayed its No. 35/3/25 vase. The numerical designation suggests that this piece was a vestige of the No. 35 line made four to five years earlier, and the number 25 refers to the plate etching, an all-over floral motif consisting of daisies.

Plate etchings were also featured in June, 1935, when the New Martinsville firm advertised its No. 103 Candy Box. This was then being marketed in

SELLS FOR ONE DOLLAR AT A PROFIT

Here's the new No. 101 nine-inch vase, made in all our beautiful colors and crystal. It is suitable to take large bunches of short or long stemmed flowers and it is an ideal dollar retailer.

The top measures seven inches in diameter. The entire vase is finely finished. It has an exceptional appearance and is a real work of art which you can turn over profitably for $1.00.

NEW MARTINSVILLE GLASS MFG. CO.
NEW MARTINSVILLE, W. VA.

*Ad from* **Crockery and Glass Journal.**

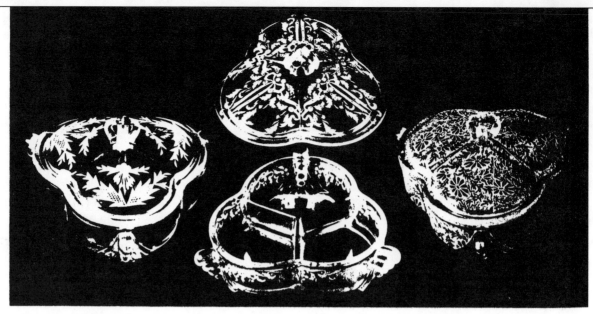

Cutting 150          Etching 103 24          Etching 103/25

# Our New Candy Box De Luxe
## Number 103

*From* **Pottery, Glass and Brass Salesman** *(June 6, 1935).*

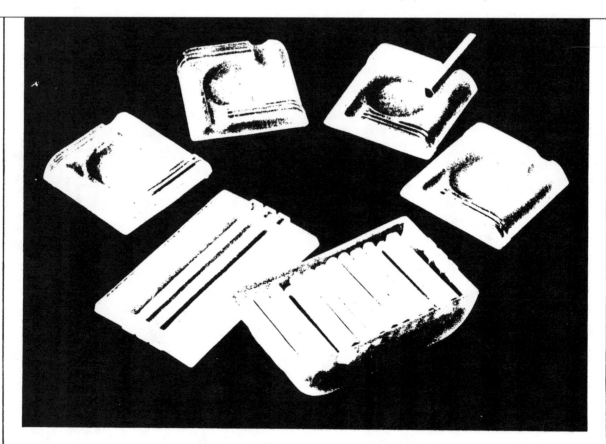

# Cigarette Set No. 105

*From* **Pottery, Glass and Brass Salesman** *(December, 1935).*

178

# Console Set in Crystal Eagle Pattern
## OUTSTANDING FOR 1936

**NO. 18**

**MODERATELY PRICED**

*From* **Crockery and Glass Journal** *(January, 1936).*

"crystal, evergreen, Ritz Blue, amber and rose [pink]" with a retail value of 98 cents. Ruby was 50% higher at $1.49. Cuttings on crystal, rose or amber were priced at $1.59, and plate etched ware in crystal, rose or amber was highest in suggested retail price at $1.98.

The streamlined No. 105 cigarette set was advertised in the December, 1935, issue of *Pottery, Glass and Brass Salesman*. These sets consisted of four identical ashtrays accompanied by a covered cigarette box. Designed to retail for one dollar, these sets came in crystal, black and blue. If the customer so desired, sets could be had with a crystal base for the cigarette box to contrast with either a black or a blue lid.

December, 1935, also marked the debut of New Martinsville's No. 18 line, which was also called "Crystal Eagle" by the firm, although this term may not have been applied to colored articles. A large bowl [see Fig. 409] with matching underplate was illustrated in *China, Glass and Lamps*. These articles were made from the same mould, but they were finished into different shapes. The large bowl and underplate were shown with a pair of "two way" candlesticks in a full-page ad in the January, 1936, issue of *Crockery and Glass Journal*. When the No. 18/728 Service Set (creamer, sugar

## No. 18 728—SERVICE SET

This nifty little item is a bit out of the ordinary. Maybe that's the reason it proved such a big success at the Pittsburgh Show. Comes in all colors, including ruby. Packed in individual cartons.

To retail for $1.00 PER SET—A BIG BUY

### NEW MARTINSVILLE GLASS MANUFACTURING CO.

New Martinsville　　:　　:　　W. Va.

*From* **Pottery, Glass and Brass Salesman** *(February, 1936).*

# NEW REFRESHMENT SET

High sales for Summer months with this new No. 36 Refreshment Set. Blown Jug, 60-oz. capacity, with stuck handle, and six 9-oz., light pressed tumblers to match. Large assortment of color including ruby—all pieces exceptionally high quality, full finished and fire polished. Packed in individual cartons and priced for quick turnover at good profit. Get your needs now!

## NEW MARTINSVILLE GLASS MFG. COMPANY

*From* **Pottery, Glass and Brass Salesman.**

a "large assortment of color" but only ruby glass was mentioned. This set was named "Oscar" in Weatherman's *Colored Glassware of the Depression Era 2* (p. 294). There may have been other articles in the No. 36 line. A No. 36 vase in New Martinsville's jade green [see Fig. 366] was decorated with a plate etching designed by Harry Barth. On October 7, 1937 New Martinsville's workers and management agreed on moves and wages for the No. 36 individual creamer and sugar.

New Martinsville's No. 2 Waffle Set was among the more utilitarian products of the company during the mid-1930s. This set consisted of a large flat tray and two covered pitchers of different sizes [see Figs. 357-358]. The larger pitcher was intended to hold the mixed batter for waffles, while the smaller was for syrup. A 1934 ad said that the set was available in "all colors except ruby." The No. 2 Waffle Set is known today in crystal, amber, cobalt blue, emerald green and rose (pink). From time to time, crystal pitchers are found with colored lids. Readers interested in this set should examine the various illustrations in the fourth edition of Florence's *Kitchen Glassware of the Depression Years* (pp. 21, 35, 63 and 82). One of New Martinsville's competitors, the nearby Paden City Glass

and salt/pepper shakers on a tray) was shown in the February, 1936, issue of *Pottery, Glass and Brass Salesman*, it was available in "all colors, including ruby" to retail for a dollar per set (see Over's *Ruby Glass of the 20th Century*, p. 48, fig. 400). A vanity set, designated No. 18/2, was also made, as was indicated earlier in this chapter.

The New Martinsville firm maintained production of many different candlesticks during the 1930s, too. Although these could be used with large bowls from various lines to form a console set, the candlesticks were also sold alone as accent pieces and often outlived other articles in their respective lines. Agreements in the files of the National Association of Manufacturers of Pressed and Blown Glassware indicate that the No. 37 three-light candlestick was in production in October, 1937. As the next chapter indicates, the No. 37/3 and other candlesticks from the 1930s were still in production in the early 1940s, too.

A rather plain No. 36 Refreshment Set, consisting of a tall, 60-ounce capacity pitcher and six tumblers, was advertised in 1935-36. One ad promised

## NEW WAFFLE SET

Modern 5-piece Waffle Set with batter jug and syrup jug (both covered) on handled tray. Flat covers on jugs make them serviceable for refrigerator use also. Available in crystal and all colors except ruby. Packed in individual shipping cartons and priced to retail at $1.00, you'll find these sets a profitable item for your department. Order a selection of this No. 2 Waffle Set today!

### NEW MARTINSVILLE GLASS MFG. CO.
NEW MARTINSVILLE, W. VA.

*From* **Crockery and Glass Journal.**

Manufacturing Company, produced similar "batter sets" about the same time (these are illustrated by Florence and may also be found in Weatherman's *Colored Glassware of the Depression Era 2*, p. 309).

## WORKERS' PERSPECTIVES

Just as the Great Depression had its impact upon the New Martinsville Glass Manufacturing Company and its executives, so too did the factory's workers feel its effects. Some glassworkers sought whatever other jobs they could find in and around New Martinsville, and most had vegetable gardens and fished or hunted game for food. When work was slack, they journeyed to other glass factories, some electing not to return if prospects for steady work seemed brighter in their new surroundings. Those who called New Martinsville home and were skillful workers caught a few turns in nearby Moundsville or Paden City as conditions in those plants permitted and hoped for better days locally.

In the mid-1920s, the American Flint Glass Workers Union had opened its own bank, The American Bank, near the union's international headquarters in Toledo, Ohio. When several other banks in Toledo failed, the American Bank toppled with them, closing its doors in August, 1931. The AFGWU lost membership as glass plants closed and workers unable to find employment left the trade for other jobs. Publication of the monthly *American Flint* magazine was suspended for a time in the early 1930s.

When Theodore Hoskins wrote for the *American Flint* in March, 1935, he said that New Martinsville was working just "three days a week," but that "two furnaces [are] in operation and two day tanks ready to start when business warrants. There are 15 press shops employed and one iron mould shop, also one new press shop to start next week." Throughout much of 1935, part-time was the rule at New Martinsville, as workers divided time and averaged about three days per week.

In the November, 1935, issue of the *American Flint*, New Martinsville glassworker A. M. McGraw had these optimistic words to say:

*This is the time of year that all glass workers look forward to as the weather gets cooler and the orders begin to pile in. Let's hope they never stop piling in, for it looks to me like we will all have to be working double time soon to meet our living expenses, considering how fast the prices are going up on groceries and meats. Ross Schwing, our genial factory manager, surely can make*

*good glass. He can make A-No. 1 glass and talk football at the same time. You know we are all football crazy down here, because we have the best high school football team in the valley. They are second to none. Since my last report we have fire in two more tanks and it looks as if the orders are coming in fast. We will probably be working full time before this letter goes to press.*

McGraw's enthusiasm was matched by the sales performance of the company's products, which, at this time, would have included the No. 37 (Moondrops) line as well as the recently-introduced No. 42 Radiance line. In the December, 1935, *American Flint*, McGraw said "we have plenty of orders for a nice long run and it looks like Santa Claus will be sure to come around this year." The plant was on half-time through the holidays, but he predicted that "quite a few new moulds coming out ... will surely make a hit on the market" (*American Flint*, January, 1936). These jubilant words, from McGraw's column in the February, 1936, *American Flint* need no elaboration:

*The big glass show is now in full swing and I understand that the buying is heavier than any time since 1928. That is very encouraging to both the workers and the manufacturers, for when we work good the first part of the year our chances are good for steady work all year. The latest report from the glass show is "we are getting plenty of orders." What a grand and glorious feeling!*

Even an Ohio River flood in early 1936 did not dampen the enthusiasm in New Martinsville among the glassworkers, although it did about $12,500 worth of damage to the factory, according to a report filed in Wetzel County Circuit Court by general manager/receiver Ira Clarke. In the April, 1936, *American Flint*, Arch McGraw reported that all were working full time with "lots of orders coming in every day." He concluded that "we have a good company to work for down here. Our factory manager treats us all equal and that's something you don't find in every factory."

A report in the *American Flint* in the January, 1937, issue was under the by-line of George Workman. He said that during the past six months "we have been going at it hammer and tongs," as workers were "getting in some real good time and have been working double shift." Another Ohio River flood in January, 1937, shut the plant down for nearly three weeks, but two shifts were put on when production resumed on February 8, 1937. Workman soon reported that there were nine shops on day turn and eight on the night turn (*American Flint*, March, 1937). The renaissance

## NEW MARTINSVILLE, W. VA.

### By Arch M. McGraw

Here we are once again boys. Conditions have taken a sudden change for the worse down here at the New Martinsville Glass Co. It is just a month since the flood waters descended on this beautiful little town and just about submerged everything in it. But after many days of uncertainty and hardships the waters receded and now you can hardly tell there ever was a flood. The factory has resumed work again after being idle for three weeks on account of the flood, but they are only working part time now. I suppose we can blame that on the flood too. But it is all in a lifetime and I suppose we are able to take it, anyway, us glass workers are accustomed to taking it on the chin with a smile. I know I am able to take it. "I'm Irish!"

Some of us fellows will be living and smiling a long time after some other fellows are dead and pushing up daisies. But then we glass workers should all be good and kind to each other, for we only have a short time to be together anyway. Our trade is slipping fast. It won't be long until the machines will push us out altogether, so why do we cut each other's throats and be mean and hateful with each other? Why not go down smiling and friendly with each other, as all good brothers should. After all, "Brotherly Love" is the highest form of Christianity.

Jim Donaldson has gone back to Morgantown, and Wm. Rice left for Columbus, Ohio. Edward Casey drifted back to Pittsburgh. Guy Wilt is operating a high class tonsorial parlor over in Hannibal, Ohio. Any of you who want a good free hair cut just drop in to see Guy if you happen to be over that way. Was sorry to see these men leave, but such is the plight of a glass worker these days. It is just "on again, off again" but mostly off again.

John Forbes passed away at his home, April 9th. He had been ill for several weeks from the effects of a stroke. It is with the deepest regrets that we see the passing of these old time Flints, and our deepest sympathy goes out to the son and daughter of this deceased brother. God, in His divine wisdom may call us most anytime, and if we have done some wrong against a brother, let's make it right before we are called.

Well, it won't be long until the favorite slogan will be "On to Newark" and don't forget, you delegates, be sure to get acquainted with Gottlieb Zinn when you get there, as I'm sure you will find him the best and squarest all-around Dutchman you ever met, and give him my best regards as I don't expect to get there. Here's wishing the trade steady work the rest of the fire, as I may be ringing off for a time. And this community wishes to thank the Morgantown Glass Co. for the large donation they sent over for the flood sufferers, and they wish to especially thank the committee from the Morgantown Glass Co., that came over here at their own expense to do relief work. They did everything on the q. t. But I'm going to tell you their names. Here they are: Edward Shay, president; Ben Pitman, secretary, and Charles Best, all from Local Union No. 77. They are surely fine fellows and they deserve a big hand along with the rest of the Morgantown Glass Co. Thanks, brothers, from the whole community.

—— ATTEND YOUR MEETINGS ——

**American Flint** (*May, 1936*).

wrought by Ira Clarke was nearly complete, and the New Martinsville plant seems to have been as busy as ever.

## GLASS PLANT FOR SALE

On April 27, 1937, Ira M. Clarke died suddenly. He had been affiliated with New Martinsville's glass enterprise from 1919 through September, 1926, and then again starting in August, 1932. The factory closed down almost immediately. In early June, 1937, the Circuit Court appointed Sheriff Frank Berger of Wetzel County as "special receiver" (*Wetzel Democrat*, June 6, 1937). Company treasurer John F. Martin, who had been affiliated with the glass firm for many years, died on June 23, 1937. The plant was soon put up for sale, and it operated sporadically for about a year before a buyer could be found.

After Clarke's death, the plant was closed for about five weeks before production resumed in early June, 1937. A few months later, glassworker William Cross wrote that work was steady enough with nine press shops and one iron mould shop "getting eight and ten turns a week" (*American Flint*, September, 1937). The Wetzel County Circuit Court sought bids for the plant on July 24 and again on September 25, but no interested parties came forward.

In November, 1937, Cross wrote that "business is not so good as a year ago," and he stated that "the company is experiencing some difficulty in obtaining enough orders to operate full time" (*American Flint*, November, 1937). On a less serious note, Cross also mentioned that local union No. 16 had planned a fish dinner at the War Memorial Building, noting that "beer will be on tap and a glassworker's idea of a good time is anticipated."

In early 1938, within an official report of the special receiver to Wetzel County Circuit Court, Sheriff Frank Berger announced that the plant had secured a valuable contract for private mould work: "arrangements were concluded with a certain large consumer for two specially designed glass pieces amounting in all to 1,080,000 pieces aggregating a total volume of business of approximately $45,000. The moulds for this particular merchandise are now under construction at the expense of the customer, and the items should be in production within four to six weeks."

The above order notwithstanding, the New Martinsville plant's workers were compelled to divide time throughout the winter and spring of

## VALUABLE GLASS PLANT FOR SALE

The New Martinsville Glass Manufacturing Plant, a plant now manufacturing table ware and glass novelties, with all real estate, buildings, machinery, tools and fixtures will be offered at public auction at the Court House of Wetzel County, in New Martinsville, West Virginia, at 10 o' clock A. M., on the 24th day of July, 1937.

TERMS OF SALE: One-third cash on day of sale, or as much more as the purchaser may elect to pay; one-third in six months and one-third in twelve months, deferred payments evidenced by interest bearing notes with security and title retained until full payment.

—A Splendid Opportunity For Investment—

**M. H. Willis, W. J. Postlethwait, Walter F. Ball, Special Commissioners**

*This description of the New Martinsville Glass plant appeared in the* American Glass Review.

1938. Apparently, some scrip continued to be issued in lieu of cash wages, too. The report of the special receiver for May 31, 1938, noted outstanding scrip totalling $4,751. In June, 1938, glassworker David White said that the employees were working only "a couple of days a week," concluding dourly that "if there is anything in the old adage 'There is no rest for the wicked,' then the glassworkers sure are improving fast" (*American Flint*, June, 1938). General manager Harry Barth resigned in June, 1938 (but he would soon be involved with the plant again), and he was succeeded by Fred Schlens, the son-in-law of the late Ira Clarke, who had experience in managing some aspects of the glass factory.

In yet another effort to liquidate the plant, the special receiver appointed by the Wetzel County Circuit Court again advertised the property and fixtures for sale in the *American Glass Review*. This time, two men from Connecticut, R. M. Rice and Carl Schultz, submitted bids totalling about $44,000 for the plant as well as its real estate, fixtures and other assets. The commissioners appointed by the Circuit Court—W. F. Ball, A. E. Larrick and W. J. Postlethwait—accepted the bids of Rice and Schultz, and the *Wetzel Democrat* reported the good news to its readers on July 21, 1938, in the midst of the city of New Martinsville's centennial celebration. Rice and Schultz were no strangers to the glass business, for both were involved with the Silver City Glass Company of Meriden, Connecticut, and had numerous con-

**$5.00** — Payable Only at the Office of the Company

New Martinsville, W. Va., MAY 2 1 1932

Sixty days after date, for value received, Without Interest, we promise

## TO PAY TO THE BEARER

REGISTERED $5 AND 00¢
F-2145

$5.00

The New Martinsville Glass Manufacturing Co.

N⁰ 6748

By _____ Treas.

Countersigned _____ Prest.

*This scrip note for $5.00, signed by company president Frank William Clark and treasurer John F. Martin, was issued to a glassworker in 1932.*

tacts with buyers and distributing firms in the trade. The *Democrat* noted that "extensive repairs are contemplated" for the plant and said further that "prospects for the continued operation of the factory [are] very good."

The sale of the plant and other assets also meant that the New Martinsville Glass Manufacturing Company, which was chartered in 1901, now ceased to exist as a corporation. Rice and Schultz soon joined forces with New Martinsville's Harry Barth, former general manager of the plant, to form a new corporation with a similar name: the New Martinsville Glass Company.

In March, 1939, the final disbursements were made to the creditors of the now-defunct New Martinsville Glass Manufacturing Company. Those who had signed the moratorium on August 3, 1932, received, all told, about 25 cents for each dollar owed them. Unredeemed scrip issued to glassworkers over the years was now worthless. The case was officially closed by Judge James F. Shipman of the Wetzel County Circuit Court on May 10, 1939. By that time, however, longtime New Martinsville glassman Harry Barth was hard at work, laying the groundwork for yet another chapter in the history of glassmaking at New Martinsville.

# CHAPTER SIX

# NEW MARTINSVILLE GLASS, 1938 - 1944

Without doubt, the *Wetzel Democrat's* report of July 21, 1938, was good news for New Martinsville. The plant had been sold to interests from New England, but the principals, R. M. Rice and Carl Schultz, intended to make needed repairs and to operate it just as before. The key person in New Martinsville after the sale of the plant was surely Harry Barth. After all, Rice and Schultz were, albeit glassmen, still outsiders, and the New Martinsville factory needed someone at the helm who was in familar territory.

Harry Barth had worked his way up from an initial job as a laborer in the packing room about 1918 to the post of assistant general manager under Ira Clarke. When he left the New Martinsville Glass Manufacturing Company in June, 1938, Barth surely did so with the knowledge that he would join with Rice and Schultz to form a new company as soon as the plant was sold by court order.

Harry Barth was born on July 10, 1900, and he graduated from Magnolia High School in New Martinsville in 1918. Endowed with considerable talent in both music and art, Barth played the saxophone as well as other instruments, and he led a locally popular orchestra/dance band dubbed the "Magnolia Serenaders." He could draw with pen and ink and paint in watercolors, and he produced some splendid woodcarvings in a home workshop.

As assistant general manager and then as general manager during the late 1930s, Barth had many responsibilities, of course, but he was deeply interested in various aspects of design in the glasshouse, especially for cuttings and the elaborate plate etchings. Unfortunately, the New Martinsville firm did not seek design patents for any of these, so it is difficult to unravel their history. Nonetheless, the memories of family members as well as the testimony of former workers leaves little doubt that Harry Barth was the creator of several, if not all, of these plate etchings: No. 26 Meadow Wreath; No. 28 Rose and Robin; No. 29 Florentine; No. 30 Wild Rose; and No. 31 Canterbury. He may also have designed another motif, called simply Wakefield, which was introduced for the 1940 sales season.

*Harry Barth, c. 1918.*

In the summer of 1938, however, the aesthetic pleasures of design were not Harry Barth's main pursuit. An entirely new corporation, the New Martinsville Glass Company, was chartered by the state of West Virginia. Schultz held 5 shares and Rice 4 shares, while Harry Barth had 1 share. As general manager, Barth was expected to re-open and operate the plant. Almost immediately, labor problems began to emerge. On August 9, 1938, Barth wrote at length to his friend Charles Voitle, executive secretary of the National Association of Manufacturers of Pressed and Blown Glassware. These excerpts from Barth's letter detail the situation in New Martinsville:

*These new owners have placed me in charge of their affairs here as of August 1. The writer was instructed ... to solict applications from the AFGWU with a view to going over them and making our plans for an organization that would be able to step into our factory and go to work as soon as we were able to get all our affairs in shape. ... A group of skilled workers of the old company called upon me and with no ceremony advised that they resented very much our asking for applications. ... They stated further that when the new Company was ready to begin operations, they would expect to move every employee of the old company back into the employ of the new Company. They implied that no other arrangement would be tolerated and that we would have nothing to say about the matter.*

*Charlie, I don't mind telling you that when we sat down and covered the situation and made up our minds that we could do something with a reorganized company in the way of operations, it was agreed that we should forget any past experiences with the old company and start from scratch. ... I am putting it to you: All this new organization bought was the land, buildings, equipment, etc. We did not buy any local agreements; we bought no workers; and we aren't going to buy any headaches.*

Despite the ominous tone of the letter above, Barth was able to move quickly to secure a force of glassworkers without much difficulty. On August 20, he wrote again to Voitle, stating with some relief that an "amicable settlement" had been reached and mentioning further that "we don't think there will be any trouble." He concluded by noting that fire had been lit in the furnaces and operations would resume shortly. The *Wetzel Democrat* (August 25, 1938) shared his optimism, for its headline read simply "GLASS FACTORY TO START NEXT MON." By November, 1938, Gus Weltz's column in the *American Flint* joined the chorus: "Conditions look better here at present than they have for some time, and we hope it continues."

In the spring of 1939, Wilda J. Hassner (now Mrs. Herbert Kappel) began work as a secretary in the offices of the New Martinsville Glass Company. For $10 per week, she took dictation from the firm's executives and typed letters, including those of Harry Barth. She recalls using a hand-cranked mimeograph machine to make multiple copies of price lists for integration into company catalogues (a series of three hole-punched sheets assembled between two covers with brass fasteners). "I was amazed at the big department stores in New York City that bought glass from us," she noted in an interview. When she left the company in 1942 or 1943, she was making $14 a week doing such tasks as preparing purchase orders and processing billings. Among her co-workers in the office were Doretta Schultz, Alice Bargerhoff, Frances Lamping Bridgeman, and Arminta Adams.

Harry Barth left the New Martinsville Glass Company in August, 1940, to join the Optical Division of the War Production Board in Washington, D. C. As part of his column for the September, 1940, issue of the *American Flint*, William Cross offered this praise:

*This article would be incomplete if I failed to pay some tribute to our former general manager, Harry Barth. This man was an asset to the New Martinsville glass factory, having charge of this plant under several different ownerships, and in every case he has shown proven ability under the circumstances. He has a wonderful knowledge of the glass business, a firm belief in unions, and is a real man among men, always firm in his belief, but beaten he would acknowledge it and take it like a man. Harry was a New Martinsville boy, graduated in our school, came from a fine religious family and he always had the interest of our town and his fellow man at heart as well as the firm which employed him. He was always cool and calm and the same everyday and by his good judgment, sound thinking and sense of fairness he gained the admiration of everyone that knows him. We are sorry to lose him, but he has gone and our very sincere and best wishes go with him.*

---

# NEW MARTINSVILLE GLASS COMPANY

## *Manufacturers of*

### HAND-MADE QUALITY GLASSWARE

o

### NEW MARTINSVILLE, W. VA.

August 31, 1939

---

**Company letterhead stationery from 1939.**

About a decade later, Harry Barth was involved with his own enterprise, called Barth Art Glass, which bought blanks from the Paden City Glass Manufacturing Company, the Viking Glass Company and other firms. Mr. O. O. Brown, who was employed as a cutter at the Paden City plant for 27 years and later had his own firm (Ohio Valley Cut Glass), also did cutting work for Barth Art Glass. He recalls Harry Barth as a talented artist and an effective salesman.

Walter Clulo came to manage the New Martinsville plant from a similar post at the Imperial in Bellaire, Ohio, and he had formerly been at the Beaumont plant in Morgantown, West Virginia. Clulo was in New Martinsville less than a year, however, when he was replaced by Orrie "Dock" Mosser. Interestingly, Mosser had been a skilled glassworker at New Martinsville in years past, before he progressed to management at the Cambridge Glass Company in Cambridge, Ohio, and the Duncan Miller concern in Washington, Pennsylvania. Mosser remained in New Martinsville for quite a few years and was well-liked by the glassworkers.

Charles Merritt, who came from Morgantown to New Martinsville, also held a managerial post in the early 1940s. Several former employees recall Merritt as a sort of "efficiency expert," keenly interested in making improvements in various areas of glass production. M. G. "Max" Biberthaler was general manager of the plant for a short time during 1943-44, but he was not among those listed in the company's personnel when the firm changed its name to the Viking Glass Company in mid-1944.

The enmity between labor and management which had been present in earlier times at New Martinsville seems to have given way to better relations, particularly under Harry Barth during 1938-40 and, later, when a number of physical improvements were made in the plant. The spirit of this renewed good feeling was captured by glassworker John Plott's column in the *American Flint* for May, 1944:

*When we came down the river to work at the New Martinsville Glass Co., several of those we were leaving behind smiled and said "Why are you going there? You will never make enough to to buy your beer, just working a day and a half a week. Why Dock Mosser or no other manager can make a go of that plant." Well, they were right in their predictions, for he has out-managed himself into general superintendent of the whole plant, has 16 shops working night and day, on the best floor that any worker has ever stood on. He also has installed two automatic lehrs with the third one on the way; two new glazers have been in operation for some time, one day tank operating and to my knowledge there are two more day tanks coming which will be equal to a four-pot furnace. Now if that is not managing, I do not know what is. We have full cooperation here between the men and supt. Mosser, who is never too busy to sit down and talk things over with us. Not that this writer is a lover of any foreman, but you do have to give credit where credit is due, and I know the members of Local 16 will back me in this.*

## STAPLE ITEMS

Although today's collectors are understandably most interested in the pattern lines and items such as figurines which were made at New Martinsville from 1938 to 1944, at least some measure of the plant's economic well-being stemmed from its continuing ability to make and market the glassware needed by soda fountains, saloons and hotels. The firm also made smoker's supplies, and some special candleabra were developed. Console sets with cuttings were also produced.

Soda fountains needed dishes in various sizes for ice cream sundaes as well as footed tall tumblers for ice cream sodas. Saloons required everthing from beer mugs, shot glasses and whiskey tumblers to graceful stemmed wines and champagne flutes. In addition to articles such as water tumblers, egg cups, sherbet dishes and punch cups, hotels needed durable condiment containers (cream and sugar sets, cruets, salt/pepper shakers and sugar pours) and glassware for serving, especially many sizes of pitchers. The New Martinsville Glass Company made them all.

The line of smoker's supplies (cigarette jars and boxes, ashtrays, pipe holders, and even a base for a lighter) made at New Martinsville between 1938-1944 was probably derived from successful private mould work then being done for various giftware enterprises. These items are rather well-designed, functional articles in heavy crystal.

Several candlesticks from previous years remained in the New Martinsville firm's line during 1938-1944; among these were No. 18 (see Index), No. 37/2 (see Figs. 410 and 444) and No. 37/3 (see Fig. 443). Two graceful candelabra, designated No. 453 and No. 425, appear in original catalogue sheets. The No. 425 was apparently quite popular for some time, and it can be found in various Viking Glass Company catalogues, too.

Console sets with several different cuttings were also made between 1938 and 1944. Many of

*(continued on p. 192)*

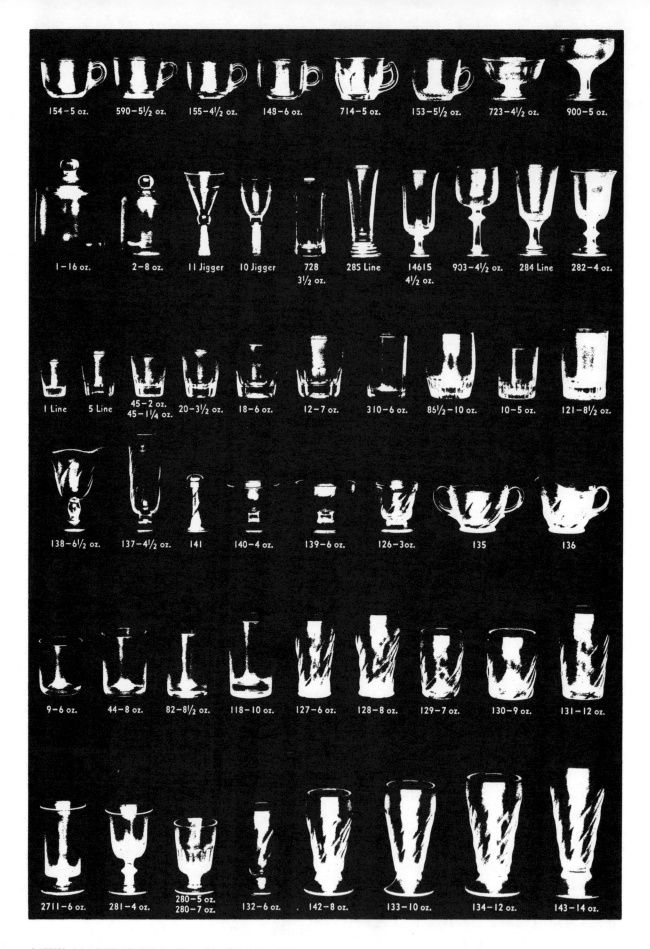

154–5 oz. 590–5½ oz. 155–4½ oz. 148–6 oz. 714–5 oz. 153–5½ oz. 723–4½ oz. 900–5 oz.

1–16 oz. 2–8 oz. 11 Jigger 10 Jigger 728 3½ oz. 285 Line 14615 4½ oz. 903–4½ oz. 284 Line 282–4 oz.

1 Line 5 Line 45–2 oz. 45–1¼ oz. 20–3½ oz. 18–6 oz. 12–7 oz. 310–6 oz. 86½–10 oz. 10–5 oz. 121–8½ oz.

138–6½ oz. 137–4½ oz. 141 140–4 oz. 139–6 oz. 126–3 oz. 135 136

9–6 oz. 44–8 oz. 82–8½ oz. 118–10 oz. 127–6 oz. 128–8 oz. 129–7 oz. 130–9 oz. 131–12 oz.

2711–6 oz. 281–4 oz. 280–5 oz. 280–7 oz. 132–6 oz. 142–8 oz. 133–10 oz. 134–12 oz. 143–14 oz.

## NEW MARTINSVILLE GLASS COMPANY
New Martinsville, W. Va.

*Assortment of saloon and soda fountain supplies from an original catalogue.*

12½ Line    17 Line    310—12 oz.    202—12 oz.    723—12 oz.    95—14 oz. / 71—12 oz.    Belled Tumblers    Straight Tumblers    Taper Tumblers

714/2—12 oz.    714/1—8 oz.    725—10 oz.    708/1—10 oz.    714/0—4 oz.    544½—8 oz.    708/1—5½ oz.    120—4½ oz.

542    9—6 oz.    910—4½ oz.    10—6 oz.    714—6½ oz. Low    714—6½ oz. High    550—7 oz.    35—12 oz.    1—14 oz. / 2—12 oz.

42—5 oz.    43—5 oz.    310—4½ oz. / 310—6 oz.    714—4 oz.    714—5½ oz.    30—6 oz.    31—4½ oz.    33—3½ oz.    37—6½ oz.

160/6—72 oz.    160/5—64 oz.    160/4—52 oz.    160/3—42 oz.    160/2—32 oz.    160/1—20 oz.

NEW MARTINSVILLE GLASS COMPANY      New Martinsville, W. Va.

*Many of these items were intended for hotel use; note the assortment of pitchers in the bottom row.*

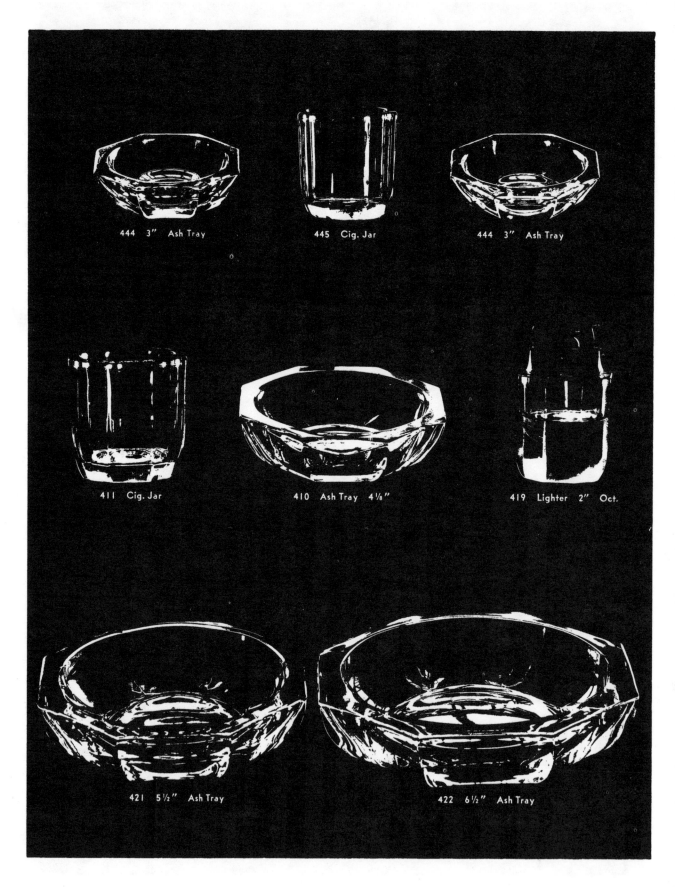

444 3" Ash Tray     445 Cig. Jar     444 3" Ash Tray

411 Cig. Jar     410 Ash Tray 4⅛"     419 Lighter 2" Oct.

421 5½" Ash Tray     422 6½" Ash Tray

MADE BY THE
NEW MARTINSVILLE GLASS CO.         VIKING         NEW MARTINSVILLE
WEST VIRGINIA

*This original catalogue sheet shows an assortment of ashtrays and open cigarette jars; note the No. 419 octagonal lighter, which needed only lighter fluid to make it operable.*

453 C/abra
5¼" High 9½" Wide

18 C/abra
6" High 7¼" Wide

37/3 C/abra
5½" High 7" Wide

425 3 Lt. C/abra
6½" High 13" Wide

MADE BY THE
NEW MARTINSVILLE GLASS CO.

VIKING

NEW MARTINSVILLE
WEST VIRGINIA

*Original catalogue sheet showing candleabra.*

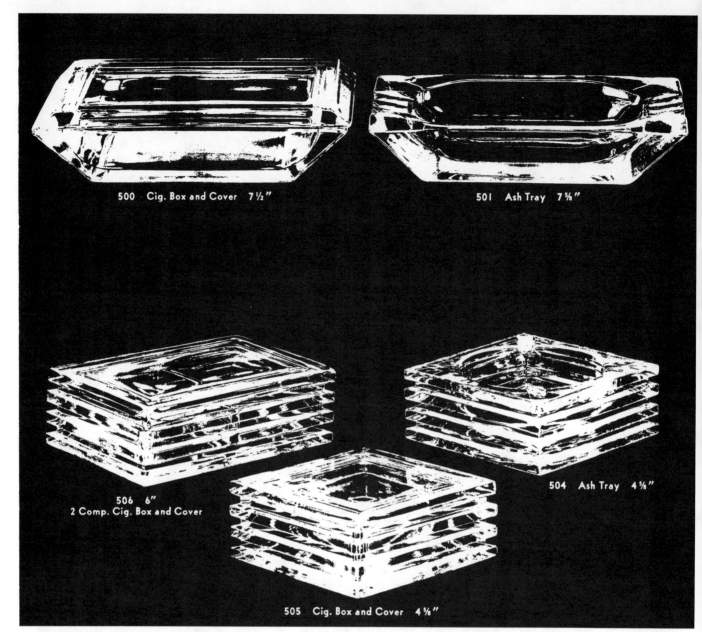

500   Cig. Box and Cover   7½"

501   Ash Tray   7⅝"

506   6"
2 Comp. Cig. Box and Cover

504   Ash Tray   4⅝"

505   Cig. Box and Cover   4⅝"

*These cigarette boxes and ashtrays were available only in crystal glass; wholesale prices ranged from $13.20 to $24.00 per dozen.*

these simply combined a pair of candlesticks (usually 4457 , but sometimes 4453) with a bowl from the No. 42 Radiance line or a bowl from the No. 45 Janice line. Attractive sets were also made when a pair of 4457 candlesticks was grouped with No. 703 13" flared bowl. Four different cuttings (457, 458, 459 and 463) are shown in original catalogue sheets.

### PATTERN LINES

In 1936, about two years prior to the sale of the plant in 1938, the New Martinsville firm had launched its No. 42 Radiance line. Like its predecessor, No. 37 (Moondrops), No. 42 Radiance was a success in terms of sales. As the previous chapter detailed, No. 42 Radiance continued in the line for some time, as several plate etchings were developed by Harry Barth between 1938 and 1940 to

add to the longevity of the pattern. In addition to the sales generated by No. 42 Radiance, the New Martinsville Glass Company benefitted from the introduction of two new pattern lines, which were known as the No. 44 (or 4400) line and the No. 45 (or 4500) Janice line.

Both the No. 44 line and the No. 45 line were in production throughout the early 1940s, and the moulds from both lines remained in the plant when the New Martinsville firm was reorganized as the Viking Glass Company in 1944. An early Viking price list dated April, 1945 (see p. 216), lists numerous pieces from these lines. From time to time between 1945 and 1986, moulds from the No. 44 and No. 45 lines were utilized by the Viking

*(continued on p. 200)*

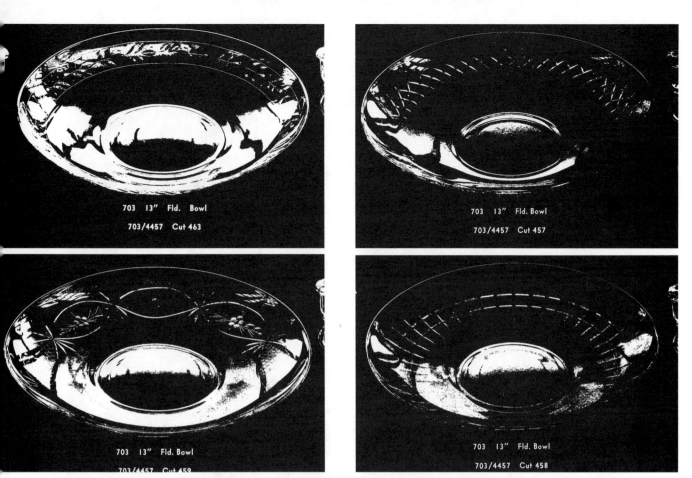

703 13" Fld. Bowl
703/4457 Cut 463

703 13" Fld. Bowl
703/4457 Cut 457

703 13" Fld. Bowl
703/4457 Cut 459

703 13" Fld. Bowl
703/4457 Cut 458

*No. 703 13" flared bowls with various cuttings.*

4453/29 6" Stick

4456/29 12" Bowl

4453/29 6" Stick

44/29 Cheese and Cracker 11"

44/29 Sugar and Cream W/Tray

*This original catalogue sheet shows several sets from the 4400 line with the No. 29 Florentine plate etching. The candlesticks from the console set in the top row remained in production for many years.*

# ETCHED No. 29 FLORENTINE PATTERN

37/29   12" 3 Compt. Relish

44/29   Cheese & Cracker

44/29   14" Plate
44/29   11" Plate

44/29   11" Hdl. Sandwich

44/29   3 Pc. Mayonnaise Set

44/29   11" Hdl. Nut Bowl

44/29   Sugar, Cream & Tray

44/29   3 Compt. Candy Box & Cover

44/29   11" Cake Salver

4457/29   2 light Candlestick

4456/29   13" Flared Bowl

4457/29   2 light Candlestick

4453/29   6" Candlestick   4454/29   13" Flared Bowl   4453/29   6" Candlestick

44/29   10" Flared Bowl
44/29   11" Plate

**NEW MARTINSVILLE GLASS COMPANY**          New Martinsville, W. Va.

*The No. 29 Florentine plate etching was available on many articles in the 4400 line, as shown in this original catalogue sheet. The 37/29 relish in the upper left is a holdover from the earlier No. 37 (Moondrops) line.*

# ETCHED No. 30 PATTERN

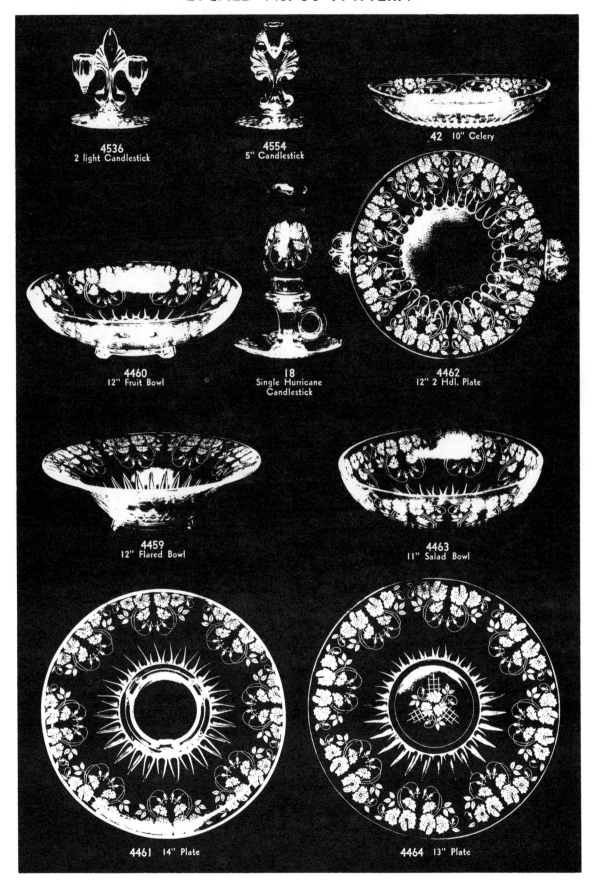

**4536** 2 light Candlestick

**4554** 5" Candlestick

**42** 10" Celery

**4460** 12" Fruit Bowl

**18** Single Hurricane Candlestick

**4462** 12" 2 Hdl. Plate

**4459** 12" Flared Bowl

**4463** 11" Salad Bowl

**4461** 14" Plate

**4464** 13" Plate

NEW MARTINSVILLE GLASS COMPANY          New Martinsville, W. Va.

*Most of the articles in this original catalogue sheet featuring the Wild Rose plate etching are from the No. 44 line.*

PREMIER SHOWING At Pittsburgh

WAKEFIELD
A new etching pattern

Also Special Promotional Items for Spring Sales

At the Pittsburgh Show you will find that Room 690 is headquarters for promotional numbers. The New Martin Crystal is introducing to its line many new items of acknowledged popularity. In addition to the promotional pieces, you will see the Wakefield etching in a full range of tableware . . . and you will see a new and delightful array of those little, quick-selling novelty items. See them January 8th to 16th, Hotel William Penn, Room 690.

*New* MARTIN *Crystal*

ALSO INTRODUCING MANY NEW NOVELTY ITEMS.

*This ad (from* Crockery and Glass Journal, *January, 1940) shows a large No. 45 Janice plate with the Wakefield plate etching; note the references to "New Martin Crystal," especially that in the lower right.*

**4543** 3 pc. Mayonnaise Set    **413** 5" Ash Tray    **418** 4" Ash Tray    **410** 4" Octagon Ash Tray    **411** 3" Octagon Cigarette Holder

**4541** 6" Candy Box and Cover    **4545** Ind. Sugar, Cream and Tray    **4561/47** Canape Set    **4548** 3 pc. Condiment Set

**4567** Guest Set    **4544** Sugar, Cream and Tray    **4554** 5" Candlestick    **412** 5 pc. Cigarette Set

**4555** 13" Flared Bowl    **4536** 2 light Candlestick    **4551** 11" Oval Bowl 8" Wide

**4550** 7" Footed Vase    **4552** 11" Handled Basket    **4565** 9" Ball Vase

NEW MARTINSVILLE GLASS COMPANY      New Martinsville, W. Va.

*Original catalogue sheet showing Janice items.*

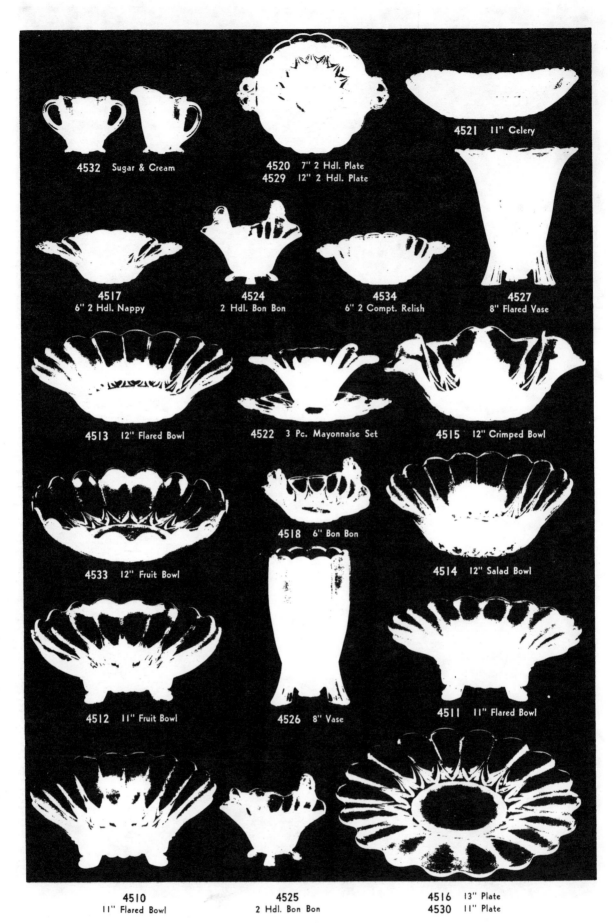

4532  Sugar & Cream

4520  7" 2 Hdl. Plate
4529  12" 2 Hdl. Plate

4521  11" Celery

4517
6" 2 Hdl. Nappy

4524
2 Hdl. Bon Bon

4534
6" 2 Compt. Relish

4527
8" Flared Vase

4513  12" Flared Bowl

4522  3 Pc. Mayonnaise Set

4515  12" Crimped Bowl

4533  12" Fruit Bowl

4518  6" Bon Bon

4514  12" Salad Bowl

4512  11" Fruit Bowl

4526  8" Vase

4511  11" Flared Bowl

4510
11" Flared Bowl

4525
2 Hdl. Bon Bon

4516  13" Plate
4530  11" Plate

NEW MARTINSVILLE GLASS COMPANY

New Martinsville, W. Va.

*Original catalogue sheet showing Janice items.*

198

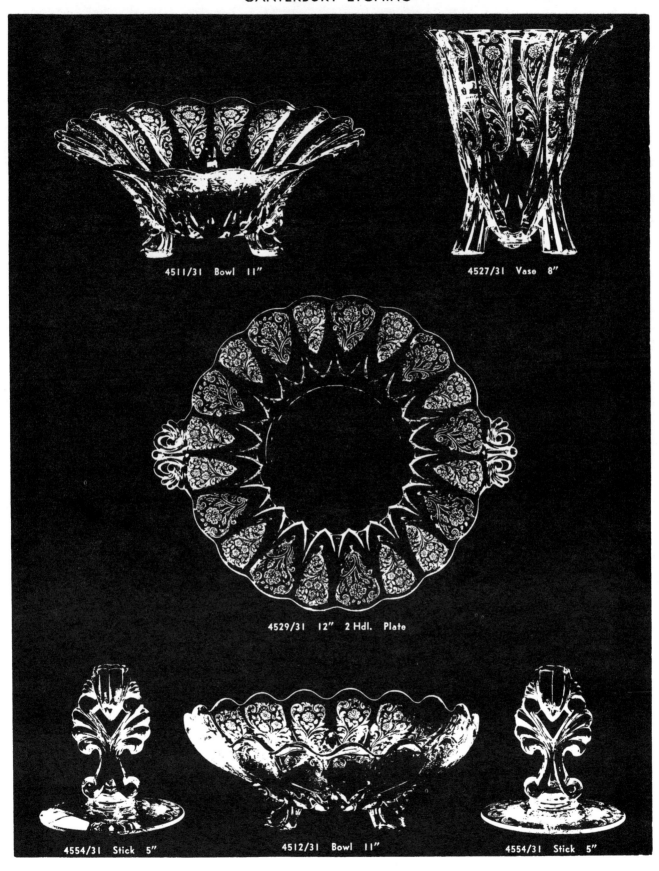

4511/31  Bowl  11"

4527/31  Vase  8"

4529/31  12"  2 Hdl.  Plate

4554/31  Stick  5"

4512/31  Bowl  11"

4554/31  Stick  5"

MADE BY THE
NEW MARTINSVILLE GLASS CO.

VIKING

NEW MARTINSVILLE
WEST VIRGINIA

*Original catalogue sheet showing Janice items with the Canterbury (No. 31) plate etching.*

Glass Company to produce various articles. Furthermore, quite a few items from the No. 42 Radiance line appear in company catalogues from the 1950s and 1960s. A plate etching called Prelude was developed by Viking about 1947-48, and all pieces with the Prelude motif, whether from the No. 42 Radiance or the No. 44 or No. 45 lines, can definitely be dated as post-1944.

The No. 44 line was probably introduced in late 1938 or sometime in early 1939. Original factory records and catalogue sheets indicate that this line was sometimes also called the 4400 line. The Millers dubbed it simply "Teardrop." Despite the fact that No. 44 (Teardrop) was a relatively lengthy line containing an assortment of items, it is generally unknown among the ranks of collectors today who are interested in depression-era glass.

The relatively plain surface of articles in the No. 44 (Teardrop) line was ideal for the plate etchings then being developed and marketed by the New Martinsville firm. Many pieces from the No. 44 (Teardrop) line were decorated with a plate etching called Florentine, which also carried the factory designation No. 29. The Wild Rose plate etching (No. 30), which had been used on the earlier No. 42 Radiance line, was also used on pieces from the No. 44 line.

Original catalogue sheets show the following articles in the No. 44 (Teardrop) line: cheese and cracker set; sugar and cream with tray; three-piece mayonnaise set; plates in various sizes (11," 13" and 14"); handled sandwich tray; handled nut bowl; three-compartment candy box with cover; and 11" cake salver. Similar catalogue sheets show some items with four-digit numerical designations; the first two digits, of course, are always "44." These pieces are listed: 4453 6" candlestick; 4454 13" flared bowl; 4456 12" bowl or 13" flared bowl; 4457 5 1/2" 2-light candleholder; 4460 12" fruit bowl; 4461 14" plate; 4462 12" 2-handle plate; 4463 12" salad bowl; and 4464 13" plate. The candlestick and candleholder (4453 and 4457, respectively) were in production for many years, and one or both appeared in catalogues issued by the Viking Glass Company for quite some time.

The No. 45 line, which also had Janice as its original name, probably debuted in 1940. This was an extensive tableware line, and, like No. 44, it was destined to remain in production for many years. One of the first ads to show No. 45 Janice appeared in the January, 1940, issue of *Crockery and Glass Journal*. Although the name of the pattern was not given, this ad showed the Wakefield plate etching and mentioned "New Martin Crystal," complete with distinctive typography and a line drawing of a martin (see p. 196).

Most of the No. 45 Janice tableware pieces were designated by four-digit numbers which always have "45" as the first two digits. Former employees often referred to Janice as the "4500 line." Original price lists and catalogue sheets show these pieces:

4510 11" flared bowl
4511 11" flared bowl
4512 11" fruit bowl
4513 12" flared bowl
4514 12" salad bowl
4515 12" crimped bowl
4516 13" plate
4517 6" 2-handled nappy
4518 6" bon bon
4520 7" 2-handled plate
4521 11" celery
4522 3 pc. mayonnaise set
4523 7" mayonnaise plate and ladle
4524 2-handled bon bon
4525 2-handled bon bon
4526 8" vase
4527 8" flared vase
4529 12" 2-handled plate
4530 11" plate
4531 10" bowl
4532 sugar and cream
4533 12" fruit bowl
4534 2-compartment relish
4535 10" fruit bowl
4536 2-light candelabra
4537 8" salad plate
4538 15" plate
4539 15" rolled edge torte plate
4540 syrup jug with dripcut top
4541 6" candy box and cover
4543 3 pc. mayonnaise set
4544 sugar, cream and tray
4545 individual sugar, cream and tray
4548 3 pc. condiment set
4550 7" footed vase
4551 11" oval bowl
4552 11" handled basket
4554 5" candlestick
4555 13" flared bowl
4561 canape set
4565 9" ball vase
4567 guest set

137 - 2SJ

452
FROSTED WITH CLEAR BALL

237 - 2SJ

4550 - 2SJ

111 - 2SJ

412 - 2SJ

443 - J

137 - 2SJ

4543 - 1SJ

4566 - J

4528 - 2SJ

662 - J

454 - SJ

456 - S - J
SET

4543 - 1SJ

498
J

**NEW MARTINSVILLE GLASS CO.**

*Note the "SJ" (Swan Janice) pieces shown here. Compare the four-digit numbers on this original catalogue page with those shown on pp. 197-198.*

4551 - 2 SJ

412 - 1 SJ

4565 - 2 SJ

443 - BJ

4521 - 1 SJ

4521 - 2 SJ

4541 - 1 CSJ

443 - RJ

443 - 1 SJ

4541 - 1 HSJ

477 - 7½"

4541 - 1 SJ

475 - 6"

4551 - 1 SJ

476 - 6"

*More items from the "SJ" portion of the 4500 line. The three articles near the bottom (Nos. 475, 476 and 477) were definitely in production in 1943.*

202

Of course, several of these pieces, such as 4526 and 4527, were made from the same mould and then subjected to different finishing techniques to alter the shape of the pressed piece. Likewise, the 4451 bowl was the basis for the 4552 basket, and the 4524 and 4525 bon bons began with the same pressed piece. The 4514 12" salad bowl was the basis for three other items—4513, 4515 and 4533. A few other articles, such as the 4528 cheese and cracker set, were soon added to the line.

Among the most interesting constituents of the No. 45 Janice line are the pieces which feature graceful swan necks. Two original catalogue pages, probably c. 1943, show more than a dozen of these, ranging from small sugar/creamer sets to covered candy boxes and large vases. Articles were designated by the typical four-digit number followed by an additional number ("1" or "2" to denote the number of swan necks) and the letters "SJ" (denoting "Swan Janice"). Thus, the 4465 ball vase becomes 4465-2SJ and the 4541 6" candy box with cover becomes 4541-1SJ. Incidentally, this may have been the beginning of the manufacture of swans at New Martinsville. A Viking Glass Company publication released in 1950, *From American Sands and Artists Hands: A Story with Pictures about the Creation of America's Hand Made Glass*, mentions "Viking's famous Swans" and illustrates several of them.

After the No. 45 Janice line was well-established, the New Martinsville firm apparently formed console sets by combining bowls from this line with a pair of candlesticks (either 4453 or 4457) from the earlier No. 44 (Teardrop) line. Several light cutting motifs—No. 401 and No. 409—which had been used on the No. 44 (Teardrop) line can also be found on pieces of No. 45 Janice. The 4520 (7" 2-handled plate) was used as the basis for an item featuring a representation of the Iams Funeral Home in New Martinsville. The creamer and sugar from the No. 45 line can also be found with decoration applied by the Lotus Glass Co. of Barnesville, Ohio (for the Lotus's "Sylvania" motif on New Martinsville's No. 45 line, see Weatherman's *Colored Glassware of the Depression Era 2*).

It is difficult to ascertain the relative success of the No. 44 (Teardrop) and No. 45 Janice lines. In the January, 1940, issue of the *American Flint*, Lloyd Prim (who was also known as "Punky") wrote that the New Martinsville plant was "sailing along on an average of about eight turns a week,

## NEW MARTINSVILLE

### By William L. Cross

Having been appointed Press Secretary, I will try and let the trade know how things are going in the Parlor City. This little city was named the Parlor City by a movie actress by the name of Gloria Swanson, and I think it is deserving of its name. We have a clean little city, good streets, good water system, own our own electric system, have good schools, and a number of good churches; two good banks, and one of the best little glass plants in the Ohio Valley. We have more English speaking citizens per capita than any city in the Ohio Valley, and everyone is proud of our Parlor City.

That much for our city, now I will get along with some news. Work here for the past few weeks has been two and three days, but the future looks better. We will get four days this week and we are told we will get at least four days a week now, at least for a while.

We have lost some of our members recently. David H. White is employed at Paden City, W. Va.; Charles Powell is employed at Williamstown, W. Va., and Lloyd Punky Prim is in Morgantown, W. Va. Thomas Haught is employed at Buffalo, N. Y. He is not working at the trade. Good luck to all the boys and we hope that circumstances will permit us to be together sometime.

We had a little trouble here recently and Guy Alexander was here to settle the dispute. Everything was ironed out and forgotten, and things are moving along in fine shape. Come again, Guy, we are always glad to see you.

We were very sorry to learn of the sad misfortune of Sim Garret. He was employed at Williamstown, W. Va., when he had a stroke and fell from his foot board. He was a blower. He is improving a little and we hope he is soon able to be out.

Well, the Democrats are happy as they have F. D. R. to vote for again for his third term, and if some of the predictions are correct, he will be our next President. Well, our convention is another paragraph in the history of our organization, and we have a few officers who have been elevated to higher positions in our trade offices and we are confident that they have the ability to perform their respective duties, and no matter how hard their task may be, we hope they will be inspired by our good and sincere best wishes that their duties will be a pleasure to them. I take this means of saying "hello" to all my friends in the trade and I am signing off for this time.

*From the* American Flint *(August, 1940).*

and we do not hear anyone complaining." A month later, he reported that the skilled glassworkers had worked just five turns in nearly three weeks, January 1-18, although the mould makers and cutters were on full time. By late summer, however, glassworker William L. Cross was quite optimistic, hoping for steady work "four days a week."

In July, 1940, Jay Ackerman registered his design for a candlestick (#121,407 granted July 9, 1940), which was assigned to the New Martinsville firm. Made for many years as the No. 415 candlestick, this graceful article was in the line quite some time, and variations of it were made by the Viking Glass Company as well as its successor, Dalzell-Viking. An original catalogue sheet, c. 1943, shows an attractive console set which combined the No. 416 rectangular bowl with four No. 415 candlesticks. In September, 1940, Cross said that the firm had started its ten-pot furnace, bringing "the capacity to twenty-two pots, and we are starting a night shift at this writing" (*American Flint*, September, 1940). Charles Merritt came from Morgantown to replace Harry Barth as general manager.

The year of 1941 was, from all reports, a good one for the New Martinsville Glass Company, although it did not begin with high hopes. In the February, 1941, issue of the *American Flint*, glassworker Harold A. Neely wrote that "this is one year that we did not hear a number of reports of a large amount of orders being received at the glass

**New Martinsville Glass Co., "Raindrops"**

*This photograph of New Martinsville's No. 1* *Raindrops line appeared in* **China, Glass and Lamps** *(May, 1942).*

show held in Pittsburgh, Pa., and we are wondering if this is a good sign, because for the last several preceding years we would hear that there were so many orders that there was no hope of filling them all." Neely recalled that 1940 had started out well, but "we would work good for a few weeks and then work would get slack," and, by the end of May, "the factory would be down to two or three days a week."

By March, Neely noted that work was "fairly good" with "10 press and 1 blow shop" turning out what Neely described as "heavy cut and polished glassware." He suggested that such ware had been

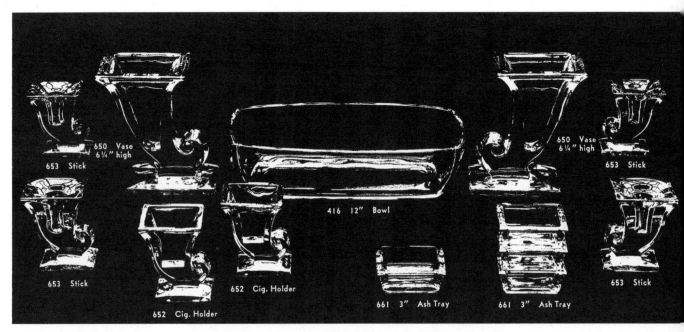

*This original catalogue sheet shows New Martinsville's "Cornucopia" line. The No. 416 rectangular bowl was also used with other candlesticks to form various console sets.*

Labels on images (top row): Cordial · C/Tail · Wine · Goblet · Sau/Champ. · Sherbet

Labels on images (bottom row): 2 oz. Whiskey · 5 oz. O.F. · 10 oz. Tumbler · 14 oz. Tumbler · 12 oz. Tumbler · 7 oz. O.F.

*Original catalogue sheet showing stemware and drinking glasses in the No. 14 line.*

imported into the United States from Europe before the onset of WWII (*American Flint*, March, 1941). In August, Edward C. Metts reported that the firm had "great expectations for this Fall and Winter," and he provided this insight into some methods of manufacture: "We have been trying a lot of new moulds and making as high as ten different shapes out of one article" (*American Flint*, August, 1941). Metts might have been discussing the 4400 (Teardrop) line, but it seems more likely that the Swedish-style "Krystal Klear" pieces were the basis for his assertion.

In December, 1941, an illustrated ad in a trade journal showed "The Three Bears" and mentioned "new decorative pieces in our heavy, lustrous VIKING CRYSTAL." The ad lists "Figures, Smoker's Ware, Cornucopias, Bowls, Vases, Candlesticks, [and] Book Ends." The "Three Bears" and the book ends are discussed later in this chapter. The mention of cornucopias indicates that the firm's "Cornucopia" line—a series

of book ends, vases, candlesticks, cigarette holders, ash trays and bowls—was in production at this time.

In May, 1942, the trade publication *China and Glass* made mention of New Martinsville's No. 14 line, which was apparently also called "Raindrop." This line is, at first glance, somewhat similar to other firm's "hobnail" styles, although New Martinsville's version is rather low and well-rounded. The "hobs" are arranged neatly in rows with little space between them.

Although the photo of No. 14 Raindrops which appeared in the trade journal showed several tableware articles, only stemware and "gift items" were pictured in the company's catalogue, which did not use the name Raindrops. The No. 14 line was primarily stemware and beverage tumblers, and six sizes of each can be found. Stemware include cordial, sherbet, cocktail, saucer champagne, wine and goblet. The range of beverage tumblers consists of a 2 oz. whiskey, two sizes of

14/6  3 Crimp.  Bon Bon  5"

14/9  3"  3 Crimp.  Vase

14/7  3½"  Ivy Bowl

14/8  6 Crimp.  Bon Bon  7"

14/5  2"  Hat

14/11  Compote
3" High  5½" Dia.

14/1  4"  Hat

14/10  Crimped Compote
3¼" High  5" Dia.

14/2
5"  Fld.  6 Crimp.  Vase

14/3
5½"  Cupt.  6 Crimp. Vase

14/4  6"  Compote

MADE BY THE
NEW MARTINSVILLE GLASS CO.

V I K I N G

NEW MARTINSVILLE
WEST VIRGINIA

*Original catalogue sheet showing gift items in the No. 14 line. The three compotes were made from moulds used for stemware, and the other articles were fashioned from various drinking glass items.*

"Old Fashioned" glasses (5 oz. and 7 oz.), and three sizes of tumblers—10 oz., 12 oz., and 14 oz. The stemware and tumblers were low-priced, ranging from $4.00 to $4.80 per dozen (wholesale), depending upon size.

The gift items in the No. 14 Raindrops line were made from moulds used for standard stemware or tumblers. The 14 oz. tumbler could be finished in various ways to produce either the No. 14/2 5" flared and crimped vase or the No. 14/3 5 1/2" cupped and crimped vase. Likewise, the saucer champagne was the basis for the No. 14/10 and the No. 14/11 compotes. The No. 14 line was made only in crystal in 1942 and for several years thereafter; items are listed as "Viking's Antique" in a price list dated April, 1945, from the Viking Glass Company. Later, pieces in a variety of colors were produced by Viking as part of the firm's "Yesteryear" line.

The January 4, 1943, issue of *Retailing* showed five articles in New Martinsville's "Krystal Klear" line. These are rather heavy crystal pieces, quite representative of the "Swedish" style to which the firm then aspired. These were identified by three-digit numbers in the 470s. The mould for the base of the No. 472 candy box was also used to create three different vases (Nos. 475, 476 and 478) as well as the No. 477 comport. Later, handled baskets and a few other articles were added to this short line, which was re-numbered as the 800 line and also called "Christina" in catalogues issued by the Viking Glass Company. There may have been additional items included within the Krystal Klear line. Occasionally, one finds a piece of New Martinsville glass, such as an animal figurine, with its Krystal Klear label intact.

*Krystal Klear label.*

In late January, 1943, the New Martinsville plant was damaged by flooding on the Ohio River. Once cleanup was finished, the firm began working "about three days per week" under new general manager Max Biberthaler (*American Flint,*

February, 1943). The 10-pot furnace was fired about a month later, and several local women joined the plant's work force as "carrying-in boys" to replace men who had entered military service.

## PRIVATE MOULDS

During the 1938-1944 period, private mould work was important to the economic well-being of the New Martinsville Glass Company. The firm's mouldmaking department sometimes made moulds for a customer and then the hot metal division produced the glassware to the customer's specifications. Sometimes, a customer's mould would come to New Martinsville from an independent mouldmaking establishment, such as Weishar's Island Mould Company in Wheeling or one of the shops operated by the Overmyer Mould Company.

Often, a mould was shipped to New Martinsville from another glass plant, for the customer who owned the mould felt that glass could be produced more economically or more efficiently by the New Martinsville firm. Because the customer owned the mould (and could move it to another glassmaking establishment as long as his financial "account" was clear), it may be difficult to determine those articles which were made for brief periods in New Martinsville or those items which were made in New Martinsville as well as in other glass plants, such as the nearby Paden City Glass Manufacturing Company.

Fortunately, several ledger-type books were kept in the mouldmaking department at New Martinsville. These records (combined with the memories of several employees) offer a picture, albeit incomplete, of the private mould activity in New Martinsville from the late 1930s to the mid-1940s. They show that much private mould work consisted of smoker's supplies, giftware or lamp parts and that numerous figurines were also made.

Many private mould customers were in the giftware business. Typically, these enterprises maintained showrooms in New York City or Chicago where prospective customers could examine the firm's giftware lines, which consisted of metal and ceramic items as well as glass. Among those listed in the mould record books are these: Warren L. Kessler, Inc.; Marks and Rosenfield; Irving W. Rice; and Wiel Freeman (a division of the Wiel Ceramic Co.).

Other private mould customers were in the lighting goods trade. For them, the New Martinsville firm produced shades and/or columns

475 Vase 6"

472 C/Box 9" High

474 Vase 6½"

478 Vase 5"

477 Comport 7½"

*The mould for the No. 472 candy box was the basis for all the other articles shown here.*

which were shipped back to the customer so that the lamps could be assembled, often with metal parts or wiring obtained from other suppliers. Among those listed in the mould record books are the following: Bertman Electric Co.; Golden Electrical Products, Inc.; Edward P. Paul Co.; and the Universal Electric Art Company. Another lighting goods customer was the Tibor firm, which shipped more than a dozen moulds for lamp parts to New Martinsville in June, 1941. About five years later, these moulds were sent to the John E. Kemple Glass Co. in East Palestine, Ohio, so that the lamp parts could be made in opal glass for Tibor by the Kemple firm.

Several former New Martinsville employees recall Theodore "Teddy" Model (pronounced "Mo-dell"), an affable, well-dressed gentleman from New York City who was "a sharp operator" in the giftware trade and visited the glass plant from time to time. The New Martinsville firm made ashtrays and cigarette boxes for Model, but he was particularly interested in figurines, especially those in the shapes of various animals. Several other private mould customers—Ebeling and Reuss (New York City) and Malcolm's House and Garden Store (Baltimore)—were also involved with animal-shaped figurines. Perhaps the successes of their private mould customers with these kinds of figurines led the New Martinsville Glass Company into this line for themselves.

In 1940-41, the New Martinsville plant received a number of private moulds from the New York firm of Henry Amdur and Son. Mould records list more than 30 different articles, chiefly ashtrays, cigarette boxes, bases for cigarette lighters and trays. These items were produced for about five years, and an entry in a mould record book notes that "All Amdur Moulds" were "shipped to New York Aug. 1, 1945."

## FIGURINES

As the previous section of this chapter has indicated, the New Martinsville firm made figurines, particularly those in the shapes of various animals, for several of its private mould customers. It seems likely that the management of the New Martinsville plant soon decided to make and market its own figurines, perhaps hoping to capitalize on the apparently strong sales realized by their private mould customers. In this regard, some moulds which belonged to private mould customers may have been purchased or otherwise acquired by the glass company. The New

Martinsville firm may, of course, also have produced new moulds which were close copies of a successful private mould figurine, since these objects were not protected by design patents.

Several figurines had, of course, been made at New Martinsville in earlier years. Among these are the Police Dog lamp base (see Fig. 324), the Elephant (both incense burner and cigarette holder; see Figs. 317 and 319) and the Dancing Lady flower frog (see Fig. 323). The distinctive dog lamp base was re-issued as a figurine and designated the No. 733 Police Dog.

Figurines became an important part of the New Martinsville Glass Company's production during 1941-1944, and many of these objects were later made in various colors by the Viking Glass Company. Incidentally, these articles were usually listed as "Book Ends" in company catalogues or price lists; the smaller figurines appear on "Miscellaneous" pages. Readers interested in various figurines made at New Martinsville and elsewhere should consult Lee Garmon's and Dick Spencer's *Glass Animals of the Depression Era* (pp. 146-166); this book is particularly valuable for its coverage of re-issues by Viking and its successor, Dalzell-Viking. The information reported below, much of which comes from original mould records and factory catalogues, will serve to establish beginning dates for the production of some figurines, especially those made from moulds which were crafted in New Martinsville's mouldmaking shop.

The first mention of New Martinsville's animal figurines can be found in a trade journal ad from December, 1941. The copy alludes to "new decorative pieces in our heavy, lustrous VIKING CRYSTAL" and mentions "Figures, Smoker's Ware, Cornucopias, Bowls, Vases, Candlesticks, [and] Book Ends." A small illustration shows "The Three Bears," a trio of solid crystal figurines now called "Papa Bear," "Mama Bear" and "Baby Bear." A "small bear" appears in the mould records (completed in June, 1941, this became the No. 487 Bear), as do No. 489 Papa Bear and No. 488 Mama bear (both were completed in August, 1941). On some catalogue sheets, each is simply called "Bear" and differentiated by size; on other catalogue sheets, the appellations "Daddy Bear" and "Mama Bear" may be found. At $36.00 per dozen (wholesale), these were among the firm's most expensive animal figurines. The No. 487 Bear was also combined with the wheelbarrow-

*This portion of an original catalogue sheet shows New Martinsville's bears.*

489 Bear 4½" High 6½" Long    487 Bear 3" High 4¼" Long    488 Bear 4¾" High 5¾" Long

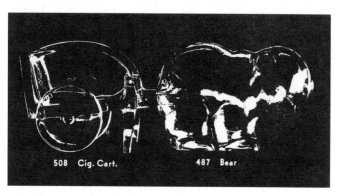

508 Cig. Cart.    487 Bear

*From an original catalogue sheet. The Bear and the Cart are separate pieces.*

like No. 508 Cigarette Cart on an original catalogue sheet devoted to "Smokers' Supplies."

A mould for small Chicks designed so that they were "Pressed 4 at a time" was completed in February, 1942, as was a mould for a "Rooster book end." These were the No. 667 Chicks and the No. 668 Rooster, respectively. A No. 669 Hen completed the group of barnyard fowl (see Garmon and Spencer, p. 151). The No. 670 Squirrel book end with base and the No. 674 Squirrel (without base) probably date from about the same time, and they are found together with the Rooster, Hen and Chicks on the same catalogue sheets. The No. 671 Shell candlestick is pictured with them.

The No. 452 Seal book end was available in crystal or with a satin, "frosted" finish (produced by hydrofluoric acid). The entire book end might be frosted, or the ball balanced on the seal's nose could be left clear. A September, 1944, ad in *Crockery and Glass Journal* illustrated the No. 452 Seal book ends, although they had surely been in production for several years prior. The mould for the Seal was modified, turning the ball into a candleholder; this article was known as the No. 452 Seal Stick, and it was apparently available only in crystal.

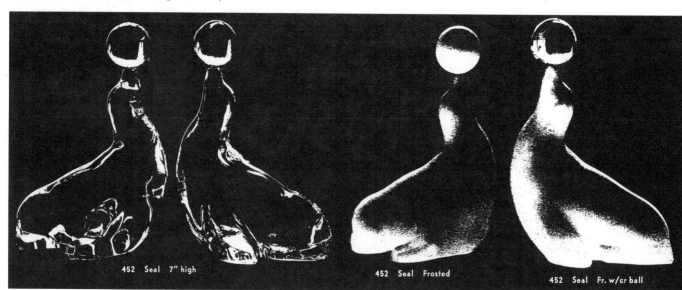

452 Seal 7" high    452 Seal Frosted    452 Seal Fr. w/cr ball

*This portion of an original catalogue sheet shows the Seal figurine.*

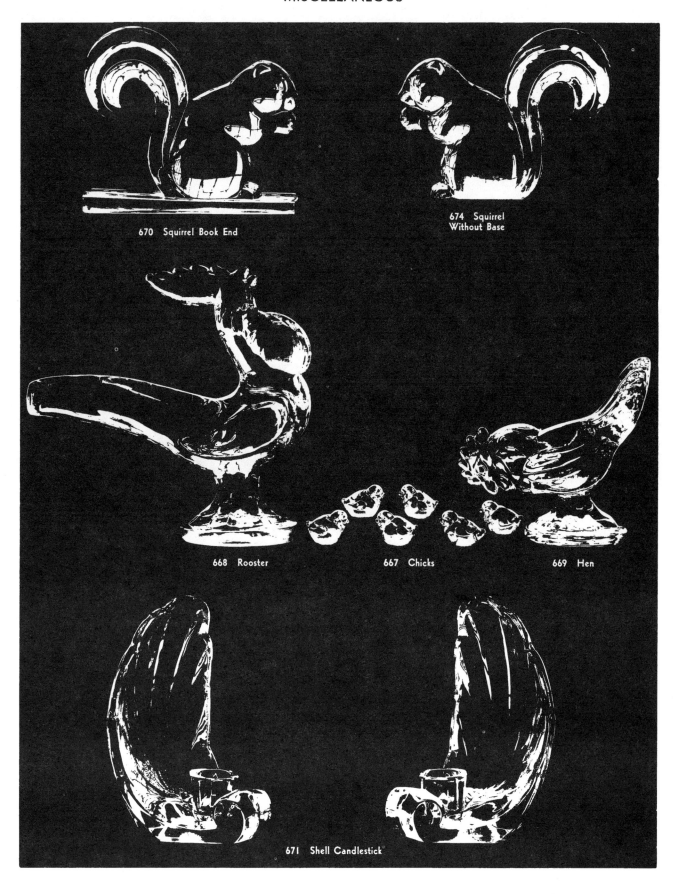

670 Squirrel Book End

674 Squirrel
Without Base

668 Rooster

667 Chicks

669 Hen

671 Shell Candlestick

MADE BY THE
NEW MARTINSVILLE GLASS CO.

VIKING

NEW MARTINSVILLE
WEST VIRGINIA

*Original catalogue sheet.*

According to original records, Ebeling and Reuss had their private moulds for a "101 Peacock" and a "1010 Bird" at New Martinsville in 1940; a "Horse Head Book End" is also listed but is neither described nor dated. A letter (dated November 22, 1944) from Malcolm's House and Garden Store in Baltimore to the New Martinsville Glass Co. indicates that Malcolm's then had four moulds in the New Martinsville plant, including "Fish Bookends" and "Gazelle Bookends" (the other two items are a "Goose Sauce Server" and the ladle for same). These same four items are listed for Malcolm's in the New Martinsville Glass Co.'s mould records, which include a note that another mould, described only as "Malcolm's Horse," was shipped to Paden City on February 12, 1943. The "Malcolm's Horse" may have been made in New Martinsville's mould shop, for an entry indicates that such a mould was completed on February 19, 1941, at a cost of $48.64.

The most extensive entries in the original mould records concern Wiel Freeman, a subsidiary of the Wiel Ceramic Company. In September, 1940, these moulds were received at New Martinsville: "Scroll Book End," "Horse Book End" and "Shell Vase Book End." The latter is surely the Nautilus Bookend (see Garmon and Spencer, p. 159). The Scroll book end may have been the New Martinsville Glass Company's inspiration for the interesting Man-In-The-Moon candlesticks (Garmon and Spencer, p. 158).

The "Horse Book End" is not described in the original factory mould records, but it is probably the rearing horse which resembles those made by the L. E. Smith Glass Company and the Fostoria Glass Company (for a comparison of these, see Garmon and Spencer, p. 231). According to "Book Ends: Summary [of] Move and Wage Agreements," a document prepared by the National Association of Manufacturers of Pressed and Blown Glassware (February 4, 1944), the New Martinsville Glass Company was making this article as early as November, 1940. Workers were required to make 200 of them in a five-hour turn, and the presser was paid $5.49; the gatherer and the finisher made $4.39 and $4.94, respectively.

A Wiel Freeman "Peacock mould" is listed, but the only information recorded is its shipment to New York on April 30, 1946. Two other Wiel Freeman moulds are, however, easily identified from the original mould records, namely, the

*New Martinsville's Horse.*

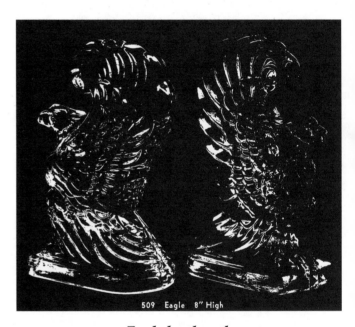

509 Eagle 8" High

*Eagle book end.*

"Tiger Book End" (see Garmon and Spencer, p. 148) and the "Eagle Book End" (see Garmon and Spencer, p. 156). The mould for the Eagle book end was made in the New Martinsville mould shop (at a cost of $163.21), and it was completed on August 5, 1941. The Tiger book end does not seem to appear in extant factory catalogues or price lists, but the No. 509 Eagle is pictured.

Another brief entry in the original mould records for Marks and Rosenfield mentions the "Book End Lady Head." The records reveal that this mould was made by the Overmyer Mould Co. and was received in New Martinsville on September 6, 1940; it was "shipped away" to some

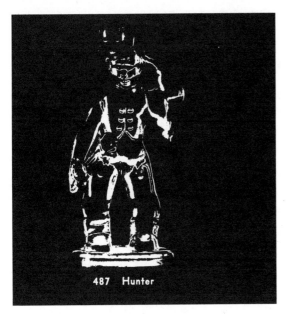

*Hunter figurine.*

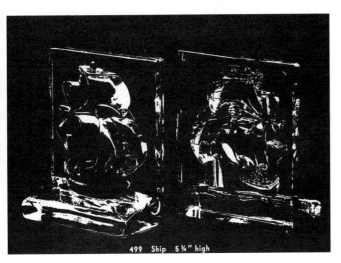

*Ship book ends.*

unmentioned destination just two years later (September 8, 1942). These are probably those called Lady Face today (see Garmon and Spencer, p. 158); they do not seem to appear in extant factory catalogues or price lists, so they may have been made solely for Marks and Rosenfield.

The so-called Woodsman was originally designated "Hunter," and an entry concerning this mould is dated November, 1941, in the mould department's records. An entry made about the same time for the "Ship Book End" is certainly the Clipper Ship book ends (see Garmon and Spencer, p. 159). Both the No. 487 Hunter and the No. 499 Ship are in factory catalogues and price lists. The No. 487 Hunter may have either a round or a square base.

Original mould records indicate clearly that the two Pelicans (see Garmon and Spencer, pp. 155-156), a Pigeon, and several Pigs (see Garmon and

Spencer, pp. 151-152) were not made until after the New Martinsville Glass Company became known as the Viking Glass Company in June, 1944. Furthermore, a Viking catalogue (c. 1947-48) illustrates the following animal figurines: No. 435 Baby Seal; No. 710 Elephant; No. 716 Wolfhound; No. 762 Large Pig and No. 763 Small Pig; No. 764 Large Rabbit and No. 765 Small Rabbit; and No. 766 Porpoise. Some of these, of course, could have been in production when the New Martinsville Glass Company became known as Viking, although this seems unlikely. Except for the No. 435 Baby Seal, all of these have been assigned ware numbers higher than those figurines known to have been made prior to mid-1944.

The Starfish book end attributed to New Martinsville by Garmon and Spencer (p. 147) was made at Paden City beginning in late 1939, according to "Book Ends: Summary [of] Move and Wage Agreements," a document prepared by the National Association of Manufacturers of Pressed and Blown Glassware (February 4, 1944). Other glass firms—such as Cambridge, Fostoria and Heisey—also made animal figurines, and a complete account of the production of all of these interesting articles has yet to be undertaken.

## VIKING GLASS IS BORN

The change of name from the New Martinsville Glass Company to the Viking Glass Company was not a sudden one. In fact, this contemplated alteration was first announced publicly nearly three years before it was finally accomplished!

A story in the December 29, 1941, issue of the magazine *Retailing* (Home Furnishings Edition) revealed that the factory was to be "completely revamped, remodeled and modernized in preparation for ... an entirely different field of glass production ...." The new venture, according to this article, was "the manufacture of hand-made, quality glassware of the heavy Swedish type." In keeping with the new lines, the article continued, "the name of the company is to be changed in the near future to the Viking Glass Co. in order that its name will be more closely identified with the kind of ware it will specialize in from now on."

For some time, the firm's advertising and catalogs had reflected that the "Viking" glass line was a key product of the New Martinsville Glass Company. Several trade marks were used. In 1943, a stylized footed drinking glass appeared with the words "Viking Glass" superimposed, along with

*(continued on p. 217)*

# this Trade-Mark means

# "made in America"

American craftsmen and manufacturers have never been long in surpassing quality and design of foreign goods, and it is to the great credit of American merchants that they have aggressively merchandized and advertised American products, FIRST. Thus we have acquired a standard of living for all far beyond any in the history of man.

## New Martinsville Glass Co.

### NEW MARTINSVILLE, WEST VIRGINIA

This is the second in a series of New Martinsville Glass Company advertisements designed to show the close relationship between the American Manufacturer, and the American Retailer.

*From* **China and Glass** *(October, 1943).*

214

West Virginia is one of the great glass states in America. It is to the credit of merchants in the United States that they have always preferred to merchandise American made goods. Their cooperation has brought about the supremacy of Our Country's manufacturers.

American quality and style has pleased the home makers in Our Land, and American artisanship has achieved a definite superiority. Advanced methods of manufacture have built volume production which in turn has rewarded the American workmen with many times the pay received in foreign countries.

# *New Martinsville Glass Co.*
## *NEW MARTINSVILLE, WEST VIRGINIA*
### DISPLAY OFFICES:

225 Fifth Ave., New York City     1466 Merchandise Mart, Chicago, Ill.     150 Post Street, San Francisco, Calif.

This is the third in a series of New Martinsville Glass Company advertisements designed to show the close relationship between the American Manufacturer and the American Retailer.

**From Crockery and Glass Journal *(October, 1943).***

# Viking Glass Company
New Martinsville, W. Va.      APRIL, 1945

ITEMS THAT MAY BE SOLD THE LAST SIX MONTHS OF 1945
All prices per dozen, net, plus regular packing charges, F.O.B. factory.

## BASKETS

| | | |
|---|---|---|
| 2 | 14" Square Basket | $24.00 |
| 136 | 11" Square Basket | 18.00 |
| 458 | 10" Basket | 24.00 |
| 471 | 12" Basket | 24.00 |
| 4552 | 11" Oval Basket | 9.90 |
| 4566 | 8½" Basket, 4-Toed | 6.60 |

## BEVERAGES

| | | |
|---|---|---|
| 10/2 | 48 Oz. Water Bottle, Light | $4.36 |
| 10/2 | 48 Oz. Water Bottle, Heavy | 5.32 |
| 11 | Double Jigger | 1.82 |
| 102 | Punch Ladle | 5.40 |
| 237 | 24 Oz. 9½" Decanter, GS, N/Hdl. | 6.00 |
| 237 | 24 Oz. 9½" Decanter, GS, W/Hdl. | 7.20 |
| 434 | 29 Oz. Decanter, GS, Plain only | 13.20 |
| 708 | 15-pc. Punch Set | 82.20 |
| 711 | 25 Oz. Decanter, GS | 15.00 |
| 711/741/735 | 10-Pc. Liquor Set | 45.00 |
| 711/742/735 | 10-Pc. Wine Set | 47.40 |
| 741 | 1½ Oz. Whiskey | 1.80 |
| 742 | 3 Oz. Wine | 2.00 |

## BON BONS

| | | |
|---|---|---|
| 4518 | 6" Bon Bon, 2 Hld. | $3.00 |
| 4524 | 5" Bon Bon, 2-Hdl., 4-Toed | 3.00 |
| 4525 | 5½" Bon Bon, 2-Hdl., 4-Toed | 3.00 |

## BOTTLES, PERFUME

| | | |
|---|---|---|
| 675 | 3/8 Oz. Bottle GS (S.C.) | $5.85 |
| 676 | ¾ Oz. Bottle GS (S.C.) | 7.20 |
| 677 | 1¼ Oz. Bottle GS (S.C.) | 9.00 |
| 678 | 4 Oz. Bottle GS (S.C.) | 11.70 |

## BOWLS

| | | |
|---|---|---|
| 416 | 12" Oblong Bowl | $13.20 |
| 426 | 8" Round Bowl | 12.00 |
| 431 | 12" Belled Bowl | 24.00 |
| 432 | 9½" Belled Bowl | 15.00 |
| 433 | 7" Belled Bowl | 9.00 |
| 439 | 9" Round Bowl | 9.00 |
| 446 | 9½" Oct. Bowl | 18.00 |
| 449 | 10½" Round Bowl | 18.00 |
| 459 | 9" Cupped Bowl, Oct. | 15.00 |
| 480 | 5½" Bowl, 8-Crimps | 18.00 |
| 481 | 6" Bowl, 8-Crimps | 18.00 |
| 482 | 12" Bowl, 8-Crimps | 15.00 |
| 484 | 11" Shallow Bowl | 15.00 |
| 493 | 12" Bowl, Rolled Edge | 10.80 |
| 654 | 8" Square Bowl | 12.00 |
| 657 | 8"Cloverleaf Bowl | 12.00 |
| 702 | 12½" Shallow Bowl, Round | 10.80 |
| 703 | 12½" Shallow Bowl, Round | 10.80 |
| 707 | 12½" Bowl w/Marie, 8-Crimps | 12.00 |
| 718 | 8½" Flower Bowl W/Block | 13.20 |
| 4211 | 12½" Bowl, Crimped | 7.25 |
| 4265 | 11" Flared Bowl | 6.60 |
| 4459 | 12" Flared Bowl | 6.60 |
| 4510 | 11" Flared Bowl, 3-Toed | 6.60 |
| 4511 | 11" Flared Bowl, 3-Toed | 6.60 |
| 4512 | 10½" Cupped Bowl, 3-Toed | 6.60 |
| 4512/CM | 10½" Cupped Bowl, 3-Toed | 13.20 |
| 4513 | 12" Flared Bowl | 7.20 |
| 4515 | 12" Bowl, 6-Crimps | 7.20 |
| 4551 | 11" Oval Bowl | 6.60 |
| 4555 | 13" Flared Bowl | 9.90 |
| 4574 | 5½" Flower Bowl, 8-Crimps | 9.00 |

## CANDLESTICKS

| | | |
|---|---|---|
| 415 | 6½" 1-Lt. Squirrel Candlestick | $6.60 |
| 425 | 6½" 3-Lt. Candelabra | 15.00 |
| 448 | 2½" 1-Lt. Oct. Candlestick | 6.00 |
| 451 | 2" 1-Lt. Candlestick, C&P | 4.80 |
| 452 | 7" 1-Lt. Seal Candlestick | 15.00 |
| 453 | 5¼" 2-Lt. Candelabra | 9.90 |
| 652 | 3½" 1-Lt. Cornu. Candlestick | 6.60 |
| 653 | 4" 1-Lt. Cornu. Candlestick | 6.00 |
| 655 | 2" 3-Lt. Candelabra | 12.00 |
| 4457 | 5" 2-Lt. Candelabra | 6.60 |
| 4457/CM | 5" 2-Lt. Candelabra | 9.90 |
| 4536 | 5" 2-Lt. Candelabra | 5.40 |
| 4554 | 5½" 1-Lt. Candlestick | 4.00 |

## CANDY BOXES AND COVERS

| | | |
|---|---|---|
| 660 | 7" 3-Part Cloverleaf Candy Box and Cover | $7.80 |
| 662 | 6½" 3-Part Candy Box and Cover | 7.20 |
| 4541 | 5½" Candy Box and Cover | 6.60 |

## CANDY JARS AND COVERS

| | | |
|---|---|---|
| 472 | 9" Candy Jar and Cover, Oct. | $15.00 |

## CELERY

| | | |
|---|---|---|
| 4521 | 11" Oblong Celery | $4.80 |

## CHEESE AND CRACKER SETS

| | | |
|---|---|---|
| 4528 | 11" Cheese and Cracker | $9.00 |

## COMPOTES

| | | |
|---|---|---|
| 477 | 5" Compote, Oct. | $15.00 |

## CONDIMENT SETS

| | | |
|---|---|---|
| 4548 | 3-Pc. Condiment Set | $6.60 |

## FIGURES

| | | |
|---|---|---|
| 435 | 4½" Baby Seal | $7.20 |
| 452 | 7" Seal | 15.00 |
| 487 | 3" Baby Bear | 7.20 |
| 488 | 4" Mama Bear | 18.00 |
| 489 | 4" Papa Bear | 18.00 |
| 667 | 1" Chicks | .72 |
| 668 | 7½" Rooster | 15.00 |
| 669 | 5" Hen | 12.00 |
| 670 | 5½" Squirrel W/Base | 12.00 |
| 674 | 4½" Squirrel No/Base | 9.60 |
| 716 | 7" Wolfhound | 15.00 |
| 733 | 5" Police Dog | 7.20 |

## LINERS

| | | |
|---|---|---|
| 1 | 6 Oz. Egg Liner | $1.33 |

## MAYONNAISE SETS

| | | |
|---|---|---|
| 4522 | 3-Pc. Mayonnaise Set | 6.60 |

## NAPPIES

| | | |
|---|---|---|
| 4517 | 6" Nappy, 2-Hdl., Crimped | $3.00 |

## PLATES

| | | |
|---|---|---|
| 42 | 14" Plate | $7.25 |
| 450 | 13" Round Plate | 18.00 |
| 490 | 5½" Bone Plate | 2.40 |
| 4516 | 13" Plate | 7.20 |
| 4520 | 7" Plate, 2-Hld. | 3.00 |
| 4529 | 11" Plate, 2-Hld. | 6.60 |
| 4530 | 11" Plate, Rolled Edge | 6.00 |
| 4538 | 15" Plate | 12.00 |
| 4556 | 14" Footed Plate, Rolled Edge | 9.90 |

## PUFF BOXES

| | | |
|---|---|---|
| 714 | 3" Puff Box & Cover | $12.00 |

## RELISHES

| | | |
|---|---|---|
| 37/5 | 10" 3-Part Relish, 2-Hld. | $7.25 |
| 507 | 4½" 2-Part, Relish, 2-Hld. | 3.00 |
| 658 | 13" 5-Part Relish, 3-Ring | 12.00 |
| 659 | 13" 5-Part, Relish, 3-Ring, 2-Hld. | 18.00 |
| 662/1 | 8" 3-Part Relish, Crimped | 4.20 |
| 4534 | 6" 2-Part Relish, 2-Hld. | 3.30 |

## SALT DIPS

| | | |
|---|---|---|
| 11 | 1½" Round Salt Dip, C&P | $3.30 |
| 112 | 2¼" Oval Salt Dip, C&P | 3.60 |
| 120 | 1¾" Square Salt Dip, C&P | 3.30 |
| 130 | Ind. Salt Spoons | .30 |

## SMOKING SUPPLIES

| | | |
|---|---|---|
| 2 | 4¾" Oct. Ash Tray, C&P | $15.00 |
| 110 | 3¼" Oblong Ash Tray, C&P | 7.80 |
| 111 | 4¾" Oblong Ash Tray, C&P | 12.00 |
| 118 | 4" Oblong Ash Tray, C&P | 6.00 |
| 118 | 5½" Cigarette Box w/Cov., C&P | 24.00 |
| 204 | 4" Round Coaster or Ash Tray | .91 |
| 410 | 4" Oct. Ash Tray | 3.30 |
| 411 | 2½" Oct. Cigarette Jar | 3.30 |
| 412 | 5-Pc. Cigarette Set | 7.80 |
| 413 | 4½" Horseshoe Ash Tray, FP | 3.60 |
| 413 | 4½" Horseshoe Ash Tray, C&P | 6.60 |
| 414 | 3" Round Ash Tray or Coaster | .96 |
| 421 | 5½" Oct. Ash Tray | 6.00 |
| 422 | 6½" Oct. Ash Tray | 9.00 |
| 436 | 4" Fish Ash Tray | 3.00 |
| 442 | 6" Horseshoe Ash Tray, FP | 6.60 |
| 442 | 6" Horseshoe Ash Tray, C&P | 13.20 |
| 444 | 3" Oct. Ash Tray | 1.80 |
| 445 | 2" Oct. Cigarette Jar | 2.40 |
| 495 | 6" Ash Tray, C&P | 18.00 |
| 500 | 7½" Cigarette Box W/Cov., C&P Top & Bottom | 12.00 |
| 501 | 7½" Oblong Ash Tray, FP | 6.60 |
| 502 | 6" Oblong Ash Tray | 3.00 |
| 503 | 5¼" Ash Tray | 3.00 |
| 504 | 4" Square Ash Tray, FP | 6.60 |
| 506 | 6" Oblong Cigarette Box W/Cov. | 9.00 |

| | | |
|---|---|---|
| 508 | Cigarette Cast | 6.60 |
| 511 | 6½" Star Ash Tray | 6.60 |
| 652 | 3½" Cornu. Cigarette Holder | 6.00 |
| 661 | 3" Square Ash Tray | 1.50 |
| 737 | Wheelbarrow | 12.00 |

## SUGAR AND CREAM SETS

| | | |
|---|---|---|
| 4532 | 2-Pc. Sugar & Cream Set | $4.80 |
| 4532 | 3-Pc. Sugar & Cream w/Tray | 6.60 |
| 4545 | 2-Pc. Ind. Sugar & Cream Set | 4.20 |
| 4545 | 3-Pc. Ind. Sugar & Cream w/Tray | 6.60 |

## VASES

| | | |
|---|---|---|
| 42 | 10" Flared Vase | $5.10 |
| 42 | 12" Flared Vase | 8.00 |
| 131 | 8" Square Vase, FP | 15.00 |
| 134 | 6" Square Vase, FP | 12.00 |
| 135 | 6" Jug or Vase, w/Hdl., FP | 15.00 |
| 423 | 6" Oct. Vase | 12.00 |
| 424 | 8" Oct. Vase | 18.00 |
| 427 | 7" Round Vase | 24.00 |
| 428 | 5½" Round Vase | 15.00 |
| 429 | 4½" Round Vase | 9.00 |
| 460 | 4½" Vase, 8-Crimps | 15.00 |
| 461 | 6" Vase, 4-Crimps | 15.00 |
| 475 | 6½" Vase, 8-Crimps | 15.00 |
| 650 | 6" Cornu. Vase | 15.00 |
| 651 | 5" Cornu. Vase Bookend | 15.00 |
| 4232 | 10" Flared Vase, 8-Crimps | 5.10 |
| 4565 | 9" Ball Vase | 9.90 |

## VIKING'S ANTIQUE

| | | |
|---|---|---|
| 14 | 9 Oz. Goblet | $2.40 |
| 14 | 6 Oz. Saucer Champagne | 2.40 |
| 14 | 3 Oz. Cocktail | 2.40 |
| 14 | 12 Oz. Tumbler | 2.40 |
| 14 | 10 Oz. Tumbler | 2.10 |
| 14 | 7 Oz. Old Fashioned | 1.80 |
| 14 | 5 Oz. Tumbler | 1.80 |
| 14/8 | 7½" Bon Bon, 6 Crimps | 3.00 |
| 14/10 | 5" Compote, 8-Crimps | 2.40 |
| 14/2 | 5" Flared Vase, 6-Crimps | 3.00 |

## ETCHED No. 26 LINE

| | | |
|---|---|---|
| 42/26 | 10" Flared Bowl | $9.00 |
| 42/26 | 7" 3-Part Candy Box w/Cov. | 12.00 |
| 42/26 | 11" Cheese & Cracker | 12.00 |
| 42/26 | 10" Oval Celery | 7.20 |
| 42/26 | 3-Pc. Mayonnaise Set | 12.00 |
| 42/26 | 11" Plate | 9.00 |
| 42/26 | 14" Plate | 12.00 |
| 42/26 | Sugar, Cream and Tray | 12.00 |
| 42/26 | 9" Tray | 6.00 |
| 42/26 | 10" Vase | 12.00 |
| 42/26 | 12" Vase | 14.52 |
| 37/5/26 | 10" 3-Part Relish, 2-Hld. | 12.00 |
| 4211/26 | 12½" Crimped Bowl | 12.00 |
| 4213/26 | 13" Flared Bowl | 12.00 |
| 4221/26 | 9" Ball Bowl | 18.00 |
| 4221/26 | 9" 5-Qt. Punch Bowl | 18.00 |
| 4222/26 | 8½" 2-Part Relish | 7.20 |
| 4223/26 | 7½" 2-Part Relish | 7.20 |
| 4230/26 | 12" Vase, 8-Crimps | 14.52 |
| 4232/26 | 10" Vase, 8-Crimps | 12.00 |
| 4265/26 | 11" Flared Bowl, 3-Toed | 12.00 |
| 4457/26 | 5" 2-Lt. Candelabra | 9.00 |

## ETCHED No. 29 LINE

| | | |
|---|---|---|
| 44/29 | 11" Plate | $9.00 |
| 44/29 | 14" Plate | 12.00 |
| 44/29 | 10" Bowl | 9.00 |
| 44/29 | 11" Cheese and Cracker | 12.00 |
| 44/29 | 3-Pc Mayonnaise Set | 12.00 |
| 44/29 | 11" Hld. Sandwich Tray | 12.00 |
| 44/29 | 10½" Hld. Nut Bowl | 12.00 |
| 44/29 | 11" Salver | 12.00 |
| 44/29 | 7½" 3-Part Candy Box w/Cov. | 12.00 |
| 44/29 | 3-Pc. Sugar, Cream w/Tray | 12.00 |
| 4454/29 | 12" Flared Bowl | 12.00 |
| 4456/29 | 13" Flared Bowl | 12.00 |
| 4457/29 | 5" 2-Lt. Candelabra | 9.00 |
| 4459/29 | 12" Flared Bowl, 3-Toed | 12.00 |
| 4460/29 | 12" Cupped Bowl, 3-Toed | 12.00 |
| 4461/29 | 13" Footed Plate, R. E. | 12.00 |
| 4462/29 | 11" Plate, 2-Hld. | 12.00 |
| 4463/29 | 11" Cupped Bowl | 12.00 |
| 4464/29 | 13" Plate | 12.00 |
| 37/5/29 | 10" 3-Part Relish, 2-Hld. | 12.00 |

FP—Fire Polished      G.S.—Ground Stopper      CM—Cut Marshall      C&P—Cut and Polished      S.C.—Spear or Crescent Stopper

*Dated April, 1945, this may be one of the first price lists issued by the Viking Glass Company.*

## NEW MARTINSVILLE, W. VA.

### By John Plott

Well, here I am back again writing for the "Old Flint Magazine" after an absence of ten years when that "Wild Irishman," Brother Pat Moriss and I, John Plott, used to write for Local 55 of the Duncan Miller Glass Company, Washington, Pa. I am now going to pick up my "poison pen" and write for Local 16 of New Martinsville, W. Va.

My first duty will be to give the list of the glass workers employed at Local 16. The following brothers are: Head Shop gathering boy, John Plott, Head Shop presser, Raymond Hoskins, Head Shop finisher, Carl Gray. Second Head Shop presser, "Cal" Tripplett, gathering boy, "Coon" Bickert, finisher, George Lynskey. "Wild Animal Shop"—Zack Boyd, presser, Carl Nice, gatherer, Louie Zohn, finisher. Cup Foot Shop:— Eddie Metts, presser, Fred Sarver, gatherer, "Dorie" Hoskins, bowl finisher and Guy Ingram, foot finisher. "Odds and Ends Shop"— Ray Ritz, presser and Bud Sarver, gatherer. "The Fancy Shop"— Jack Dayton, presser, Dave Potts finisher and Leo Dubois, gatherer. On that "sweet smelling perfume shop" our presser is Owen Medley, Lawrence Nice, bowl finisher, patent-tool finisher, this writer's fancy brother-in-law, Earl Burch, gatherer, Otis Travis. We have on the blow shop, Gus Theret, blower, Charley Pyle, gatherer, Bernard Boyd, blocker, and Doc Twyman, finisher. We also have with us on other shops "mouse" Helms, presser, Odd Mason, gatherer, Ray Crumbly, presser, Adam Smith, gatherer, "Henney" Zohn, presser, Otis Workman, gatherer. Bert Bailey, presser, Jim Bartrug, gatherer, and Bill Zohn, finisher. On our "fancy stopper shop" we have Andy Drinko, presser, Bud Frye, gatherer, Amos Johnson, finisher. Our handlers are Mack Schwing, and June Stackhouse. (If I have overlooked a brother, please excuse me). Our Works Manager is "Doc" Mosser, day bosses are Reader McCoy and John Yeager, night bosses are Ed Angus and ex-brother Grover Frye.

No doubt you have all heard that I have "tied the knot." Married life is certainly a pleasant one. Brothers, this Ohio Valley is one wonderful place to work, if you don't believe me ask Tom Tucker. You will hear more from me and about old brothers I am working with and the ones I previously worked with at Local 55. A couple of bosom brothers from Local 15 will know whom I mean when I start to write about them in our magazine.

Here's closing 'til next time. Buy more WAR BONDS! Buy Union-made goods!

*This column from the* **American Flint** *(February, 1944) mentions many workers then at New Martinsville.*

"hand made" below the foot and "New Martinsville West Virginia Glass." Also in 1943, a round logotype featured the word "Viking" in reverse type with "New Martinsville Glass Co. New Martinsville, W. Va." around the circumference.

When the stockholders of the New Martinsville Glass Company met on June 1, 1944, they voted to change the name of the enterprise to Viking Glass Company. The firm's advertising notices reflected the new name immediately, although it was not officially recorded in the records of Wetzel County for nearly five years (Deed Record, April 11, 1949).

*Crockery and Glass Journal* (November, 1944) announced the corporate name change and went on to identify the firm's officers:

*G. R. Cummings, President and Secretary; C. T. Swartling, Executive Vice-President and Treasurer. Mr. Swartling is a Certified Public Accountant and was formerly associated with Seward & Monde of New Haven, Connecticut; O. F. Mosser, Vice-President. Mr. Mosser is very well known throughout the glass industry. He was formerly associated with the Cambridge Glass Company and Duncan & Miller; E. W. Wren, Assistant treasurer; Mr. Wren was formerly with H. F. Ferguson Company; Mr. Fred H. Gardner has been appointed Advertising Counsel.*

The Viking firm retained the moulds used by the New Martinsville Glass Company, of course, so today's glass collectors may well ponder whether a given article was made under the "New Martinsville" or the "Viking" corporate name. Indeed, some articles may have been made under the aegis of the original New Martinsville Glass Manufacturing Company (1901-July, 1938), as well as the New Martinsville Glass Company (August, 1938-May, 1944) and then were continued by the Viking Glass Company. Other articles may have begun as private mould work and later became part of the line under one or more of the firms which operated the New Martinsville plant.

This book has attempted to document the various tableware lines and novelty items made by the first two firms, the New Martinsville Glass Manufacturing Company (1901-1938) and the New Martinsville Glass Company (1938-1944). The history of the Viking Glass Company (1944-1986) and its successor, Dalzell-Viking Corporation, has yet to be written.

# BIBLIOGRAPHY

Angus, Fern. "The Glass of New Martinsville," *The Antique Trader Weekly*, June 15, 1977, pp. 48-49.

Archer, Margaret and Douglas, *The Collector's Encyclopedia of Glass Candlesticks*. Paducah, KY: Collector Books, 1983.

Archer, Margaret and Douglas, *Glass Candlesticks*. Paducah, KY: Collector Books, 1975.

Archer, Margaret and Douglas, *Glass Candlesticks Book 2*. Paducah, KY: Collector Books, 1977.

Barnett, Jerry. *Paden City: The Color Company*. N. p.: privately printed, 1978.

Florence, Gene. *The Collector's Encyclopedia of Depression Glass*, revised tenth ed., Paducah, KY: Collector Books, 1992; revised eleventh ed., Paducah, KY: Collector Books, 1993.

Florence, Gene. *Elegant Glassware of the Depression Era*. Paducah, KY: Collector Books, 1983; revised fifth ed. Paducah, KY: Collector Books, 1993.

Florence, Gene. *Kitchen Glassware of the Depression Years*, fourth ed. Paducah, KY: Collector Books, 1990.

Florence, Gene. *Very Rare Glassware of the Depression Years*. Paducah, KY: Collector Books, 1988.

Florence, Gene. *Very Rare Glassware of the Depression Years*, 2nd Series. Paducah, KY: Collector Books, 1991.

Garmon, Lee and Spencer, Dick. *Glass Animals of the Depression Era*. Paducah, KY: Collector Books, date??

Gaston, Mary Frank. *Collector's Guide to Art Deco*. Paducah, KY: Collector Books, 1989.

Heacock, William. *Collecting Glass*, volumes 1-2-3. Marietta, OH: Antique Publications, 1984-1986.

Heacock, William. *The Glass Collector*, issues 3 and 6. Marietta, OH: Antique Publications, 1982 and 1983.

Klamkin, Marian. *The Collector's Guide to Depression Glass*. New York: Hawthorn Books Inc., 1973.

Lafferty, James R. *The Forties Revisited*, volume II. N. p.: n. p., 1969.

Miller, Addie and Everett. "New Martinsville Glass," *Rainbow Review*, Vol. III, No. 11 (November, 1973).

"The New Martinsville Glass Story," *Antiques Today*, Vol. I, No. 2 (Spring, 1973), pp. 52-57.

Over, Naomi L. *Ruby Glass of the 20th Century*. Marietta, OH: Antique Publications, 1990.

Peterson, Arthur G. "New Martinsville Glass Manufacturing Co., Part I," *Hobbies* (Nov., 1968) 122-123.

Peterson, Arthur G. "New Martinsville Glass Manufacturing Co., Part II," *Hobbies* (Dec., 1968) 98X-98Y.

Pierce, Bob. "Favorite Pieces: New Martinsville Janice," *Glass Collector's Digest* (August/September, 1992), pp. 80-81.

Stout, Sandra McPhee. *Depression Glass III*. Des Moines, IA: Wallace-Homestead, 1976.

Weatherman, Hazel Marie. *Colored Glassware of the Depression Era 2*. Ozark, MO: Weatherman Glassbooks, 1974.

Weatherman, Hazel Marie. *Price Trends 2 for Colored Glassware of the Depression Era Book 2*. Springfield, MO: Glassbooks, Inc., 1979.

Whitmyer, Margaret and Whitmyer, Kenn. *Bedroom and Bathroom Glassware of the Depression Years*. Paducah, KY: Collector Books, 1990.

# INDEX

A-B-C plates 74
    illustrated 112
Ackerman, Jay 204
Adams, Arminta 186
Amdur, Henry and Son 209
American Art Glass Co. (Byesville, Ohio) 15
animal figurines 207, 209-213
ashtrays 74-78, 141
    illustrated 46, 75-78, 114, 127, 132, 141, 190, 192

Baird, David 8, 21
Baker, David 13
Ball, W. F. 183
Banner, see Floral Oval
Bargerhoff, Alice 186
Barth Art Glass 187
Barth, Harry 55, 130, 139, 154, 160, 180, 183-187, 192, 204
    pictured 162, 185
Beaded Diamond, see No. 200
bear figurines, see Three Bears
Beaumont Glass Co. (Morgantown, W. Va.) 187
beer mugs 139, 141
    illustrated 141
Belford, W. R. 13
Berger, Sheriff Frank 182
Bertman Electric Co. 209
Bess, J. C. 13
Biberthaler, M. G. 187, 207
Bishop, William 13
bobeche
    illustrated 114
Bond, Frank 152
Bonita Art Glass Co. (Wheeling, W. Va.) 142
Bowden, C. 152
Bowers, A. L. 13
bowl with flower frog 81-82
    illustrated 82, 131
boy A-B-C plate 74
    illustrated 112
Braun, Julius 47
Bresock, George 13, 152
Bridgeman, Frances Lamping 186
Brown, O. O. 187
Bruhey, Julia 54
Buckeye Glass Co. (Martins Ferry) 1
Burkett, F. 152
By-the-Sea night lamp, see No. 800 night lamp
Byesville Glass Co. (Byesville, Ohio) 15

Call of the Wild silver deposit 146-147 (Lotus Glass Co.)
    illustrated 130
Cambridge Glass Co. (Cambridge, Ohio) 84, 87, 187, 213
candelabra 187
    illustrated 191
Carlyle, T. 152
Carnation, see No. 88
Cat lamp
    illustrated 138
Celtic, see No. 100
Chaplin, Callie 27
Chaplin, Delia 27
Chaplin, Olia 27
Charleton, Al 47
Charton, Albert 13
Cheffy, Frank 13
Chesterfield smoker's set, see No. 149 smoker's set
Chicks, see No. 667
Christina 207
    illustrated 114
Chuffy, Frank 152
Clark, Frank W. 2-3
Clark, Josephus 3-4, 16
Clarke, Ira M. 39, 47, 52-55, 59, 64-65, 67, 70, 73-75, 79-80, 82-83, 85, 87-89, 139-140, 153-157, 182-183, 185
Clarke, William P. 87-88
Clipper Ship bookends, see Ship
Clulo, Walter 187
Collins, James W. 1-3, 5, 7-8
Colonial Girl powder box 151
Colonial Line, see No. 728
Combs, Robert H. 13, 19
Conroy, M. J. 47
console sets 71-72, 187
    illustrated 71-72
Cooper, James 1
Cooperative Flint Glass Co. (Beaver Falls, Pa.) 14
Cornucopia line 205
    illustrated 204
Creased Waist, see No. 58
Creighton, John 47
Crescent, see Diamond Point Disc
Crimmel, George C. 13, 151
Crist, Howard 152
Cross, William 88-89, 152, 182, 186, 203-204
Cummings, G. R. 217

Curly Locks, see No. 56
Curtsy figural powder jar 151
Curved Body 17
    illustrated 17, 102
cut ware 59-65
    illustrated 59-65, 131, 193

Dancing Lady flower frog 149, 209
    illustrated 127
Daugherty, M. R. 89
decorated ware, hand-painted 64-65
    illustrated 124, 126, 129
Deighton, William M. 13, 152
Diamond Glass-Ware Co. (Indiana, Pa.) 87
Diamond Match Company 75, 129, 141
Diamond Point Disc 69
    illustrated 69
dog A-B-C plate 74
    illustrated 112
Douglass, Mark 1-3, 14
Dover, Becky 27
Duncan Miller Glass Co. (Washington, Pa.) 187

Eagle book end 212
    illustrated 212
Ebeling and Reuss 209, 212
Edmonds, Frank 33, 36
electric shades, see shades
Elephant cigarette holder 149, 209
    illustrated 127
Elephant incense burner 149, 209
    illustrated 127
Elite, see No. 558
Ellson, George 54
Elson, G. W. 13
Embassy, see No. 726
Emch, Russell C. 88-89, 152
Express, see No. 723

Federal Glass Co. (Columbus, Ohio) 153
Fenton Art Glass Co. (Williamstown, W. Va.) 87, 130
figurines 209-213
    illustrated 210-213
Fish bookends 212
Fisher David 1-2, 7, 13, 21, 35, 44, 47, 52, 65, 69, 139 pictured 7, 22
Fisher, Samuel 47
Flapper Girl 151
    illustrated 130
floor lamp 54, 83
    illustrated 83

Floral Oval 69
    illustrated 111
Floral Panel, see Rock Crystal
Flower Basket plate etching, see Meadow Wreath
flower baskets 64
    illustrated 62
flower frog, patented 81-82
    illustrated 82, 131
Flowering Vine 7
    illustrated 101
Forbes, Jack 152
Forbes, J. F. 13
Forbes, John 38, 47, 52-53, 87
Forbes, William 13, 152
Fort Pitt (Dithridge) Glass Works (Pgh., Pa.) 14
Fortuna, see Perkins
Fostoria Glass Co. (Moundsville, W. Va.) 87, 212-213
Fox, Bertha 27
Fox, Henry 14
France, Harry 14
Frey, Charles 89
Frizzell, F. 89
Frontier, see No. 718
Frye, George 87, 152
Fuller, E. 152

Gaffney, Michael 14
Garrett (George G.) Decorating Co. 27, 29
Garrett, George 14, 27
Garrett, W. T. 14
Garrett, Thomas 27
gas shades, see shades
Gazelle bookends 212
German mug 13
Gillett, John 14
Gillooly, Joseph 89
Glenn, Miss Mary 52
Golden Electrical Products, Inc. 209
Goodwin, J. 152
Grandon, Cyrus 14
Gruntz, John 14
Gunto, M. 152

H. Northwood and Co. 3
Hamilton, William 1
hand lamps 7
Haskins Glass Co. (Martins Ferry, Ohio) 15
Hassner, C F. 14
Hassner, W. D. 14
Hassner, Wilda J. 186

Hat Match Holder 39
    illustrated 101
Haught, Thomas 152
Heart in Sand, see No. 724
Heather, see No. 800
Heisey, A. H., and Co. (Newark, Ohio) 87, 213
Hen, see No. 669
Herrigan, John 14
Higbee [J. B.] Glass Co. (Bridgeville, Pa.) 52-53,
    65, 68-69, 74, 87
Highland, see No. 517
Hill, Arch 55, 83, 88, 152
Hommell, C. R. 14
Horse 212
    illustrated 212
Horseshoe Medallion, see No. 707
Horstman, Ed 89, 151-152
Hoskins, Elam 152
Hoskins, J. 152
Hoskins, Raymond 89, 152
Hoskins, Theodore 152, 181
hotel glassware 187
    illustrated 189
Houze Convex Glass Co. (Pt. Marion, Pa.) 147
Howell, Anthony 152
Huggins, C. N. 14
Hunter 213
    illustrated 213

Iams Funeral Home 203
Icicle and Window, see No. 43
Imperial Glass Co. (Bellaire, Ohio) 87, 153, 187
Indiana Glass Co. (Dunkirk, IN) 146
Ingram, Guy 152
inkwells
    illustrated 45-46
Iris night lamp
    illustrated 101
Island Mould Co. (Wheeling, W. Va.) 207

Jackie, see Flapper Girl
Jacobs, Jackson 14
Janice (No. 45 or No. 4500 line) 192, 200, 203
    illustrated 114, 136-137, 196-199, 201-202
Japanese Iris, see No. 716
Johnson, Charlie 152
June Bug cutting 64
    illustrated 64

Kappel, Mrs. Herbert, see Hassner, Wilda J.
Kavanaugh, Daniel 14

Kavanaugh, Martin J. 14, 16, 19, 92
Kemple Glass Co. (E. Palestine, Ohio) 209
Kern, Henry 14
Kessler, Warren L., Inc. 207
Kilgore, Alex 152
Kirrig, Paul 52
Koontz, Jacob 2-3
Krystal Klear 205, 207
    illustrated 133, 208
Kunzler, William 14

Lacy Daisy 69
    illustrated 68 (see also Floral Oval)
Lady Face bookend 212-213
Lamberton, W. 14
lamps 7, 39
Lanam's Foundry 145
Landberg 69
    illustrated 68 (see also No. 524)
Larrick, A. E. 183
Leaf and Star, see No. 711
Leaf Drooping 17
    illustrated 101
Lehew, D. L. 14
Lenoir, see No. 715
Libbey Glass Co. 14
library lamps 39, 51
    illustrated 43
Lincoln Hat, see Hat Match Holder
Lincoln Theatre 147-148
List, Carrie 27
List, Lewis 14
Lively, Dave 152
Local Union No. 16 (AFGWU) 2, 21, 31, 36, 88-
    89, 139, 151-152, 181-182, 203, 217
Long, Inez 27
Long, "Polly"
    pictured 32
Lorraine, see No. 722
Lotus Glass Co. (Barnesville, Ohio) 130, 142-143,
    146-147, 203
Lusitania, see No. 708

Malcolm's House and Garden Store (Baltimore,
    Md.) 209, 212
Man-in-the-Moon candlesticks 212
Marks and Rosenfield 207, 212-213
Many Petals, see No. 55
Marshall, P. 152
Martha Washington trinket box
    illustrated 127

Martin, John F. 182
Martin, Paul 89
Martin, Samuel R. 1-3, 18, 47
Mason, Charles 151-152
Mason, Oliver 152
Matheny, George L. 1-3, 18
Mauretania, see No. 702 (Horseshoe Medallion)
McCormick, W. E. 14
McEldowney, Robert 47, 52, 55, 89, 139-146, 148-
    149, 154
    pictured 139
McFadden, A. 152
McGrail, D. J. 47
McGraw, Arch 181-182
Meadow Wreath, see No. 26 plate etching
measuring cups 56
    illustrated 56
Medley, Joseph 14
Melrose water tray, see No. 523
Merritt, Charles 187, 204
Metts, Edward C. 205
Miller, Elzie (E. E.) 2, 14, 52, 152
Miller, Eugene 53
Miller, Frank 14
Mirror Star, see No. 719
Model, Theodore 209
Mooney, E. D. 1, 7, 16, 19, 92
Mooney, George 14
Mooney, Thomas 2, 18
Mooney, W. L. 14
Morgan, F. 152
Morris, P. D. 1
Mosser, Frank 152
Mosser, Orrie 187, 217
Mound Valley Glass Co. (Kansas) 8
mounting glassware 44
    illustrated 44
Muranese ware 3, 14-17
    illustrated 16, 91-93
Murry, S. M. 14

Nautilus book end 212
Neely, Harold A. 204
Nelson, Carl 14
New Martinsville Board of Trade 3
New Martinsville peachblow, see Muranese
Nice Kitty beverage set 84, 86-87
    illustrated on back cover
night lamps 7
No. 2 Waffle Set 180-181
    illustrated 129, 180

No. 6 ashtray
    illustrated 76
No. 7 smoker's tray
    illustrated 76
No. 9 mint jar 65
No. 9-3000 mint jar
    illustrated 126
No. 10 cake plate 64
    illustrated 63
No. 10 candlestick 71, 147
    illustrated 122
No. 10 candy box
    illustrated 62, 64, 116
No. 10 Hall Boy jug 64, 83
    illustrated 61
No. 10 molasses can 64
No. 10 pen tray 55-56
    illustrated
No. 10 Plain Pattern 38, 48
No. 10 plate and cheese compote 64
    illustrated 62
No. 10 plates
    illustrated 123
No. 10 relish dish 74
    illustrated 73, 117
No. 10 sandwich tray 64
    illustrated 61, 63, 131
No. 10 souvenir plate 74
    illustrated 112
No. 10-1-282 wine set
    illustrated 115
No. 10-2 candlestick 71
No. 10-2 cigarette set
    illustrated 121
No. 10-2 console set 70-71
    illustrated 72
No. 10-2 dresser set, see Queen Anne
No. 10-2 octagon sandwich tray 62, 70
    illustrated 70
No. 10-2 water bottle 83
No. 10-2-3000 smoker set
    illustrated 124
No. 10-2-3004 candlestick
    illustrated 126
No. 10-3 candlestick 71
    illustrated 122
No. 10-3 liquor set 83
    illustrated 84
No. 10-4 candlestick 71
    illustrated 129-130
No. 10-4-3004 candlestick
    illustrated 126

No. 10-10 console set 71
　illustrated 117
No. 10-12 console bowl
　illustrated 131
No. 10-12 console set 71
　illustrated 120
No. 10-12-3004 console bowl
　illustrated 126, 129
No. 10-21 console set 71
　illustrated 117
No. 10-728 smoker's set 75
　illustrated 77
No. 10-3016 smoker's set 77
　illustrated 124
No. 12 candlesticks
　illustrated 114
No. 13 ashtray
　illustrated 76
No. 14 ashtray
　illustrated 76
No. 14 beer mug
　illustrated 141
No. 14 candlestick
　illustrated 65
No. 14 Raindrops line 205, 207
　illustrated 133, 204-206
No. 15 ivy ball 141-142
　illustrated 142
No. 15 vanity set 150-151, 165
　illustrated 128, 150, 166
No. 16 candlestick
　illustrated 65
No. 16 line 154-156
　illustrated 155
No. 17 candlestick
　illustrated 65
No. 18 candelabra 187
　illustrated 191
No. 18 Crystal Eagle 179-180 165
　illustrated 132, 179
No. 18 saucer candlestick 71
　illustrated 71, 127
No. 18-2 vanity set 165
　illustrated 128, 132, 166
No. 18-728 service set
　illustrated 179
No. 20 ashtray 141
　illustrated 121, 127
No. 21-9 candlestick 71
　illustrated 73
No. 25 beer mug
　illustrated 141

No. 25 vanity set 165
　illustrated 166
No. 26 Meadow Wreath plate etching 166-167,
　177, 185
　illustrated 132, 174-175
No. 28 Rose and Robin plate etching 177, 185
　illustrated 168-169
No. 28 vanity set 165
　illustrated 166
No. 29 Florentine plate etching 185, 200
　illustrated 193-194
No. 30 (Fan in Oval)
　illustrated 27, 112
No. 30 Wild Rose plate etching 176-177, 185, 200
　illustrated 176, 195
No. 31 Canturbury plate etching 185
　illustrated 199
No. 33 Modernistic 144-147, 149, 151
　illustrated 128-131, 144-146
No. 34 (Addie) 146-149, 154
　illustrated 130, 147
No. 34 (Statesman) 43
　illustrated 44
No. 35 (Fancy Squares) 147-149, 154, 177
　illustrated 130, 148
No. 36 Jeff pitcher 43
　illustrated 41
No. 36 refreshment set 180
　illustrated 180
No. 36 vase
　illustrated 130
No. 37 (Moondrops) line 148, 154-162, 166-167,
　177, 180-181, 192
　illustrated 129, 131-134, 154-159
No. 38 line 138, 160-163
　illustrated 160-163
No. 38 punch bowl 56
No. 39 punch bowl 56
No. 40-2-82 beverage set 164
　illustrated 164
No. 42 Radiance 166-177, 181, 192, 200
　illustrated 129, 132, 135, 167-176
No. 42 Roly Poly 163-164
　illustrated 133, 164
No. 43 (Icicle and Window) 43
　illustrated 44
No. 44 (Teardrop) line 192, 200, 203
　illustrated 137, 193-195
No. 45 line, see Janice
No. 46 Mutt pitcher 43
　illustrated 41

No. 49, see Rock Crystal
No. 52 17
  illustrated 101
No. 53 (Scroll Two Band) 17
  illustrated 94, 102
No. 54 (Palmette Band) 17
  illustrated 94, 102
No. 55 Fern comport
  illustrated 138
No. 55 (Many Petals) 17
  illustrated 94, 101
No. 56 (Curly Locks) 17
  illustrated 94, 101
No. 57 (Vining Rose) 17
  illustrated 94-95, 102
No. 58 (Creased Waist) 17
  illustrated 94
No. 60 molasses can
  illustrated 95
No. 61 (Rose Viking) 17
  illustrated 94-95, 102
No. 62 (Vine with Flower) 17, 102
No. 63 (Tall Aster) 17, 102
No. 64 (Palm Tendril) 58
  illustrated 58
No. 65 (Plume Band) 58
  illustrated 58
No. 66 (Footed Four Petal) 58
  illustrated 58
No. 69 saloon salt 17
  illustrated 94
No. 82 tumbler
  illustrated 115
No. 88 Carnation 8, 10, 13, 38, 48
  illustrated 8-10, 24, 26, 103, 108, 113
No. 97 Old Colony 38, 48, 56, 66-67, 70
  illustrated 37-38, 66, 104-105, 107
No. 100 (Celtic) 6
  illustrated 6, 97, 105, 113
No. 100 night lamp 147
  illustrated 100, 150
No. 101 flower vase 177
  illustrated 132, 177
No. 103 candy box 178-179
  illustrated 178
No. 105 cigarette set 178-179
  illustrated 178
No. 107 three-compartment candy box 74
  illustrated 74
No. 108 punch bowl 177
No. 113 tumbler
  illustrated 115

No. 116 (Zipper Cross) 70
  illustrated 70, 113
No. 140-1 guest jug and tumbler 64, 83
  illustrated 61, 115
No. 146 38
No. 147 (Star in Bullseye) 38
No. 148 38
No. 149 (Monitor) 70-71
  illustrated 70
No. 149 (Plain Arches) 39
  illustrated 39
No. 149 Allah smoker's set 75, 150
  illustrated 78, 129, 132
No. 149-2 candy jar
  illustrated 116
No. 149-2-3019 cigarette holder
  illustrated 124
No. 149-3 candy jar 64-65
  illustrated 61, 116, 127, 129, 132
No. 149-3-3002 candy jar
  illustrated 126
No. 149-4 cigarette holder 77, 147
  illustrated 78, 121
No. 149-4-3020 cigarette holder
  illustrated 124
No. 150 3
No. 150 molasses can
  illustrated 95
No. 150 (Oriole) 58
  illustrated 58
No. 150 sweet pea vase 65
No. 150-3010 sweet pea vase 87
  illustrated 124
No. 155 3
No. 160 lamps
  illustrated 99
No. 160 (Vining Rose) molasses can
  illustrated 95, 113
No. 160-6 iced tea jug and cover 64
No. 160-8 plate
  illustrated 117
No. 160-10 console set 71
  illustrated 71
No. 160-12 salad set 74
  illustrated 117
No. 160-3019 lemon plate 87
  illustrated 124
No. 190-0 molasses can 64
  illustrated 60
No. 190-4 jug 87
  illustrated 115

No. 198-7 jug 87
illustrated 115
No. 200 (Beaded Diamond) 5-6
illustrated 96
No. 237-61 liquor set 163
illustrated 163
No. 310 (Mansion) 38, 48, 56
illustrated 56
No. 312 (Panelled File)
illustrated 113
No. 314 (Long Buttress)
illustrated 113
No. 400 6
illustrated 96
No. 401 cutting 172, 177, 203
illustrated 172
No. 409 cutting 173, 177, 203
illustrated 173
No. 425 candelabra 187
illustrated 191
No. 435 Baby Seal 213
No. 452 Seal 210
illustrated 210
No. 453 candelabra 187
illustrated 191
No. 472 candy box 207
illustrated 208
No. 474 vase
illustrated 208
No. 475 vase 207
illustrated 208
No. 476 vase 207
No. 477 comport 207
illustrated 208
No. 478 vase 207
illustrated 208
No. 487 Bear 209
illustrated 210
No. 487 Hunter 213
illustrated 213
No. 488 Mama Bear 209
illustrated 210
No. 489 Papa Bear 209
illustrated 210
No. 500 Wetzel 6-7, 10, 38, 48, 67-68
illustrated 7-8, 24, 37, 67, 112
No. 501 ice tub 69
No. 502 Paris 69
No. 508 Cigarette Cart 209-210
illustrated 210
No. 509 Eagle bookends 212
illustrated 212

No. 511 bud vases 64
No. 511-3055 bud vase
illustrated 125
No. 517 Coarse Zig Zag 69
No. 524 Landberg 69
illustrated 68
No. 530 Star A-B-C plate 74
illustrated 112
No. 531 A-B-C plate (boy) 74
illustrated 112
No. 532 A-B-C plate (dog) 74
illustrated 112
No. 553 (Helio) 69
No. 556 Royal 38, 48
No. 557 line
illustrated 68
No. 557 (Salem) 38, 48
illustrated 37
No. 558 (Elite) 38, 48
No. 600 3, 6
illustrated 98-99, 131
No. 601, see Diamond Point Disc
No. 603 puff box, see Martha Washington
No. 608 shaving mug 69
illustrated 69
No. 610 shaving mug 69
No. 667 Chicks 210
illustrated 211
No. 668 Rooster 210
illustrated 211
No. 669 Hen 210
illustrated 211
No. 670 Squirrel bookend 210
illustrated 211
No. 671 Shell candlestick 210
illustrated
No. 674 Squirrel 210
illustrated 211
No. 677 perfume bottle
illustrated 133
No. 678 perfume bottle
illustrated 133
No. 700 lamp 51
illustrated 40
No. 700 (Pleated Oval) 8, 10, 21
illustrated 8-9, 24
No. 701 lamp
illustrated 40
No. 702 lamp 39, 51
illustrated 40, 42
No. 702 (Long Leaf Teasel) 10, 21, 67
illustrated 11, 67, 113

No. 703 flared bowl
  illustrated 193
No. 704 (Placid Thumbprint) 10, 13, 21, 23
  illustrated 12, 101, 104-107, 112
No. 705 Klear Kut 10, 13, 19-21, 38, 48, 68
  illustrated 12, 21, 24, 67-68, 105, 109, 112
No. 705 lamp 39
  illustrated 41
No. 706 lamp 51
  illustrated 40
No. 707 (Horseshoe Medallion) 23, 29-30
  illustrated 23-24, 26, 37, 105-106, 108
No. 708 Lusitania 23, 36, 38, 43, 49
  illustrated 23, 31, 113
No. 708 Pullman creamer 58
No. 709 lamp 51
  illustrated 40
No. 711 (Leaf and Star) 23-25, 27, 30, 38, 49, 67, 70
  illustrated 24-27, 30-31, 66, 104, 107, 112
No. 712 (Placid) 23, 25, 30, 38, 49, 67-68
  illustrated 25, 27, 30, 37, 67
No. 713 (Pleated Medallion) 25-26, 38, 49, 67-68
  illustrated 25-26, 30, 37, 67, 113
No. 714 (Chateau) 25-27, 30, 38, 43, 49-50
  illustrated 25, 103, 114
No. 715 Lenoir 27, 29
  illustrated 28, 33, 106-107
No. 716 Rebecca 27, 29
  illustrated 28-29, 108
No. 717 (Horseshoe Daisy) 23, 29, 38, 50, 68
  illustrated 29, 30, 67-68, 103, 106
No. 718 (Frontier) 29-30, 38, 50
  illustrated 29-31, 33, 37, 104-105, 112
No. 719 Old Glory 30-31, 38, 50, 65
  illustrated 30-31, 33, 35, 66, 103, 105
No. 720 Florene 30-31, 38, 50
  illustrated 31, 33, 104-105, 107
No. 721 (Studio) 35
  illustrated 34-35, 103, 107
No. 722 (Lorraine) 35, 38, 51
  illustrated 33-35, 106, 109
No. 723 Bridge Sugar and Cream Set 74
  illustrated 73-74, 127
No. 723 (Express) 35-37, 51
  illustrated 35-36, 113
No. 723-8 bud vase 64
  illustrated 115
No. 724 (Heart in Sand) 35-38, 51
  illustrated 37, 109-110
No. 725 cigarette jar
  illustrated 122

No. 725 fan vases 87
  illustrated 120
No. 725 Plain Colonial 38, 51, 66
No. 725 tobacco jar
  illustrated 122
No. 726 (Embassy) 38, 65-66
No. 727 hotel water tray 64, 83
  illustrated 61
No. 727 lamps 59, 82-83
  illustrated 40, 82
No. 727 store fixtures 58-59
  illustrated 59
No. 728 ashtray
  illustrated 122
No. 728 candy jar 65
  illustrated
No. 728 Colonial Line 38, 69-70
  illustrated 69-70, 113
No. 728 guest set 65, 83
  illustrated 123, 130
No. 728 liquor set 83-84
  illustrated 85
No. 728 match stand
  illustrated 122
No. 728 plate
  illustrated 117
No. 728-12 salad set 74
  illustrated 117
No. 728-3006 guest set
  illustrated 125, 127
No. 728-3011 candy jar
  illustrated 126
No. 758/742/735 wine set
  illustrated 114
No. 767 candelabra
  illustrated 132
No. 800 night lamp (By the Sea) 7
  illustrated 100-101, 113
No. 800 (Heather) 6
  illustrated 24
No. 900 39, 51
No. 1000 cone holder 56
  illustrated 57, 114
No. 1059 candlestick
  illustrated 127
No. 1926 143-144
  illustrated 130, 144
No. 1926 candy box
  illustrated 123
No. 1926 vanity set 65, 79
  illustrated 80, 119

No. 1926-2 vanity set 79
  illustrated 79-80
No. 1926-3 vanity set 79
  illustrated 80-81
No. 1926-3001 vanity set
  illustrated 125
No. 1926-3003 candy box
  illustrated 126
No. 2001 vanity set 65, 79
  illustrated 80, 119, 125
No. 2003 smoker set
  illustrated 121, 124
No. 2051E console set 71
  illustrated 71
No. 4400 line (see also No. 44) 192, 200, 203
  illustrated 137, 193-195
No. 4500 line (see also Janice) 192, 200, 203
  illustrated 114, 136-137, 196-199, 201-202

octagon 62, 143
  illustrated 131, 143
O'Donnell, Thomas 14
Oelschlegar, J. 152
Ohio Valley Cut Glass (Paden City, W. Va.) 187
Old Glory, see No. 719
Oldham, C. W. 14
Oneacre, Henry 14
Oneacre's Drug Store 148
Overmyer Mould Co. 207, 212

Paden City Glass Mfg. Co. (Paden City, W. Va.)
  47, 142, 154, 180-181, 187, 207, 212-213
Palmette Band, see No. 54
paperweights 55-56
  illustrated 46, 55
Paris
  illustrated 111
Paul, Edward P., Inc. 209
peachblow, see Muranese
Peach Melba 52, 81, 86, 142
Pegg, G. W. 14
percolator tops 39
Perkins
  illustrated 111
Phoenix Glass Co. (Monaca, Pa.) 14
Pillar and Flower 17
  illustrated 102
Pittsburgh Cut Glass Co. (Beaver, Pa.) 87
Plain Colonial, see No. 725
Plott, John 187, 217

Police Dog, No. 733 149, 209
  illustrated 127
Postlethwait, W. J. 183
Potts, Dave 152
Powel, C. 89
Powell, Charlie 152
Powell, Rachel 27
Prelude plate etching 200
Prim, Lloyd 203
Princess, see No. 10-2
private mould work 142, 207, 209

Queen Anne dresser or vanity set 79, 150
  illustrated 118, 127-128

Radiance, see No. 42
Rebecca, see No. 716
revolver 74
Rexford 69
  illustrated 111
Rice, Irving 207
Rice, R. M. 183-185
Rider, Wilbur 89
Ridge, Ivy May 27
Ritz, R. 152
Riverside Glass Co. (Wellsburg, W. Va.) 8
Rock Crystal (Floral Panel) 3, 5-6
  illustrated 5, 93, 97, 101
Rockhill, Charles S. 47
Romona 69
Rooster, see No. 668
Rose and Robin, see No. 28 plate etching
Rose Relievo 17
  illustrated 101
Rose Viking, see No. 61
Rose Viking hand lamp
  illustrated 113
Royal, see No. 556
Ruble, Harold 151, 165
Ruggles, R. 2

saloon glassware 187
  illustrated 188
St. Mary's Glass Co. (St. Mary's, W. Va.) 142
Saladin, Theodore 14
Salem, see No. 557
Sawyer, O. 152
Schlens, Fred 154, 183
Schulte, Charles 52
Schultz, Carl 183-185

Schultz, Doretta 186
Schultz, Frank 89
Schwing, Clark 152
Schwing, Max 152
Schwing, Ross 55, 89, 181
Schwing, Theodore 55, 89
scroll book end 212
Scroll Two Band, see No. 53
Scully, Ed 151
Seal bookend or figurine, see No. 452
Seelback, Ed 151
shades (gas/electric) 6-7, 16-17
    illustrated 100
shell vase book end, see Nautilus
Shell candlestick 210
    illustrated 211
Ship book end 213
    illustrated 213
Shipman, Judge James F. 184
Shurtliff, C. E. 14, 31
Shurtliff, Howard 14, 31, 33
    pictured 32
Silly Toby 149
    illustrated 148
slipper 39
    illustrated 39
Smith, Emma 27
Smith, G. E. 14
Smith, John 14, 152
Smith, L. E., Glass Co. 212
Smith, Miss 52
Smith, William 14
smokers' accessories 74-78
    illustrated 75-78, 190, 192
soda fountain glassware 56, 66-67, 187
    illustrated 56-57, 188
Specialty Glass Co. (E. Liverpool, Ohio) 1
sponge cups
    illustrated 46
Squirrel, see Nos. 670 and 674
stand lamps 6
stamp plates
    illustrated 46
Star of David, see No. 500 Wetzel
Starfish book end 213
Statesman, see No. 34
stationers' glassware 55, 139-
    illustrated 45-46
Stender, John 2
store fixtures, see No. 727
straw jar
    illustrated 56

sugar pour
    illustrated 57
Sullivan, C. 152
Sunburst, see Muranese
Sunglow, see Muranese
Sunlite, see Muranese
Sunray, see Muranese
Sunrise, see Muranese
Suter, Carl 151
Swan Janice articles 203
    illustrated 201-202
Swaner, Clyde 14
Swartling, C. T. 217
Swirl Rib 7
Sylvania decoration by Lotus 203

Tall Aster, see No. 63
Tarentum Glass Co. (Tarentum, Pa.) 14
Thomas, Robert 47
Three Bears 209
    illustrated 210
Tibor 209
Tiger book end 212
Tisher, Ida 47
Toole, Ann
    pictured 162
Top Hat, see Hat Match Holder
Tyler County Glass Company 14

Universal Electric Art Co. 209

vanity sets 79, 149-151, 165-166
    illustrated 79-81, 128, 150, 165-166
Vickers, Joseph 14
Victoria, see No. 10-2
Viking Glass Co. 213-217
Vine with Flower, see No. 62
Vining Rose, see No. 57
Vining Rose molasses can, see No. 160
Voitle, Charles 87, 89, 185-186
Volstead Pup beverage set 84, 86-87, 149
    illustrated 86, 114

Wade, Lee 152
Waffle Set, see No. 2
Wakefield plate etching 185, 200
    illustrated 196
Ward, Charles E. 88
Washington, Martha, see Martha Washington
Webb Decorative Glass Works (Coudersport, Pa.)
    14

Webb, Hugh Fitzroy 14-15
Webb, Joseph 3, 14-16, 19, 92
Wells, F. C. 2
Weltz, Gus 186
West Virginia Glass Co. (Martins Ferry) 1
West Virginia Optical Glass Co. (Wheeling, WV) 3
Wetzel, see No. 500
White, David 152, 183
Wiel Freeman 207, 212
Wilson, Lenora 27
Wilt, Guy 89, 152
Wiltse, Ivy 27
Wiltse, Minnie 27
Wise Owl 149
    illustrated 127, 148
Witten family 1
Wolfe, Kenneth 152
Woodcock, G. B. 1
Woodsman, see Hunter
Workman, George 89, 152, 181
Wren, E. W. 217

Zipper Cross, see No. 116
Zohnd, Louis 87, 152

# New Martinsville Glass, 1900-1944

compiled by James Measell et al.

## Value Guide, 1994-95

This is the first comprehensive price guide to the glassware made at New Martinsville from its inception until the time it was renamed the Viking Glass Company in 1944. Some articles of New Martinsville glass, such as the early Muranese (formerly called "Peachblow") pieces and pattern lines decorated with ruby stain, have been popular with glass buffs for quite some time.

As collectors' enthusiasm for American-made, Depression-era glass has risen dramatically over the past decade, the best-known New Martinsville patterns—particularly No. 37 (Moondrops), No. 42 Radiance and No. 45 Janice—have become much sought after, especially in those colors (such as ruby or cobalt blue) which may have been made only for brief periods. The collectibility of kitchen glassware and vanity sets, some of which were made at New Martinsville, has been stimulated by several recent books devoted to these subjects.

Publication of this book brings to light many patterns and numerous items made at New Martinsville which have heretofore been unidentified and/or unattributed (or wrongly attributed). Increased knowledge begets interest, of course, and collectors will now begin to seek items such as New Martinsville's smoker's articles or pieces in the firm's No. 33 Modernistic line more avidly than they have in the past.

Prices given are for pieces in mint condition without chips, cracks or other defects. Decorated articles should be free of blemishes in the hand-painting, ruby stain, etc.

Neither the publisher nor the author can be liable for losses incurred when using this guide as the basis for any transaction.

| | | | |
|---|---|---|---|
| A-$275 | 5-225 | 26-85 | 47-45 |
| B-175 | 6-250 | 27-110 | 48-100 |
| C-110 | 7-100 | 28-325 set | 49-25 |
| D-130 pr. | 8-200 | 29-95 | 50-25 |
| E-60 | 9-225 | 30-110 | 51-40 |
| F-195 | 10-100 | 31-250 | 52-40 |
| G-40 | 11-95 | 32-125 | 53-35 |
| H-12 | 12-100 | 33-275 | 54-20 |
| I-125 | 13-125 | 34-175 | 55-30 |
| J-55 | 14-100 | 35-110 | 56-40 |
| K-100 | 15-115 | 36-125 | 57-30 |
| L-75 | 16-175 | 37-125 | 58-45 |
| M-250 | 17-275 | 38-125 | 59-55 |
| N-90 | 18-90 | 39-125 | 60-65 |
| O-75 | 19-195 | 40-95 | 61-25 |
| P-75 | 20-120 | 41-125 | 62-25 |
| | 21-120 | 42-125 | 63-25 |
| 1-$250 | 22-125 | 43-125 | 64-25 |
| 2-90 | 23-95 | 44-100 | 65-25 |
| 3-300 | 24-85 | 45-175 | 66-25 |
| 4-90 | 25-125 | 46-200 | 67-30 |

| | | | |
|---|---|---|---|
| 68-25 | 116-55 | 164-55 | 212-35 |
| 69-25 | 117-195 | 165-80 | 213-125 |
| 70-25 | 118-85 | 166-65 | 214-250 |
| 71-25 | 119-150 | 167-85 | 215-150 |
| 72-60 | 120-85 | 168-250 | 216-100 |
| 73-45 | 121-40 | 169-60 | 217-350 |
| 74-40 | 122-50 | 170-110 | 218-125 |
| 75-20 | 123-275 | 171-60 | 219-175 |
| 76-40 | 124-225 | 172-225 | 220-125 |
| 77-45 | 125-65 | 173-80 | 221-250 |
| 78-60 | 126-35 | 174-60 | 222-150 |
| 79-45 | 127-200 | 175-125 | 223-65 |
| 80-25 | 128-125 | 176-45 | 224-125 |
| 81-25 | 129-55 | 177-55 | 225-120 set |
| 82-35 | 130-225 | 178-45 | 226-200 |
| 83-20 | 131-55 | 179-175 | 227-85 |
| 84-25 | 132-250 | 180-125 | 228-125 |
| 85-25 | 133-40 | 181-60 | 229-175 |
| 86-45 | 134-125 | 182-60 | 230-55 |
| 87-25 | 135-35 | 183-25 | 231-35 |
| 88-50 | 136-100 | 184-65 | 232-45 |
| 89-45 | 137-45 | 185-150 | 233-65 |
| 90-25 | 138-65 | 186-25 | 234-25 |
| 91-45 | 139-50 | 187-45 | 235-35 |
| 92-25 | 140-100 | 188-45 | 236-45 |
| 93-55 | 141-175 | 189-25 | 237-75 |
| 94-55 | 142-225 pr. | 190-125 | 238-60 |
| 95-25 | 143-30 | 191-100 | 239-35 |
| 96-40 | 144-90 | 192-60 | 240-40 |
| 97-25 | 145-85 | 193-75 | 241-90 |
| 98-50 | 146-200 | 194-60 | 242-20 |
| 99-60 | 147-75 | 195-175 | 243-25 |
| 100-65 | 148-40 | 196-150 | 244-20 |
| 101-25 | 149-60 | 197-75 | 245-25 |
| 102-60 | 150-200 | 198-75 | 246-35 |
| 103-50 | 151-45 | 199-125 | 247-50 |
| 104-25 | 152-125 | 200-65 | 248-50 |
| 105-45 | 153-55 | 201-125 | 249-45 |
| 106-45 | 154-210 | 202-175 | 250-45 |
| 107-50 | 155-60 | 203-125 | 251-75 |
| 108-45 | 156-30 | 204-125 | 252-20 |
| 109-25 | 157-55 | 205-150 | 253-35 |
| 110-45 | 158-25 | 206-65 | 254-30 |
| 111-50 | 159-90 | 207-275 | 255-35 |
| 112-155 | 160-35 | 208-250 | 256-35 |
| 113-45 | 161-35 | 209-65 | 257-20 |
| 114-135 | 162-50 | 210-250 | 258-20 |
| 115-225 | 163-60 | 211-125 | 259-55 |

| | | | |
|---|---|---|---|
| 260-75 | 308-55 | 356-60 | 404-75 |
| 261-75 | 309-45 | 357-40 no lid | 405-35 |
| 262-20 | 310-50 | 358-55 | 406-65 |
| 263-45 | 311-75 | 359-15 | 407-45 |
| 264-15 | 312-65 set | 360-15 | 408-125 |
| 265-25 | 313-85 set | 361-10 | 409-75 |
| 266-25 | 314-25 | 362-125 set | 410-20 |
| 267-25 | 315-40 | 363-15 | 411-25 |
| 268-45 | 316-12 | 364-15 | 412-20 |
| 269-55 | 317-200 | 365-35 | 413-40 |
| 270-25 | 318-200 | 366-NP | 414-110 set |
| 271-65 | 319-200 | 367-35 | 415-20 |
| 272-65 | 320-110 set | 368-125 | 416-12 |
| 273-70 | 321-35 | 369-35 | 417-10 |
| 274-65 | 322-45 | 370-35 | 418-12 |
| 275-55 | 323-400 | 371-20 | 419-15 |
| 276-35 | 324-150 | 372-15 | 420-30 |
| 277-35 | 325-60 set | 373-12 | 421-35 |
| 278-50 | 326-100 | 374-6 | 422-18 |
| 279-55 | 327-115 | 375-7 | 423-75 |
| 280-30 | 328-25 | 376-30 | 424-20 |
| 281-35 | 329-195 set | 377-35 | 425-25 |
| 282-45 | 330-35 set | 378-135 set | 426-60 |
| 283-45 | 331-60 set | 379-10 | 427-50 |
| 284-30 | 332-160 set | 380-10 | 428-35 |
| 285-45 | 333-85 set | 381-10 | 429-30 |
| 286-35 | 334-75 set | 382-10 | 430-30 |
| 287-45 | 335-90 set | 383-5 | 431-20 |
| 288-45 | 336-125 set | 384-5 | 432-40 ea. |
| 289-25 | 337-20 | 385-25 | 433-55 |
| 290-35 | 338-20 | 386-12 | 434-15 |
| 291-30 | 339-20 | 387-12 | 435-10 |
| 292-20 | 340-110 set | 388-135 | 436-45 |
| 293-15 | 341-75 set | 389-20 | 437-30 ea. |
| 294-35 | 342-85 set | 390-75 | 438-20 |
| 295-15 | 343-110 set | 391-125 | 439-60 |
| 296-10 | 344-35 | 392-75 set | 440-65 |
| 297-15 | 345-25 | 393-125 set | 441-45 |
| 298-15 | 346-50 | 394-55 | 442-30 |
| 299-35 | 347-30 ea. | 395-40 | 443-50 |
| 300-30 | 348-75 | 396-30 | 444-40 |
| 301-75 set | 349-25 | 397-45 | 445-85 |
| 302-35 | 350-35 | 398-25 | 446-30 |
| 303-55 | 351-35 | 399-12 | 447-25 |
| 304-35 | 352-55 | 400-12 | 448-30 |
| 305-15 ea. | 353-35 | 401-35 | 449-20 |
| 306-35 | 354-15 | 402-35 | 450-20 |
| 307-50 | 355-20 | 403-75 | 451-15 |

| | | | |
|---|---|---|---|
| 452-55 | 467-10 | 482-18 | 497-35 |
| 453-20 | 468-15 | 483-15 | 498-75 set |
| 454-80 | 469-25 | 484-20 | 499-20 |
| 455-45 | 470-20 | 485-22 | 500-35 |
| 456-175 | 471-45 | 486-20 | 501-65 set |
| 457-60 | 472-30 | 487-75 | 502-50 set |
| 458-110 | 473-45 | 488-175 | 503-65 set |
| 459-15 | 474-55 | 489-25 | 504-20 |
| 460-55 | 475-20 | 490-30 | 505-55 |
| 461-40 | 476-10 | 491-20 | 506-75 |
| 462-80 pr. | 477-10 | 492-15 | 507-110 |
| 463-20 | 478-60 | 493-10 | 508-30 |
| 464-20 | 479-50 | 494-90 pr. | 509-NP |
| 465-25 | 480-70 | 495-25 | 510-450 |
| 466-15 | 481-15 | 496-85 | 511-60 |

in Booth ACROSS Artie May Harlaw
She is the Realtor on Mildreds
Duplex

234

234